P9-DOF-939

THE
BEST "WORST PRESIDENT"

THE
BEST "WORST
PRESIDENT"

WHAT THE RIGHT GETS WRONG
ABOUT BARACK OBAMA

MARK HANNAH

ILLUSTRATIONS BY
BOB STAAKE

DEY ST.
AN IMPRINT OF
WILLIAM MORROW *PUBLISHERS*

HarperCollins books may be purchased for educational, business, or sales promotional use. For information please e-mail the Special Markets Department at SPsales@harpercollins.com.

First Dey Street hardcover published 2016

FIRST EDITION

Designed by Ashley Tucker
Illustrations copyright © 2016 by Bob Staake

Library of Congress Cataloging-in-Publication Data has been applied for.

ISBN 978-0-06-244305-2

16 17 18 19 20   RRD   10 9 8 7 6 5 4 3 2 1

—

In memory of my father, Stephen,
for teaching me how to debate.

In dedication to my wife, Jennifer,
for teaching me how not to.

—

TABLE OF DISCONTENTS

—

PROLOGUE

When I met Barack Obama in the spring of 2004, I didn't see either the halo or the horns. But then again, I wasn't looking for them. I wasn't paying him much attention at all, for that matter. It was three months before a stirring speech at the Democratic National Convention would catapult him onto our country's political radar, but at the time, hardly anyone had heard of him. For me, he was the least prominent and most accessible of a pack of politicians huddled backstage at a Chicago Hyatt: we both stood over six feet tall, but we were the two "little guys" standing with a few political giants. I was a low-level staffer on John Kerry's presidential campaign, producing political events across the country. Obama was a lanky candidate for the junior Senate seat in Illinois who just a decade earlier had been a newly married law school lecturer with no elective experience and lots of student loan debt. And yet there we were, standing with Senator Kerry, Chicago's dynastic mayor Richard Daley, and Illinois's beloved senior senator Dick Durbin who, just a few years earlier, had been rumored to be on Al Gore's vice presidential short list.

Or rather, Senator Durbin was supposed to be there.

Hundreds of well-heeled, well-dressed donors had finished their dinners and were waiting for the speaking program to begin, but Durbin's people had called to say he was running late. Our campaign's fund-raising staff kept glancing over at me impatiently: these donors weren't used to delays. After a few more agonizing minutes, Durbin finally entered the backstage area and I began to rattle off my briefing. "Welcome, Senator Durbin. Now, Mr. Obama, you'll be introduced onto the stage first and after your remarks you'll introduce Mayor Daley—" But my spiel was promptly drowned out. Kerry, Durbin, and Daley hadn't seen each other in some time and were garrulously catching up. After a few other feeble attempts to get their attention— "Gentlemen, please, the donors have finished their dinners. We're running behind"—Obama shot me a sympathetic grin and then interrupted his colleagues. With one self-assured hand on the shoulder of the mayor on whose turf we stood and another on the shoulder of his party's presumptive nominee for president, the little-known senatorial candidate exclaimed in a booming baritone, "Guys, guys! Let the young man speak!"

Stunned, Kerry, Durbin, and Daley whipped their heads around to examine the interrupter. "Who the hell is this guy?" was written all over their faces. But those expressions quickly turned to "Well, I guess we *should* get this show on the road." The four of them turned to me. In the spirit of the awkward moment, I stammered through my briefing and (finally!) cued the offstage introduction.

I learned later it was at this Chicago fund-raiser that Kerry decided to invite Obama to give the keynote speech at the Democratic National Convention.[1] That decision was reportedly based on Kerry's respect for Obama's eloquence as a public speaker; it might have also had something to do with the electoral importance of Illinois or of showcasing a rising African American star within the party. In *The Audacity of Hope,* Obama writes "the process by which I was selected . . . remains something of a mystery."[2] But regardless of how it came to be, the speech channeled Americans' frustration with our increasingly partisan political culture. "There's not a liberal America and a conservative America," Obama insisted. "There's a United States of America." With this speech he became a star within the Democratic Party, and a likely contender for the party's future presidential nomination.

It's worth repeating that no one quite knows how history works, and I may certainly be deluded in thinking I had any part in it. But I can't help wondering if John Kerry's selection of Barack Obama as the keynote speaker was maybe influenced in some tiny, tiny way by the impression Obama made when he spoke up for Kerry's bumbling junior staffer. In any case, I'm sure the reaction I saw on John Kerry's face in that moment wasn't affront: it was a mixture of admiration and apprehension. And it was precisely this mixed reaction that Barack Obama would soon elicit from the country as a whole.

I found Obama's little intercession on my behalf was one of the kinder things anyone had done for me—frankly, he struck me as a nice and genuine guy. But because it seemed like he came out of nowhere, voters and pundits didn't know what to make of him. (And kindness isn't the only thing you want out of a president, after all.) As time passed, Obama became a sort of Rorschach test upon which the American people projected their own hopes and fears. Ultimately, dueling narratives about him emerged, which persisted throughout his presidency. Four years after he self-assuredly inserted himself into the conversation at the Chicago fund-raiser he inserted himself into the presidential race with the same distinguished confidence. This self-assurance is now interpreted by supporters as decisiveness and by critics as arrogance or vanity. As a senatorial candidate, he was quick to dispense with small talk backstage at that Chicago Hyatt—just as he dispensed with schmooze sessions on Capitol Hill after taking presidential office. This has led supporters to label him as independent but has led critics to label him as aloof and disengaged. There might not, in fact, be a liberal America and a conservative America. But there is a liberal idea of Barack Obama and a conservative idea of him.

The conservative idea found one of its many mouthpieces in former vice president Dick Cheney, who, in an interview with CNN's Jake Tapper in the summer of 2014, called President Obama "the worst president in [his] lifetime." A year later, as if trying to outdo himself, Cheney went on to insinuate the president might actually be conspiring to undermine the country he leads. When asked by conservative radio host Hugh Hewitt whether he thought the president was naive, Cheney suggested that "if you had somebody as president who wanted to take America down, who wanted to fundamentally weaken our position in the world and reduce our capacity to influence events, turn our back on our allies and encourage our adversaries, it [sic] would look exactly like what Barack Obama's doing."

Interesting stuff, and not just because it's terrifically hard to imagine why a president would want to sink his or her own ship. Even if they muddle his historical legacy, these competing ideas about President Obama can be productive in helping us understand the different values that underpin this era in our political life. After all, our democracy was founded on an unbridled competition of ideas—and some of the ideas that swirled around more than two hundred years ago when the Constitution was framed were as ludicrous as the idea that our own president wasn't actually born in the United States or that he is trying to "take America down."

We could also say that theories about anything—birth certificates, education policy, drone strikes, everything the president has done and everything we've thought about him, positive or negative—are meant to be tested with the application of observable facts. In the following pages I aim to take the conservative theory of President Obama and debunk it by systematically examining it in light of the relevant facts. Fear not that this will be tedious: we'll be examining some marvelous hypocrisies, shedding light on some fantastic fibs, and showcasing some of the Obama administration's surprisingly underappreciated triumphs.

I should add that, as someone who briefly worked and twice voted for Barack Obama—and who sometimes advocates for his public policies as a TV talking head—I wouldn't dare claim that I'm a dispassionate analyst. This book isn't a work of social science or objective journalism. It's more like a kind of written wrangling. I stand by the factual accuracy of everything in these pages, though I freely admit I've retrieved these facts to support my own liberal argument and refute the conservative one.

So I write in good faith (and perhaps some naïveté) when I say that I hope two groups of people will read (and enjoy!) this book. The first group is other liberals and progressives who are tired of hearing attacks on President Obama from conservative friends and family members. Let this be the handbook that arms you with the evidence and anecdotes to support your position. Let it prepare you for the next family gathering at which you're seated next to your conservative uncle and you want to explain to him why Obamacare is not, in fact, an unmitigated disaster. Or for the party where you can finally have a ready response for your friend who goes on and on about how the tragedy in Benghazi spurred a grand cover-up by the White House.

My hope that it will be useful at home, with family and friends, is genuine—and also personal. I've long experienced the joy of connecting over political disconnects. When I was growing up on Cape Cod, I worked alongside my father, a carpenter who kept the radio tuned to Rush Limbaugh's right-wing talk show on a daily basis. Every night at the dinner table, he and I would delve into spirited debates about Bill Clinton's job performance. My two younger brothers provided color commentary and kept score while my mother diplomatically tried to change the subject. The experience instilled a passion for politics in me and helped me appreciate that political disagreement that is fueled by facts (and, crucially, mutual respect) can turn people on to politics more than it turns them off.

This is of course another way of saying I hope conservatives will also read this book, including those who, like Vice President Cheney, think President Obama is one of the worst presidents we've ever had. For you, let this be an explanation of how anyone in their right mind (if you'll grant me the distinction) could support this president. I'm sure you have a liberal coworker or a neighbor or cousin who baffles you by continuing to support him. Let this be your guide to how they can possibly think the way they do. I hope you'll come across information that surprises you or helps you consider President Obama in a new light. After all, nothing is as important in politics as the ability to, in Saint Augustine's words, "hear the other side." But even if I'm not able to change your mind and convince you to sign up for the Barack Obama fan club, I promise conservative ideas will be dispelled but not disparaged. In the process of putting some choice anti-Obama excerpts to the test, this book merrily mimics the tone of the criticism lobbed at the president. But that mimicry is not mockery. If I didn't respect the conservative narrative on some level, I wouldn't spend my time writing an entire book to feud with it.

As we will see—and we won't stop there—the first two years of the Obama presidency accomplished quite a bit. Congress passed the president's economic stimulus, which prevented a nationwide economic collapse. Two iconic American car companies were rescued. The president expanded affordable health care to all Americans, something seven previous presidents (both Democrat and Republican) tried and failed to accomplish.[3] The Dodd-Frank Act was signed into law, reforming Wall Street's addiction to the risky "swaps" and "derivatives" that led to the financial crisis of 2008. And student loan interest rates were reined in while valuable education tax credits were expanded to all families making less than $180,000 a year.

Let's not forget that President Obama was sworn into office at a precarious time for our country. A culture of greed and permissiveness had placed America on the brink of economic catastrophe. The economy was hemorrhaging jobs and many people's life savings had swiftly evaporated. A culture of hubris and deceit had thrown America's military into a vague and unnecessary war in Iraq, which cost us too many lives and too much money. Our country's moral leadership and credibility were being questioned openly by our allies. But after eight years of President Obama's leadership, America remains the world's sole superpower and the model for freedom-seeking people everywhere.

The sky might have more drones in it than many of us would like, but it hasn't fallen. The sea level might be rising at a disconcerting rate, but a second Great Flood hasn't risen. President Obama might not have united the country as he and we had hoped. It's true that continued polarization leaves our rich political traditions bruised. But it hasn't left them broken.

The next president will take the oath of office while our country tackles some pretty vexing challenges. Increased partisan tension, a rising national debt, and violent extremism in the Middle East will still loom. But, as will become clear throughout the following pages, he or she is taking over at a time when our country is in significantly better shape than it was eight years ago. Our economy has been stabilized after a deep recession; a federally guaranteed right to affordable health care exists; two Supreme Court justices were appointed who helped rule that marriage is a constitutionally protected right for same-sex couples; nearly six million immigrants were protected from deportation; we are normalizing relations with Cuba after a half century of failed policies; Iran's nuclear ambitions have been suspended for the next decade; and America's public enemy number one, Osama bin Laden, is no longer.

Though they disagree heartily over the legacy of President Obama, one thing on which liberals and conservatives can agree is that his presidency was indeed consequential. Was he the best president, or the worst? Has he helped or hurt the country? Does he leave a positive or negative legacy in his wake? These should be lively and healthy arguments, and I hope this book will help them along. And in some small way, I hope it will encourage everyone—little guys, big guys—to speak up.

AUTHOR'S NOTE
ON THE ILLUSTRATIONS

Readers knowledgeable about America's political heritage will appreciate that the language of politics is frequently a visual language. Aside from visual metaphors that writers often deploy (familiar examples include "in the arena," "a marketplace of ideas," or "on the national stage"), some of the most effective displayers or disputers of political ideas have been our nation's artists and illustrators. In the 1870s, Thomas Nast's cartoons depicting the corruption of Tammany Hall and its Boss Tweed appeared regularly in *Harper's Weekly*, fueling the popular revulsion that brought down New York's powerful political machine.

Fifty years later, James Montgomery Flagg dreamed up and illustrated the famous Uncle Sam character (using himself as a model) for political posters that would recruit young Americans into military service through two world wars. During the Eisenhower presidential campaign of 1952, the candidate's most influential television advertisement was arguably not the biographical reports of the war hero, but a cartoon spot developed by Roy Disney and Disney Studios called

"We'll Take Ike (to Washington)." And we can't forget how, more recently, street artist Shepard Fairey's "Hope" poster inspired and energized Barack Obama's supporters.

So it's in this tradition that this book includes some original illustrations by one of our generation's most talented political illustrators, Bob Staake. Many readers will be familiar with Bob's graphic style from the *New Yorker* where, over the past eight years, his covers have compellingly portrayed key moments in President Obama's presidency. The most iconic of these appeared in November of 2008, right after Barack Obama had been elected. Entitled "Reflection," the solemn and celebratory cover shows the Lincoln Memorial illuminated by the moon, which doubles as the *O* in the *New Yorker* masthead. Of course the *O* also conjures the surname of this other Illinois lawmaker who was set to embody Lincoln's legacy and inherit Lincoln's office. As of this writing, it remains the best-selling cover in the magazine's history.

Like me, Bob has noticed how so many of the conservative criticisms seem to caricaturize this president—both his personality and his policies. So what better way to reveal those criticisms' ridiculousness than to illustrate these caricatures so vividly? That's exactly what Bob has done, and I think the effect is both powerful and provocative.

—

PART 1

THE
MAN

—

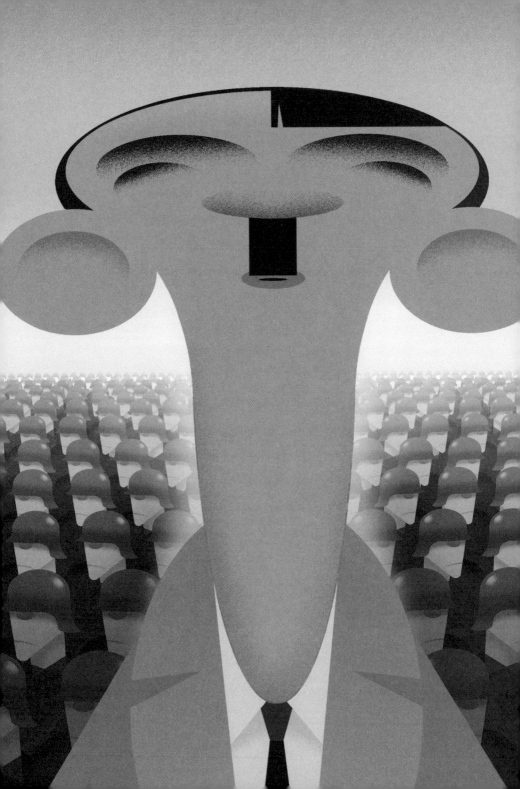

1
—
THE
DICTATOR
—

In the year before his reelection, President Obama met one-on-one with Russian president Dmitry Medvedev on the eve of a global nuclear security summit. The United States had recently set up missile launch facilities in Europe, and Medvedev called upon the Obama administration to prove it wasn't targeting Russia. In an exchange caught on tape by reporters, Obama could be heard saying, "It's important for [incoming Russian president Vladimir Putin] to give me space. . . . This is my last election. After my election, I have more flexibility."[1]

Republicans and the media pounced. Why is the American president whispering stealthy messages to the Russian president? Republican presidential candidate Mitt Romney called Obama's remarks "alarming and troubling"[2] and insisted "the American people have a right to know where *else* he plans to be 'flexible' in a second term."[3]

To most foreign policy experts, the president's comments were, at best, a savvy diplomatic maneuver that helped the missile program move forward without Russian objections or, at worst, a frank statement about the limits of conducting sensitive international negotiations amid the *gotcha!*-style politics of an election year. But to his critics, the unscripted comments were evidence of the president's systematic abuse of executive authority. The president was incapable of working cooperatively with Congress, and so he boxed out the people's elected representatives and "ruled by fiat."

Though liberals might dismiss it, this line of argument actually began to resonate with the American people. In 2015, the Pew Research Center asked hundreds of Americans to describe the president in one word. The fourth most common response was . . . (drumroll) . . . "dictator" (preceded indecisively by: "good," "incompetent," and "intelligent").[4] In this chapter, we explore whether the United States has, under President Obama, morphed from a representative democracy to a dictatorship. Spoiler alert: it hasn't! But let's explore (and explode) the case to the contrary.

—

EXECUTIVE ORDERS
THE CHARGE

President Obama has abused his authority, issuing tons of executive orders that range from raising the minimum wage of government workers to granting amnesty to millions of undocumented immigrants. Senator Jeff Sessions, a Republican from Alabama, insisted President Obama "undermined . . . the moral integrity of immigration law, and even the constitutional separation of powers."[5] In an interview with Megyn Kelly on Fox News, Sessions stated flatly, "The president has no authority to do this. It's against the law."[6] When the president announced, in his 2014 State of the Union address, he would use his executive authority to raise the minimum wage for government contractors to $10.10 an hour, conservative radio host Glenn Beck took to the airwaves and exclaimed that "over and over again, [the president] said he would use his executive power to get his way. . . . This was the State of the Union where our president declared he would become America's first dictator."[7] Later on, House Speaker John Boehner dispatched his spokesman to claim "Emperor Obama" would leave a "legacy of lawlessness."[8]

THE REALITY

Everyone who ever watched *Schoolhouse Rock!* as a kid knows it's Congress's job to create laws, not the president's. The problem is, for much of President Obama's term, Congress simply didn't do its job. The two sessions of Congress that convened from 2011 to 2014 were among the least productive[9] in modern history, leading pundits to resurrect the Truman-era title "the Do Nothing Congress." Instead of taking on the major public policy issues of the day, Republicans in Congress spent their energy on things like voting (unsuccessfully) more than sixty times to repeal or restrict Obamacare.

Believe it or not, this dithering was part of a longer-term political strategy. The leader of the Senate Republicans, Mitch McConnell, straight-up told an interviewer, a couple months before this period began, "The single most important thing we want to achieve is for President Obama to be a one-term president." They obviously failed in that endeavor, and four years later, when his party gained control of the Senate, he told the *Washington Post* he was trying to ensure that the Republican party avoids appearing "scary" to voters ahead of the 2016 presidential contest, and "to not mess up the playing field, if you will, for whoever the nominee ultimately is." The Republican leadership basically admitted that pursuing a Republican agenda would reflect poorly on their eventual nominee. Some conservatives eventually got fed up with the inaction. The *Weekly Standard*'s Stephen Hayes lamented the fact that, despite attaining a majority in the House of Representatives, Republicans were not advancing a "bolder agenda" and were dragging their feet on ripe conservative issues like tax reform.[10]

Confronted by a stubborn and stagnant Congress, President Obama has not been bashful about his use of executive orders. In that 2014 State of the Union, he asserted, "America does not stand still—and neither will I. So wherever and whenever I can take steps without legislation to expand opportunity for more American families, that's what I'm going to do."[11] He promised to make that year a "year of action" and confidently reminded Congress he wielded "a pen and a phone" to assist him when Congress would not. Sure enough, by the end of that year, the president had issued more than eighty new executive actions designed to shore up the economic recovery, mitigate climate change, and bring some overdue sanity to our immigration enforcement. Each of these topics will be discussed in detail in this book, but for now, the core question remains: Has President Obama abused his executive powers by issuing so many executive orders?

Let me answer this with a fun fact that makes my conservative friends' heads spin: President Obama has actually made fewer executive orders per year than any president since Grover Cleveland left office in 1897.[12] If Obama's critics think *he's* overreaching, I wonder what they think about Calvin Coolidge and Franklin Roosevelt and all of the other presidents of the first half of the twentieth century, each of whom issued roughly five times as many executive orders as Obama.

Of course, the sheer number of executive orders doesn't tell a full story about a president's use of executive authority. Executive orders can address minor bureaucratic issues or more substantive policy issues. Many of them simply reverse a previous president's executive order while some substantially set new precedent. President Obama has indeed exercised bold action on the immigration, environmental, and economic fronts. Because of his intervention, law enforcement has prioritized the detention of "felons, not families" and 97 percent of undocumented immigrants who are now detained are criminals or recent border crossers.[13] Because of his initiative, China and the United States (the world's two biggest air polluters) have signed a pact agreeing to aggressively reduce their carbon emissions. And because of his influence, more than a dozen states have increased their minimum wage, improving the standard of living for roughly seven million American workers.[14]

A few legal challenges have arisen to some of the president's initiatives. These checks and balances between the judiciary and the executive branches are, in fact, a wonderful thing. They're part of the self-regulating system our founding fathers designed. But one of the decisive features of this system is that, ultimately, it is a *presidential* (as opposed to a *parliamentary*) system of democracy. Our country's leader gains democratic legitimacy by being chosen directly by our citizenry (not by other politicians, as it works in the UK and elsewhere). He (or she!) is therefore independent from, and acts as a coequal check upon, the legislative branch. Alexander Hamilton explained why our Constitution grants strong powers to the chief executive in the *Federalist Papers*. "Energy in the executive is a leading character in the definition of good government," Hamilton wrote, and proceeded to explain that a strong president provided the best guard against "foreign attacks" and against the "assaults of ambition, of faction, and of anarchy."[15]

Most democracies aren't like ours. They have parliaments which select a prime minister whose power is limited to carrying out the laws that parliament passes. Any institution that's as insulated as a congress or a parliament is given to some degree of "groupthink" or "mob rule." So as every civics teacher knows, the presidential system compels compromise, exercises discretion in the execution of laws, and protects individual liberties (especially the rights of minorities)—even when doing so isn't politically popular.

President Obama isn't abusing his executive authority. He's just using it. The legislative branch that sometimes criticizes him for doing so might be populated by many more voices, which together can make a lot more noise. But it doesn't have more power. Ultimately, the specific powers of the legislature and the executive derive from the Constitution. As a former professor of Constitutional law, the president spent his early years teaching young people about the intricacies of our Constitutional democracy. How many true dictators began their political careers that way?

AUTO INDUSTRY BAILOUT

THE CHARGE

One of the first things Barack Obama did as president was to unilaterally give the automobile industry roughly $80 billion of our tax dollars under the guise of trying to "rescue" American car companies. In fact, this was a gift to the United Auto Workers (UAW) union to reward them for helping Obama get elected. Congress is supposed to have the "power of the purse" and make appropriations like this, so the president once again bypassed them. When the huge bailout wasn't enough to prop up the struggling auto industry, President Obama "sold Chrysler to the Italians who are going to build Jeeps in China,"[16] as Mitt Romney quipped on the campaign trail. For Obama, it's not enough that Americans are ruled by fiat, but an iconic American car company has to be ruled by Fiat too!

THE REALITY

When President Obama took the oath of office in January of 2009, the American economy had hit the skids. Nowhere was this pain felt more than in Detroit. That year, American automakers would sell fewer cars than at any time since 1982. Ford Motor Company and Chrysler hemorrhaged money, and private banks and investors were so anxious about their own liquidity amid the recession that they were tightwadding their cash. At the time, giving aid to car companies that faced bankruptcy was a politically unpopular move.[17] Yet the president's economic advisers recognized that letting GM and Chrysler go bankrupt would have a ripple effect. Aside from the jobs of all the employees of these two companies, jobs also would be axed across adjacent industries: auto parts providers, metal and rubber manufacturers, car dealerships. According to one industry group, even if GM alone had gone belly up, nearly two million American workers would have found themselves jobless in 2009 and 2010.[18]

And it wasn't just President Obama who foresaw this. To his credit, in the final days of his presidency, President Bush authorized a temporary bailout of the automakers (but kicked the decision for any longer-term aid package to his successor). Speaking to a trade group representing car dealers after his presidency, Bush explained, "I didn't want history to look back and say, 'Bush could have done something but chose not to do it.'"[19] Obama gave a hat tip to President Bush at the time, calling the decision "a necessary step to avoid a collapse of our auto industry."[20] Republicans who argue a president doesn't have the authority to selectively bail out specific industries and interfere with free markets in times of economic crisis are conveniently forgetting President Bush did exactly that.

The question remains: If Congress is the branch of government that's responsible for spending our tax dollars, how did the White House get $80 billion to bail out the car companies? The answer, in short, is Congress. In the final months of the Bush presidency, Congress passed the Troubled Asset Relief Program (TARP) essentially authorizing the president (and the next president) to lend hundreds of billions of tax dollars to help stabilize the economy. The Auto Industry Financing Program, which was part of TARP, was a loan, not a giveaway. Of the $80 billion lent to the carmakers, about $70 billion was recovered by the end of the program.[21] So, were we, the taxpayers, bamboozled out of the remaining $10 billion?

Not so fast. The government might not have retrieved all the money it lent, but it got back more than most economists predicted it would.[22] Moreover, if we had taken the advice of some free market purists and let the auto industry implode, the ultimate cost to taxpayers—in lost tax revenue from the car companies as well as unemployment insurance, food stamps, and medical care for laid-off workers—would have exceeded $100 billion.[23] Pensions would have dried up, economic opportunity would have stagnated, and the American Midwest would have spiraled into economic disarray. In the words of Treasury Secretary Jack Lew, the loan program was "a crucial part" of preventing "a second Great Depression."[24] When you consider $10 billion translates into about $3 for every individual living in the United States (roughly the cost of a pungent Pine tree air freshener), I'd say it was a fair trade-off.

How is the American auto industry doing today? Sales of American cars have rebounded to their prerecession levels, seeing seven years of straight growth. In fact, more American cars were sold in 2015 than at any time in the past decade. With the assistance of the temporary taxpayer support, GM and Chrysler became independent of the government and profitable in just two years. And instead of widespread unemployment, the auto industry has generated fifty thousand new jobs between 2010 and 2015.

In January of 2014, Vice President Biden paid a visit to an auto show in Detroit. Biden, a proud owner of a 1967 Corvette (and a ubiquitous pair of Ray-Ban Aviators), is the closest thing the administration has to a spokesman for American car culture. "I'm like a kid in a candy store," the vice president quipped while he hopped into a Ford-150 pickup truck, a Chrysler 200 sedan, and, yes, a new Corvette.

The visit came just a month after the U.S. Treasury sold its remaining shares in the car companies. The atmosphere was triumphant. "We bet on American ingenuity," Biden beamed. "We bet on you and we won."[25]

IRS POLITICAL TARGETING "SCANDAL"

THE CHARGE

Annoyed with the Tea Party activism that spoke out against him in 2010, President Obama unleashed the IRS to harass and investigate these grassroots conservative organizations. In 2013, an IRS employee revealed that, in reviewing the tax-exempt status of new 501(c)(4) non-profit groups, the agency had been systematically singling out conservative groups with the words "tea party" or "patriots" in their names for closer scrutiny. Darrell Issa, the chairman of the House Oversight and Government Reform Committee, who led the investigation, asserted the IRS actions were politically motivated, "directly being ordered from Washington."[26] He even told Fox News's Carl Cameron his investigation would "provide evidence to prove . . . that he can get it right up all the way into the White House."[27]

THE REALITY

The IRS controversy resonated so strongly with Obama's critics because it fit the narrative of a lawless and vindictive president who wanted to punish or disable his political enemies. This narrative found its most dramatic expression in a 2013 blog post by the *Wall Street Journal* columnist and former Reagan speechwriter Peggy Noonan:

> *Might targeting the tea-party groups—diverting them, keeping them from forming and operating—seem a shrewd campaign strategy in the years between 2010 and 2012? Sure. Underhanded and illegal, but potentially effective.*[28]

The problem with this narrative is, well, the problem with any juicy narrative. In trying to tell an enticing story, facts yield to fantasy and details defer to drama. The facts are these: Lois Lerner, who headed up the tax-exempt review process for the IRS, publicly acknowledged her agency used conservative keywords to scan applications and apologized for the practice. In a press conference, the president said "this is pretty straightforward. If, in fact, IRS personnel . . . were intentionally targeting conservative groups, then that is outrageous, and there is no place for it, and they have to be held fully accountable. . . . You should feel that way regardless of party."[29]

People did, in fact, feel that way regardless of party. During an era of deep partisan division, misbehavior by the never-popular IRS was one thing that could spur outrage on both sides of the aisle. Republican senator Marco Rubio penned a letter to Treasury secretary Jack Lew stating "no government agency that has behaved in such a manner can possibly instill any faith and respect from the American public."[30] Democratic senator Harry Reid took to Twitter to say that "targeting any group based on its political stance is completely inappropriate"[31] and swiftly supported bipartisan demands for an investigation.

Three separate investigations would eventually take place. The Justice Department, the inspector general (IG) of the Department of the Treasury and the Republican-led Congress each looked into the allegations. In fact, six congressional committees opened inquiries, and to restore public confidence in the agency, the president installed a new leader at the IRS who, in turn, replaced three deputies who were in charge of the tax-exempt division.[32] After the IRS turned over 500,000 pages of documents, and spent roughly $15 million and 98,000 personnel hours responding to subpoenas, investigators found no evidence the IRS screening process was politically motivated.[33]

What did they find, then? The IRS had been flooded with new 501(c)(4) applications, which more than doubled between 2010 and 2012.[34] Lerner's department was understaffed and overwhelmed. They created criteria for automatically searching through applications based on keywords that were listed in "be on the lookout" (or "BOLO") documents. These documents did include conservative keywords like "tea party" and "patriot," but to the bewilderment of many Republican accusers, they also included liberal terms like "progressive" and "occupy."[35] The Treasury IG, however, focused on conservative groups in his report because, according to his spokesman, Darrell Issa asked them "to narrowly focus on Tea Party organizations."[36] Though ostensibly interested in uncovering political targeting within the IRS, Issa himself had engaged in the kind of political targeting he lambasted.

According to an analysis of IRS documents obtained by the Center for American Progress through a Freedom of Information Act request, progressive groups were targeted more frequently than conservative groups. The twenty-two BOLO lists distributed to IRS staff during the height of the controversy "included more explicit references to progressive groups, ACORN successors, and medical marijuana organizations than to Tea Party entities."[37] So Darrell Issa's two main accusations of the IRS—that its targeting was politically motivated and that it focused exclusively on conservative groups—both turned out to be false.

The new head of the IRS eventually did away with the now infamous BOLO lists. These investigations showed, however, that the lists were not a tool of political persecution but a faulty shortcut for determining which groups applying for tax-exemption were likely to be disqualified for participating in political activity. This was the IRS's mandate, after all. As this story unfolded, it shocked many to learn the IRS employee who was responsible for using the "tea party" keyword in the first place was a self-professed "conservative Republican" in the agency's Cincinnati office.[38]

If the IRS was guilty of anything, it was guilty of sloppy management. The Treasury IG report detailed "confusion about how to process the applications, delays in the processing of the applications, and a lack of management oversight and guidance."[39] Basically, it found the IRS guilty of every cliché we'd previously attributed to them. But the IRS was decidedly not guilty of political targeting.

The suggestion that the White House was somehow involved just turned out to be a fantasy of one of President Obama's most zealous critics. Darrell Issa, who had previously asserted this "was a targeting of the president's political enemies," changed his tune after the revelation that progressive groups had been targeted. Speaking to CNN's Dana Bash, he claimed, "I've never said it came out of the office of the president or his campaign. What I've said is, it comes out of Washington."[40] But Issa couldn't help himself. Moments later in the very same interview, he said, "For years, the president bashed the Tea Party groups. . . . And on his behalf—perhaps not on his request—on his behalf, the IRS executed a delaying tactic against the very groups he talked about."

President Obama and the Tea Party are indeed political adversaries. They have different visions for the country they love and there are very few policy positions, if any, on which they agree. But they're both products of popular, grassroots social movements. Contrary to what Congressman Issa, Peggy Noonan, and other conspiracy theorists claim, the president has no interest in deploying an independent agency like the IRS to rip off those who disagree with him. He wants to out-compete them in the free marketplace of ideas. That's where he has more valuable currency.

OBAMACARE "SHOVED DOWN OUR THROATS"[41]

THE CHARGE

President Obama couldn't get bipartisan support for his health care overhaul and so he and Nancy Pelosi pushed it through the House of Representatives without the support of even a single Republican. Obama was so eager to get the law passed while Democrats had a so-called supermajority in the Senate (i.e., sixty Democratic senators, which prevented the Republicans from filibustering) that the vote was held for Christmas Eve in 2009. Obamacare was foisted upon the American people and has been unpopular from its inception.

THE REALITY

No House Republicans voted in favor of the Obamacare law when it passed. But this united opposition was more a product of politics than of principles. Mitch McConnell, then the leader of the Senate's Republican minority, explained why defections would not be tolerated: "It was absolutely critical that everybody be together because if the proponents of the bill were able to say it was bipartisan, it tended to convey to the public that this is O.K."[42]

Ironically, some of the Republican senators who decried Obamacare for requiring people to purchase health insurance or pay a penalty at tax time (aka the "individual mandate") were the same ones who actually supported a health care bill containing an individual mandate back when Bill Clinton was president.[43] At that time, President Clinton tried to mandate all *employers* provide insurance, but Republicans thought a requirement on individuals was more consistent with their philosophy of personal accountability and keeping businesses less regulated. The individual mandate had been supported by Republicans for more than two decades, the concept having been first conceived by a 1989 report of the conservative Heritage Foundation entitled "Assuring Affordable Health Care for All Americans."[44]

It's fair to say Obamacare passed along partisan lines, but this is at least partly because Republicans, with a partisan strategy of obstruction, turned their backs on policy ideas they once championed.

Also, let's not forget the Democrats got their partisan advantage from the collective will of the American people. President Obama and Democrats in Congress were elected by wide margins in 2008, and one of the key promises they made on the campaign trail was to do everything within their power to pass some form of universal health care. Ever since Harry Truman sought a "universal" health care insurance program in 1945,[45] and Ted Kennedy called for health care "as a right and not a privilege" in 1978,[46] Democrats had tried—and failed—to pass a health care law that covered the millions of uninsured Americans.

As a candidate, Obama was clear about his intention to pass health care reform as soon as he got into office. He elevated the issue during the Democratic primaries, stating plainly, "I am absolutely determined that by the end of the first term of the next president, we should have universal health care in this country."[47] In his first presidential debate with John McCain, Obama was asked about the "priorities" he would bring to the presidency. One of the first things he said was, "We have to fix our health care system, which is putting an enormous burden on families. . . . They are getting crushed, and many of them are going bankrupt as a consequence of health care."[48] This, folks, was truth in advertising.

And the American people liked what they heard. When we elected Barack Obama, we elected more than just a person. We elected a set of policy priorities, a set of prescriptions for the country's ills. We elected the creation of a health care model that would ensure affordable insurance was broadly available, not just up to the whims of one's employer. We got what we were promised. Did everybody get what they wanted? Of course not. The most liberal Democrats wanted "Medicare for all" or a "single-payer" plan which would have nationalized our health care marketplace. The most conservative Republicans didn't want government to be part of the solution at all.

In the final analysis, the Obamacare law was an extensive compromise between patient advocacy organizations, doctors' groups, hospital associations, and insurance and pharmaceutical companies. It was a reconciliation of Republican and Democratic policy ideas that expanded both free market–based and government-subsidized health insurance. And it was supported and passed by a majority of the people's elected representatives in Congress. It might have been a slim majority, but it was a majority no previous president had been able to attain. The idea that the Obamacare law was hastily assembled and "shoved down our throats," as many critics claimed, doesn't square with reality. The law was the product of decades of research, advocacy, and compromise. It was supported by a majority of our lawmakers who were, in turn, supported by a majority of their constituents. This is precisely how representative democracies—not dictatorships—work.

There's been some yammering to the contrary, it's true. Trey Gowdy is a Republican from rural South Carolina who surfed into Congress on the wave of Tea Party anxiety during the 2010 midterms. He has been a constant and conspicuous critic of the president. This quickly made him a darling of conservatives and got him frequent invitations on conservative media outlets. In an interview with the Fox Business Network's Lou Dobbs, Congressman Gowdy touted the idea of repealing or de-funding Obamacare, accusing the law of being "wildly unpopular" and "a train wreck as described by the people who voted for it."[49]

But the law is neither "wildly popular" nor "wildly unpopular." Although there are some polls which show the public has a slightly more negative than positive attitude toward Obamacare, public opinion is largely split along party affiliation. The vast majority of Democrats support the law and the vast majority of Republicans don't like it.[50] But as people learn about what's in the law, they like it more. In 2013, the nonpartisan Kaiser Family Foundation found that "while most of the law's individual provisions remain popular, many of the most well-liked elements are the least well-known among the public."[51]

The wave of Tea Party opposition to Obamacare crested in the 2010 midterm. By the 2014 midterms, Republican voters were still enthusiastic to vote against President Obama and the Democratic Party platform but, when asked to give a reason why they were so energized, merely 3 percent mentioned Obamacare.[52] Citing public opinion polls, a spokesman for the Democratic Party pointed out, "One thing that is much more unpopular than the Affordable Care Act is repealing the Affordable Care Act."[53]

AMNESTY TO MILLIONS OF "ILLEGAL IMMIGRANTS"

THE CHARGE

President Obama was unable to persuade Congress to support his plan for immigration reform, so he took matters into his own hands. In 2014, around Thanksgiving, Obama announced he would grant amnesty to about five million unauthorized immigrants, doling out work permits to people who crossed the border illegally. The Heritage

Foundation put out a report showing the president's immigration action would cost American taxpayers $2 trillion dollars in order to cover things like food stamps and welfare. According to Sarah Palin, President Obama was "giving the middle finger" to voters.[54] But don't just take Palin's word for it. In May of 2015, a federal court found the president's executive action illegal and, as this book goes to print, the case is being argued before Supreme Court.

THE REALITY

President Obama *did* work with Congress on comprehensive immigration reform. In 2013, after months of negotiation, a group of four Republican and four Democratic senators (delightfully called the Gang of Eight) actually got the Senate to pass a bipartisan immigration reform bill. It was a motley crew of lawmakers, uniting staunch conservatives like Marco Rubio and John McCain with avowed liberals like Chuck Schumer and Dick Durbin. It was as if the Hatfields and the McCoys got together to build a shared tree house for their children. The bill was a colossal compromise that included increased border security, workplace verification systems for employers, and a thirteen-year pathway to citizenship. As Vice President Biden presided over the Senate vote, young immigration reform activists watched excitedly from the balcony that overlooks the Senate floor. Biden had instructed them to remain silent, but when they tallied the final vote with a majority of the Senate in support (including "yea" votes from fourteen Republican senators), they couldn't contain themselves. The spectators burst into chants of "Yes we can!"[55]

Except they cannot. Hailed by the press as a rare moment of bipartisan compromise, the Senate bill was blocked in John Boehner's House of Representatives. Republicans in the House were so scared of either giving President Obama a victory on one hand or alienating Latino voters on the other that they refused to let the Senate bill come up for a yes-or-no vote. The president gave the House a year and a half to take the bill up for a vote before he resorted to his executive action.

While still politically divisive, immigration has become less of a problem in recent years as a practical matter. President Obama noted in 2011 that his administration had improved border security by "putting more boots on the southern border than at any time in our history, and reducing illegal crossings to their lowest level in forty years." CNN fact-checked these claims and gave them a thumbs-up.[56] Such statistics should please conservatives, even if they don't fit a preconceived idea of Obama as soft on immigration. But one statistic shouldn't please anybody: in the same year the president made that statement about border security, more than forty-six thousand parents of U.S. citizen children were deported.[57] Deportations have surged in the past decade, tearing apart families and destabilizing communities.

Which is why the Obama administration reformed its immigration enforcement policies while Congress dilly-dallies. Dispatching the slogan "deport felons, not families," the White House directed all Homeland Security officers be trained in priorities for enforcement.[58] The administration wasn't so preoccupied with trying to deport every undocumented immigrant who might be working hard as a busboy or hotel housekeeper. And why should it be? Imagine the state of the American bedsheet if our high school kids were the only ones tasked with delousing them. Every president must prioritize who gets deported. In 1987, after Congress passed an amnesty bill that he signed,

President Reagan acted unilaterally to give deportation protection to the children of newly legalized immigrants. Four years later, husbands and wives of those immigrants would receive protection with an executive action by President George H. W. Bush.[59] Since 1956, every single U.S. president has used executive action to offer deportation protection to some group of immigrants or another.[60]

There is a fundamental legal idea behind all these presidents acting independently of Congress on the immigration issue. It's called "prosecutorial discretion." It is the reason most legal experts argue President Obama's executive action (and those of previous presidents) is neither "illegal" nor "unconstitutional."

Even some of the most conservative legal minds agree. A recent gathering of the Federalist Society drew conservative lawyers from all over the country. The main attractions were appearances by two of the most conservative members of the Supreme Court at the time: Antonin Scalia and Samuel Alito. John Baker Jr., a Georgetown law professor who once accused President Obama of trying to "destabilize the republic," acknowledged the historical importance of granting the chief executive latitude in the execution of the nation's laws. Baker explained, "If Congress wants to restrain the discretion of the president, they are supposed to do what the separation of powers encourages them to do: write the statute tightly so that it will be actually administered the way you want it administered." Christopher Schroeder, a conservative professor at Duke Law School, beat back the suggestion that President Obama's executive action could be illegal solely because it protected a greater number of immigrants than either Reagan's or Bush's action. After conceding it might make many conservatives "uncomfortable" with the legal reality, Schroeder said, "I don't know where in the Constitution there is a rule that if the president's enactment affects too many people, he's violating the Constitution." He concluded, "The roots of prosecutorial discretion are extremely deep."[61]

According to a report by the nonpartisan Congressional Research Service, "the executive branch's authority to exercise prosecutorial or enforcement discretion has traditionally been understood to arise from the Constitution."[62] In other words, detractors have it backwards. President Obama's power to "deport felons, not families" isn't unconstitutional. That power *derives directly from* the Constitution.

So, maybe President Obama's executive action isn't illegal. But it's still going to cost taxpayers a fortune when immigrants start claiming government benefits, right? After all, that Heritage Foundation report concluded taxpayers would foot the $2 trillion costs for things like food stamps, welfare, and public health insurance. It would be a troubling conclusion except for the fact that Obama's executive action doesn't grant undocumented immigrants access to these services in the first place.[63] Conservative economist Stephen Moore, the man who would later become the Heritage Foundation's own chief economist, told Fox News the report "leaves the impression" that "immigrants are a cost to the economy. That is one thing almost all economists disagree with."[64] The conservative Cato Institute criticized the report, noting that a "flawed methodology produced a grossly exaggerated cost to federal taxpayers of legalizing unauthorized immigrants while undercounting or discounting their positive tax and economic contributions."[65] Haley Barbour, the Republican former governor of Mississippi, characterized the report more bluntly: "It's a political document. It's not serious analysis."[66]

President Obama's immigration action, if it is upheld by the courts, will be a boon, not a burden, for the economy. According to one analysis, when immigrants are able to work legally, they gain access to new jobs that pay fairer wages, which, in turn, increases the amount of money they inject into the economy through spending more and paying more in taxes. This analysis estimates that, over the next ten years, President Obama's immigration executive order will create nearly thirty thousand jobs for *all* Americans and increase the country's gross domestic product (GDP) by $230 billion.[67] A report by the president's Council of Economic Advisers put the GDP growth at a more conservative $90 billion but predicted the labor force participation would increase by 150,000 workers during the same ten-year period.[68] Whatever the particulars, the consensus among economists is that immigration reform—whether through legislation or executive action—will have a positive economic impact.

Reader, I want to let you in on a little secret. The Republican Party knows this and actually wants immigration reform too. It's something well known among political insiders. You'd never know this by listening to Republican rhetoric though. Whether it's Donald Trump making incendiary comments about Mexicans, Marco Rubio's disavowal of the Gang of Eight Senate bill he helped negotiate, or Jeb Bush recanting his previous support for granting current immigrants "legal status,"[69] all of the 2016 Republican primary election candidates were beholden to the most xenophobic tendencies of their party. Republicans will proudly tell you they're the party of fiscal responsibility and then privately admit the sloppiness of our immigration laws are fiscally irresponsible. They see the changing demographics of the electorate. The number of eligible voters who identify as Latino is climbing rapidly. Two days after Barack Obama won reelection over Mitt

Romney with 70 percent of the Latino vote, Sean Hannity took to the radio airwaves and announced he had "evolved" on the immigration issue.[70] After reiterating his support for a more secure border, Hannity, who for years had said we needed to deport "illegals," humbly proposed a new plan in which "you create a pathway for those people that are here—you don't say you've got to go home."

This isn't just a crass political calculation for Republicans, though. For many of them—as for Americans of all kinds and creeds— immigration reform is a moral imperative. Evangelical Christian pastors, for whom immigration is an urgent humanitarian issue, are among the most outspoken supporters of immigration reform.[71] They understand many immigrants who seek refuge in the United States have fled unimaginable living conditions. They sought economic opportunity when all they had known was coercion and stagnation. They sought religious freedom and social justice when all they had known was oppression. When all they had known was a regime led by an actual, factual dictator, they had succeeded, if only for the time being, in seeking out a political system led by a president of a democracy.

2

—

THE
SOCIALIST

—

Before President Obama was, in the eyes of his critics, a dictator, he was a socialist. One congressman even boasted in a fund-raising letter of being "the first Member of Congress to call [President Obama] a socialist."[1] Many saw the president's desire to improve public education, strengthen labor unions, and achieve universal health care as symptoms of a secret ideological commitment to Marxist-Leninist policies. The president's calls to "level the playing field" or require wealthy Americans "pay their fair share" in taxes weren't nods to equal opportunity or commonsense tax reform, they were socialist slogans intended to overthrow capitalism and get the working class to take back the means of production!

President Obama has been called a lot of names, but "socialist" seemed to be the epithet du jour during his first term. By the time the 2012 reelection campaign rolled around, Republican also-rans Michele Bachmann, Rick Perry and Newt Gingrich seemingly coordinated their name-calling strategies: they all invoked the slur to describe the president and his policies.[2] Even Mitt Romney, who sought to keep above the fray during the campaign, couldn't help himself. He wrote in his campaign book, *No Apology*, "It is an often remarked-upon irony that at a time when Europe is moving away from socialism and its many failures, President Obama is moving us toward that direction."[3]

It was at a campaign rally in Roanoke, Virginia, in the summer of 2012, when President Obama really stepped in it. While making a point about the importance of public education and public infrastructure, Obama described success as a product of more than intelligence and hard work. In contrast to Republicans who regularly romanticized "rugged individualism," the president spoke of "wealthy, successful Americans who agree with me" and who know they "didn't get there on their own." They profited from the mentorship of a good teacher or the easy movement of goods and services enabled by modern infrastructure. "Somebody invested in roads and bridges. If you've got a business—you didn't build that. . . . The point is, is that, when we succeed, we succeed because of our individual initiative, but also because we do things together."[4]

But that final point got lost. Did the president just say business owners hadn't built their own businesses? To the millions of people watching attack ads produced by the Romney campaign or Karl Rove's political action committee, it would seem so. Because those ads took the "if you've got a business, you didn't build that" quote out of context and ran it incessantly. The White House tried to clarify that, in his off-the-cuff remarks, the president referred to the roads and bridges.[5] But it was too late. The sound bite meshed too well with the Obama-as-socialist meme.

Calling a progressive politician a "socialist" is hardly an original move. When Franklin Roosevelt passed Social Security in the 1930s, they labeled him a socialist. A generation later, conservatives would hurl the term at Lyndon Johnson for helping to create Medicare. Long before, Horace Greeley, the abolitionist editor of the *New York Tribune,* was dubbed a "socialist" by his proslavery opponents before the Civil War.[6] One could say we have a rich tradition of dismissing progressive political ideas as "socialist." Or one could say it's a poor tradition. Or one could say we should abolish such distinctions between "rich" and "poor" and assert that this tradition lacks class.

EXPANSION OF THE FEDERAL GOVERNMENT

THE CHARGE

President Obama is just another tax-and-spend liberal who wants to expand the size and scope of the federal government. He thinks government is the solution to, rather than the cause of, society's problems. So he's beefed up regulations and rolled out the red tape in a way that cripples innovation and crushes the spirit of capitalism. Obama inherited an economy in decline, but he could have improved the pace and performance of economic recovery if he hadn't initiated so much government spending and hired so many more government workers. As Paul Ryan wrote on his website, the president has "doubled the size of government since he took office." This rapid growth in spending drives up annual budget deficits that contribute to the national debt.

THE REALITY

Three years into his presidency, Barack Obama became the first president since Ronald Reagan to reduce the number of government jobs[7] and the first president since Richard Nixon to actually oversee a reduction in the size of the government sector of the economy.[8] Allow that to sink in. Critics will counter the president took office amid an historic recession, and it was *state and local governments* which shed jobs in order to balance budgets. *That's* what accounts for these statistics, not some super smart strategy to make government more lean and efficient! Well, both of these factors played a part. Significant personnel cutbacks have occurred at the federal level as well, and the president has consolidated federal agencies to reduce the size of government.[9] Paul Ryan's above-mentioned claim the president actually "doubled the size of government" relied on out-of-date data and faulty calculations and the nonpartisan fact-checking website PolitiFact gave Ryan the distinction of "Pants on Fire" (as in, "Liar, liar . . .").[10] It was quietly removed from Congressman Ryan's website shortly after this public scolding. Still no word from PolitiFact on whether Ryan still owns those singed khakis.

The shrinkage of the government sector isn't all good news. Public sector employees include firefighters and teachers and local environmental officials, all of whom make valuable contributions to our society and to our economy. But it does dispel the conservative criticism that President Obama has increased the size of government.[11]

Maybe the number of government employees has decreased, but surely this president has sought to pay for his socialist agenda by ramping up the rate of government spending, right? Wrong. Under President Obama, federal spending has increased more slowly than at any time since the 1950s.[12]

There are two ways economists typically measure government spending: as a percentage of GDP (the country's total economic output) or as a per capita calculation (spending per person). The first measurement accounts for fluctuations in the economy as a whole and the second accounts for population growth. By either of these metrics, the Obama administration has been extraordinarily frugal. Spending on domestic and defense programs—aka "discretionary spending"—has steadily declined as a percentage of GDP since 2010. That's when the economic stimulus peaked federal spending at 9.1 percent of GDP (a rate that's not much higher than the forty-year average of 8.4 percent). The government now spends significantly less than that long-term average. The Congressional Budget Office projects within six years spending will drop to 5.3 percent of GDP.[13] As for the annual growth in government spending per capita? The Obama administration has kept it below 2 percent.[14] The only other president to have achieved such fiscal restraint in the past forty-five years? Bill Clinton. You know, the guy we always think fondly of as the president with so much restraint.

So, what about that enormous budget deficit? The president has in fact cut the annual budget deficit by two-thirds since he first took office in 2009. In that year, amid the height of the Great Recession, the U.S. government spent nearly $1.5 trillion more than it took in through tax revenue. The amount of the annual shortfall has decreased every single year of the Obama presidency and by 2015 it was down to $439 billion (which is on par with prerecession levels).[15] As Treasury Secretary Jack Lew pointed out, "The president's policies and a strengthening U.S. economy have resulted in a reduction of the U.S. budget deficit of approximately two-thirds—the fastest sustained deficit reduction since World War II."

Upon close inspection, President Obama has even defied the stereotype that he's in love with government regulation. Sure, he's used regulatory authority to curb carbon pollution and offer new protections to hospital patients. But the Obama administration has also sought to rollback senseless or duplicative regulation. In 2011, Obama issued two executive orders requiring government agencies to review all their rules and develop plans to reform them.[16] As a result of this, the Department of Agriculture will streamline poultry inspections, saving taxpayers $1 billion. The Department of Health and Human Services proposes a reduction on unnecessary paperwork for hospitals which will save us $5 billion. Obama's regulatory czar Cass Sunstein wrote in the *Chicago Tribune* that the number of rules issued by federal agencies during the first three years of the Obama administration "was actually lower than during the first three years of the Bush administration."[17] The president hasn't proved to be such a heavy-handed regulator after all.

It's unclear how Comrade Obama can continue to be accused of trying to centralize and expand the role of government when, under his watch: government jobs have declined, government spending has slowed, government deficits have shrunk, and government regulations have decreased. George Orwell used the word *doublespeak* to refer to language that inverts the actual meaning of words and is designed to confuse the public. He used the term mostly to criticize the propaganda of the Soviet socialist regime. Directed at Obama, Orwell might have found the use of the term "socialist" as, itself, an example of doublespeak too.

—

NATIONALIZING BANKS
THE CHARGE

When the financial crisis hit, the president and his economic advisers actively debated having the government take over and nationalize large banks like Citigroup and Bank of America. However, administration officials were too afraid this move would reveal their socialist ideologies, so they decided to continue the Bush administration's bank bailouts via the Troubled Asset Relief Program. In continuing TARP, which was basically corporate welfare run amok, the Obama administration rewarded the big banks that caused the financial crisis and stuck taxpayers with the bill. They might as well have nationalized the banking sector, since the bailouts were coupled with burdensome financial regulation and banks struggle to keep up with the paperwork. Scott Tipton, a Republican congressman from Colorado, complained many local bank workers "feel they are no longer working as a banker, but they're working for the federal government."[18]

THE REALITY

Flashback to the winter of 2009. The financial crisis is in full swing. Hundreds of billions of dollars have been injected into the banks to try to jump-start the economy, but the banks aren't lending. Paul Krugman, a Nobel Prize-winning economist and columnist, calls the bailed-out banks "wards of the state" and insists an "explicit, though temporary, government takeover" of the banking sector is "the obvious solution" to our financial sector woes.[19] Support for nationalizing banks seems to grow. A Harvard professor, writing for the *New York Times* website, reminds us the British and Irish governments "have nationalized huge swaths of their financial systems" and even Ronald Reagan nationalized one of the largest American banks and hundreds of smaller ones.[20]

Barack Obama has just begun his first year as president and he is huddling up with his economic advisers. Tim Geithner is the new Treasury secretary and Geithner's old mentor, Larry Summers, is the head of the president's National Economic Council. The three men are attuned to the public frustration with the banks. Bank employees continue to receive extravagant bonuses even while they are pinching pennies with borrowers. According to a book that Geithner would publish later, Summers did urge Obama to nationalize big banks or publicly shame them into decreasing their bonuses.[21] Geithner, and ultimately Obama, disagreed with nationalizing these insolvent "zombie" banks. They opted instead to require banks to undergo "stress tests" to ensure their ability to protect taxpayer dollars as they continued to compete in the marketplace.[22]

When asked by Terry Moran of ABC News why he opposed nationalizing the banks, the president responded with a tale of two countries. Both Japan and Sweden had gone through financial crises in recent years, the president recounted. Japan's government "kept on pumping money in" to its financial sector and experienced no growth. Conversely, Sweden nationalized its banks and was back in business within a few years. The president would have seemed to be making the case for nationalization. Until he drew this important distinction: "Sweden had like five banks. We've got thousands of banks. You know, the scale of the U.S. economy and the capital markets are so vast . . . our assessment was that it wouldn't make sense." Lest anyone still think the president harbored an anticapitalist ideology, it's worth sharing what Obama said next: "Obviously, Sweden has a different set of cultures in terms of how the government relates to markets and America's different. And we want to retain a strong sense of that private capital fulfilling the core investment needs of this country."[23] So much for the president's European-style socialist tendencies!

Reasonable minds can and likely will always disagree about what kind of precedent is set when the government bails out certain industries amid desperate times. The bipartisan Dodd-Frank financial reform law that was passed in 2010 outlaws government-funded bailouts going forward. But serious economists of all political stripes agreed the systemic problems facing the banking industry would have spelled economic catastrophe if the government hadn't stepped in with its short-term loans to help the banks stay afloat. Ronald Reagan once joked "the nine most terrifying words in the English language are: I'm from the government and I'm here to help."[24] Amid the banking industry meltdown, these nine words didn't seem so terrifying after all.

When President Bush enacted the TARP program in 2008, it authorized $700 billion to be spent in cleaning up toxic assets. In the end, roughly $425 billion of that was actually disbursed with about $245 billion going to banks. This is still an enormous figure, and some outrage ensued when "Big Government" came to the rescue of "Big Banks" while ordinary citizens were losing their life savings to the stock market nosedive or losing their homes to widespread foreclosures. People took little consolation in the fact that the real estate market would stabilize and the stock market would rebound because of the bailout. This outrage would translate into the antigovernment activism of the Tea Party and the anticorporate activism of Occupy Wall Street.[25] And these two movements both polarized our political debates even while they both sprouted from the same populist, antiestablishment seeds.

Ultimately, the TARP program proved to be a profitable investment for taxpayers. Keeping in mind the $425 billion injected into private companies was intended merely to stabilize the economy and not necessarily yield a profit, it's impressive the government eventually reclaimed more than $440 billion through selling its shares and collecting interest payments. As President Obama told supporters at a reelection campaign stop in New Hampshire in 2012, "We got back every dime used to rescue the banks."[26]

According to the Brookings Institution's Doug Elliott, the benefits of TARP "in stabilizing the financial system and the economy as a whole were worth hundreds of billions of dollars, and yet it turned out to be essentially free." Elliott concluded TARP was the "best large federal program ever to be despised by the public."[27] The bank bailout might have been unpopular with both conservatives who loathed government intervention and liberals who lambasted "corporate welfare." But at a time when several mainstream economists and commentators, including at least one of his senior advisers, were encouraging

President Obama to turn insolvent banks into state-run enterprises, the president invested in a market-driven, capitalist—not socialist—solution. And it paid dividends.

—

THE UNACCOUNTABLE "CONSUMER PROTECTION" AGENCY

THE CHARGE

President Obama *did create* new regulation with the creation of the Consumer Financial Protection Bureau. According to Senator David Perdue (R-GA), the CFPB is a "rogue agency that dishes out malicious financial policy and creates new rules and regulations at whim without real congressional oversight."[28] There's no question the financial industry needs more accountability and maybe even a watchdog group. After all, deceptive lending practices played a huge role in precipitating the economic crisis. But the CFPB is a largely unaccountable agency with a budget that can't be controlled by Congress. Since it is situated within the Federal Reserve, which is independent of the White House, it doesn't even receive presidential oversight.

The CFPB was designed to do two things: help consumers and rein in big banks. Yet, as a result of its overzealous regulation, it has backfired on both fronts. The agency has restricted the availability of consumer credit and given a competitive advantage to the largest banks who, unlike smaller banks, can afford to comply with the regulation. This is why Senator Ted Cruz introduced legislation to abolish the CFPB, stating, "The only way to stop this runaway agency is by eliminating it altogether."[29]

THE REALITY

In the summer of 2007, an essay appeared in a little-known progressive quarterly journal called *Democracy*. It began:

> *It is impossible to buy a toaster that has a one-in-five chance of bursting into flames and burning down your house. But it is possible to refinance an existing home with a mortgage that has the same one-in-five chance of putting the family out on the street—and the mortgage won't even carry a disclosure of that fact to the homeowner.*[30]

The difference between the toaster and the mortgage? Regulation. According to the essay, "the 'R-word' supports a booming market in tangible consumer goods" but credit products are governed by an outmoded and disorganized set of federal and state laws.

The essay presaged the mortgage meltdown that would come to pass within the year. It began to circulate. When policymakers drew up the Dodd-Frank financial reform law in 2010, they modeled a new agency based on the description, in the essay, of a "financial product safety commission." A young Treasury Department official who helped to start up the agency, then located in the basement of his office building, passed out copies of the essay as a way to recruit new employees.[31] He was kind of like a nerdy, bureaucratic version of Thomas Paine trying to start a revolution on the frontiers of consumer finance.

The core idea of this essay had become a reality within just a few short years. Its author, a Harvard professor who'd fought against banking sector abuses for years behind the scenes, stepped into the spotlight. Elizabeth Warren suddenly became a star. She was the Obama administration's first choice to lead the newly created CFPB, but after Republicans in Congress signaled their refusal to confirm her, the White House settled on the more centrist former attorney general of Ohio, Richard Cordray. A model civil servant, Cordray once used the prize money from a winning streak on *Jeopardy* in the late 1980s to pay down his law school debts.[32] Warren, for her part, went on to win the U.S. Senate seat from Massachusetts once held by Ted Kennedy and has emerged as one of the most progressive voices within the Democratic Party.

Is the CFPB unaccountable to Congress and the president? Yes and no. It's funding is, by design, insulated from the political branches of government. Protected within the independent Federal Reserve, it is beyond the reach of the political influence of the financial services lobby that would, frankly, like to see it destroyed. The people who created the CFPB understood that the agency's beneficiaries (i.e., customers who'd been misled by their lenders) wouldn't stand a chance if they were at the mercy of the banking lobby's beneficiaries (i.e., members of Congress who receive generous campaign contributions).

While its funding is independent of Congress, the CFPB's director must be approved by the Senate. Its operating budget is tied to a flat figure from the Fed. Any new regulations must receive public responses before they can go into effect. Any overreaching regulation can be challenged in the courts. It is the only banking regulator to be subject to veto power by the Treasury Department's Financial Stability Oversight Council and required to submit semiannual reports to Congress. In short, "The CFPB is subject to more oversight than any other banking regulator."[33]

What about the charge the agency actually hurts small banks that can't afford to keep up with the regulation? It's a myth. Banks and credit unions with less than $10 billion in assets are exempt from CFPB supervision. Not only are they free from CFPB regulation, but they are also actively protected from other regulatory agencies by the CFPB. Part of the CFPB mandate is to identify "unduly burdensome regulations" facing smaller banks. It does this by persuading state regulators to minimize unnecessary rules and red tape.[34]

In the aftermath of the financial crisis, many Americans opened their credit card statements with a sense of dull dread. They knew they were responsible for the debt they took on and they knew there wasn't much that could be done about interest rates jumping up on them. Many people who had defaulted on their credit cards were prepared to deal with the consequences. But they couldn't have imagined those consequences would include their bank selling their debt to third parties that would use illegal tactics to track them down or go after the incorrect balances. But that's exactly what happened to some customers of JPMorgan Chase, which basically stopped one step short of selling their debt to the mob. Working with the attorneys general of forty-seven states and the District of Columbia, the CFPB curbed this behavior and compelled Chase to refund its customers at least $50 million and permanently halt collections on half a million accounts.[35]

The CFPB also went after Corinthian College, the for-profit college chain that is widely suspected of issuing predatory student loans and granting worthless degrees. Corinthian's slogan might as well have been "Student loan debt without the hassle of education!" Teaming up with the Department of Education, the CFPB secured roughly $480 million in debt relief for Corinthian's swindled students.[36] In all, CFPB's enforcement activity has yielded more than $10 billion for American consumers.[37]

The real value of the agency extends beyond the restitution it secures for the victims of bad lending and collection practices. The value exists in the assurance it gives consumers that markets operate in an honest and fair way. By policing abusive and irresponsible lenders, and rooting out unscrupulous practices which could otherwise infect the credit markets again, the CFPB makes America safe for consumerism. Not exactly what neo-Marxists dream about.

—

GOVERNMENT HANDOUTS RUN AMOK

THE CHARGE

President Obama has become the "food stamp president," doling out ever more government freebies and undermining the longstanding American ethic of self-reliance. In the 1990s, Bill Clinton and Republican lawmakers struck a compromise to reform welfare and incentivize its recipients to get back to work. President Obama, however, put forward a plan to, in the words of a Romney campaign advertisement, "gut welfare reform by dropping work requirements." In an Obama administration, being poor is an extravagance! Not only do you get to cash your welfare check and have taxpayers foot your grocery bill, but the government will also kick in a cell phone—aka an "Obamaphone"—free of charge! Why would anyone bother to work?

THE REALITY

People who aren't poor often have a caricaturized impression of people who are. Despite the fact that the majority of welfare and food stamp recipients are white,[38] often living in rural or suburban areas, the Reagan-era motif of the Cadillac-driving "welfare queen" persists. More recently, video footage of the "Obamaphone lady" made its way around right-wing media outlets. There's a certain glee with which Republicans tout the video, which zooms in on an overweight African American woman exclaiming "everybody in Cleveland got an Obamaphone. . . . Keep Obama in president, he gave us a phone [sic]!"[39] The way in which the anecdote was cited as evidence of political patronage had grim racial overtones. A Tea Party campaign ad used the clip to suggest the Obama administration had "enslaved Americans."[40]

Still, regardless of the ugly identity politics surrounding this issue, why is President Obama wasting our tax dollars to pay for poor people's cell phones? He's not. The federal program that subsidizes landline phone service for low-income people is called Lifeline and it was created in 1984 under President Reagan and expanded under President Clinton in the 1996 telecommunications law.[41] In the last year of the Bush administration, the Lifeline program branched out to include cell phone service.[42] The funding for it comes not from tax dollars, but from the cell phone companies themselves (which sometimes pass the cost along to their customers as a separate fee).[43]

The Telecommunications Act of 1996 created a "universal service" mandate designed to "ensure all Americans, including low-income consumers and those who live in rural, insular, high cost areas, shall have affordable service and [to] help to connect eligible schools, libraries, and rural health care providers to the global telecommunications network."[44] The so-called Obamaphone program, which actually started under Bush, was designed to make sure people living in rural or urban areas can call their doctor if they're sick or be reached if their kid's school needs to get in touch. We've long acknowledged access to advanced information services is an integral part of modern life. The 1996 law took its precedent for "universal service" from the Telecommunications Act of 1934, passed under President Franklin Roosevelt, which was, in turn, an outgrowth of an agreement reached between the telecommunications industry and President Woodrow Wilson.

So why are these phones associated with Obama instead of Woodrow Wilson or, for that matter, George Bush? I've been told it has something to do with those spammy Internet advertisements (you know the ones: "Obama wants you to refinance your mortgage" or "Cut your credit card debt with a special law Obama passed"). Apparently, phony promotions and pop-up ads are what informs our political debates these days.

When food stamp rolls more than doubled between 2008 ($38 billion) and 2013 ($80 billion),[45] critics of the program suggest its expansion should be blamed on mismanagement. Representative Rick Crawford (R-AR) said, "Throughout the Obama presidency, we've seen the food stamp program grow exponentially because the government continues to turn a blind eye to a system fraught with abuse."[46]

A more clear-eyed analysis would account for another variable, something that occurred between 2008 and 2013 . . . that pesky recession! As it happens, the growth in the number of people receiving food stamps tracks fairly closely with the growth of the number of people whose income is low enough to qualify for them (130 percent of the poverty level or below).[47] The Center on Budget and Policy Priorities found the steep rise and persistence in long-term unemployment also contributed to the increase in food stamps, since "workers who are unemployed for a long period are more likely to deplete their assets, exhaust unemployment insurance, and turn to [food stamps] for help."[48] In other words, many people turned to food stamps as a last resort. And what of the fraud and abuse? According to the most recent data available, increased oversight and the use of the more trackable electronic benefits transfer (EBT) cards have shrunk the fraud rate from 4 percent in the early 1990s to just 1 percent today.[49] Despite the media portrayals to the contrary, not everyone on food stamps is a beach bum buying lobster and sushi between catching their big waves.

Finally, we're left with the charge that the Obama administration gruesomely "gutted"—or, granted waivers for—the welfare work requirement. Does the federal government seriously want to promote government dependency by passing out welfare checks to people who aren't even trying to get a job? Of course not. What the Obama administration did is allow states more flexibility in distributing welfare as long as they show how their process will be a "more efficient or effective means to promote employment."[50] Welfare recipients are not receiving waivers that allow them to avoid job hunting as Mitt Romney insinuated. Instead, states receive waivers that allow them to adjust the work requirements (as long as they improve job placement overall) and avoid time-wasting paperwork and reporting requirements. This is why the Republican staffer who designed welfare reform and its work requirement "enthusiastically supports" the waivers.[51] He points out that, under the waiver program, states could incentivize welfare-to-work by cutting welfare checks to employers who hire welfare recipients instead of the recipient directly. State governors appreciate the flexibility, which is why twenty-nine Republican governors—*including Massachusetts governor Mitt Romney*—signed a letter in 2005 requesting precisely the type of waiver program that many of them are now criticizing.[52] After all, it wouldn't have been coming from a socialist president back then.

SOCIALIZING EDUCATION

THE CHARGE

President Obama has spent a lot of time in schools, both as a student and then as a law school lecturer. So it's no surprise he has strong opinions about education. But his education initiatives smack of a federal government takeover. The Common Core standards have imposed a national curriculum on local schools, which is a hassle for teachers and students alike. This is why Louisiana's governor, Bobby Jindal, has sued the Obama administration, insisting it has "hijacked and destroyed the Common Core initiative."[53] And Senator Ted Cruz is on the record saying, "We need to repeal every word of Common Core."[54]

The president's administration has been intruding into higher education as well. Senator Tom Cotton (R-AR) pointed out how the

Obamacare bill was coupled with a lesser-known bill that overhauled the student loan program and thus "Obamacare nationalized the student loan industry."[55] If that wasn't enough, the president unveiled a plan to make community college "free" for two years. We all know nothing is free. The president's plan would use $60 billion of federal tax dollars to cover 75 percent of the tuition costs and pressure the states to foot the remainder. This is just one more of Obama's schemes to redistribute wealth in this country.

THE REALITY

Let's take a look at these three accusations—Common Core, nationalizing student loans, and free community college—one at a time.

Ted Cruz has repeatedly called for a "repeal" of Common Core, which his spokeswoman describes as "a federally created curriculum that the state's 'Race to the Top' grants are tied to."[56] Here's the thing: Common Core is neither a law (so it can't be "repealed"), nor was it "federally created" (governors and top education experts in forty-eight states developed the initiative),[57] nor is it an actual "curriculum" (it's a set of basic standards for what students should know in math and "English language arts"—reading and writing—at each grade level).[58]

The Department of Education's Race to the Top Initiative, which granted $4 billion to nineteen states that committed to improving their schools, gave credit to those states that voluntarily adopted common standards. But out of 500 points on their application, a mere 40 were related to collaborating to create some set of shared standards across state lines.[59] As Education Secretary Arne Duncan explained:

At the time, no one knew how many groups of states would come together to create their own set of common standards. It turned out to be one big group of 46—but it could have been several, or even many, groups of states uniting around different sets of standards. So this notion of our pushing for one set of standards was never correct. In fact, we were totally agnostic on the number of state consortia. We just didn't want 50 states to continue to work in complete isolation from each other.[60]

A set of Common Core standards was ultimately the happy by-product of, not a requirement for, the competition for the Race to the Top grants.

Common Core promises to unify the learning outcomes of kids across the country, and arm students in Mississippi with the same basic knowledge as students in Massachusetts. Yet it has been viciously attacked by the left as well as the right. While conservatives see it as an unwarranted imposition by the federal government, liberals fear it will cripple creativity in the classroom and tie teacher evaluations to test scores.[61] Most of the criticism, as well as the anxiety of teachers and confusion of parents, is caught up in a whirlwind of myths and misperceptions.

As the debate over Common Core began to heat up within Republican primary campaign, Chris Wallace, the host of *Fox News Sunday*, hosted a debate between Bill Bennett, a Common Core supporter who served as President Reagan's secretary of education, and the Republican governor of Texas Greg Abbott. Texas is one of the few states not to adopt Common Core, and Abbott has been a fierce critic. Bennett, who had started off the debate acknowledging there were a lot of wacky conspiracy theories floating around ("... that it requires teaching of Islamic radicalism, you have to read all of Barack Obama's speeches . . .") became exasperated after Governor Abbott told viewers to Google certain words to see how Common Core taught addition (the query directs to a right-wing website). Bennett's response would serve as good advice for anyone who cares about this issue:

> *It's an easy way to resolve this. . . . Here is what you can really do. Download the standards themselves. The common core standards . . . Not what someone said the standards were. Not what Google reported. Not what some citizens group decided was common core, but the actual standards themselves. They are public. And anybody can examine those standards. You tell me what's wrong with saying, kids should learn how to parse and diagram sentences, memorize, read the Declaration of Independence. That's what I want to know.*[62]

You too can view the standards here: www.corestandards.org/read-the-standards/. I think you'll agree that one would have to be trying pretty hard to find some cause for controversy.

Let's move on to higher education. What about the fact Obama weaseled a government takeover of the student loan industry into the Obamacare legislation? Not so. Students can continue to get private education loans from private banks. The Obama administration simply took the federal student loan program (which has been a government program since its inception in 1965) and cut out private lenders that effectively acted as middlemen between students and the government agencies that guaranteed their loans.[63] Previously, the government—and, by extension, the taxpayers—were bearing the loan program's risks without benefiting from its rewards. By replacing guaranteed loans with direct loans, President Obama will have saved, according to the Congressional Budget Office, $61 billion through-out the decade.[64] Of that savings, $36 billion will go to increases in Pell Grants to low-income students and more than $10 billion will help reduce the deficit.[65] You can say the government is taking over a student loan program that was serviced by private lenders. Or you could more accurately say the government has kicked aside the private lenders that were intercepting the profits of what was already the gov-ernment's own student loan program.

Some people who support the administration's restructuring of the student loan program still balk at the idea of government bankroll-ing a community college "free for all." Sure, we have a national interest in improving technical skills and job readiness, and of course students are drowning in student loan debt. But is another government hand-out, at a price tag of $6 billion a year, the answer? Why don't we leave the management of community colleges to cities and states? These are fair questions, which the president and his team will have to address in their final attempts to get their plan funded. Although the federal government wouldn't be "managing" community college, it would in-centivize states to participate in the program by offering 75 percent of the tuition costs and requiring states to kick in the other 25 percent.

This arrangement is designed to do two things. First, it wants to get states to stop pulling money out of public education.[66] When the recession hit, states made steep cuts to community colleges and public universities, and they failed to restore funding during the recovery. By 2014, every state except Alaska and North Dakota still spent less per student than before the recession (23 percent less on average).[67] The community college plan gets states to invest in public higher educa-tion again. The second thing this arrangement does is ensure commu-nity colleges offer "occupational training programs with high graduation rates and lead to in-demand degrees and certificates."[68] In other words, it guarantees community colleges can show their students are actually able to get good jobs and that this investment pays off for the economy more generally. The president has already cracked down on for-profit colleges that lure students with glossy advertisements but then provide them with little more than outsize student loan debt.[69] When those students of expensive for-profit colleges go bankrupt, their government-backed student loan payments are picked up by taxpayers. By extending an ethic of accountability to community colleges and covering the tuition, the president would be simultaneously improving the value of community colleges, students' educational and professional opportunities, and the quality of the workforce as a whole.

Finally, it's worth noting that President Obama's plan wouldn't extend free community college to just poor people. Anybody could take advantage of it, from the middle-class middle-age guy who just got laid off and needs new job skills to the wealthy young woman who graduates from high school and wants to save her parents money before she parlays her community college degree into a four-year college. Part of the problem with community colleges is they attract mostly poor students (and programs that primarily service poor people are politically unpopular and poorly funded). But it wasn't always this way. Between 1982 and 2006, the proportion of affluent students attending community colleges dropped while the number of poor students rose. President Obama's plan would restore economic diversity on community college campuses and curb states from divesting public colleges, so all students have an equal opportunity to develop skills that help them compete in a modern, technology-driven, market-driven, nonsocialist economy.

3
—
THE
OUTSIDER
—

Who is this exotic character on the stage of the Democratic National Convention sweet-talking millions of television viewers about uniting our country? It says he's a senator but I've never seen his picture in the paper or read anything about him online. Is this a joke that his middle name is "Hussein"? We just captured Saddam Hussein six months ago! Any relation? And his last name rhymes with the first name of America's public enemy number one (Osama!). This guy gives a good speech—but he's come out of nowhere and now he's a big lefty star? Something's afoul.

People who had this reaction to Barack Obama's speech at the 2004 convention would find cognitive consonance in a press release sent out just two weeks after the speech, which informed us "Obama is a Muslim who has concealed his religion."[1] The information in the press release, though widely discredited by the mainstream press, instantly made the rounds among conservative pundits. It was amplified in dark corners of the Internet. Its author was a loony fellow who once ran for Congress in Connecticut (as a Democrat) who promised to "exterminate Jew power in America."[2] Still, right-wing radio hosts who were determined to stop this new liberal star from rising eagerly passed this anti-Semitic Obama-hater the microphone.

As Senator Obama planned a run for the presidency, a new crop of conspiracies was sown and harvested. This time, the scandal seekers took aim at Obama's nationality, not his religion. If he had not actually been born in Hawaii, then he would be disqualified from being president under the "natural born citizen" clause of the Constitution. What a tempting tale for starry-eyed conservatives: something that both confirms Obama is unqualified to be commander in chief *and* invokes the sacred text of the United States Constitution to say so? These accusations, like the attempts by billionaire blowhard and future presidential candidate Donald Trump, to suggest Obama faked his college degrees were all part of a pattern of political behavior that desperately and deceptively tried to delegitimize a president who reinvigorated the progressive movement.

The portrayal of Barack Obama as an "outsider" or a "stranger" fits into the conservative fantasy that someone so liberal, so wonky, and so cosmopolitan just couldn't represent America. This is the flip side of some of the liberal attacks on George Bush's legitimacy, in the wake of the 2000 recount, which were similarly propelled by the idea that someone so conservative, so folksy, and so provincial just couldn't represent America. The truth is, to paraphrase Walt Whitman,

America is large; it contains multitudes. Included in those multitudes are some beliefs about Barack Obama that are simply untethered to reality. Let us try to re-tether them.

—

BORN IN THE U.S.A.?

THE CHARGE

There's an e-mail circulating out there which shows President Obama was actually born in Kenya. Or, at least, there isn't any proof he was born in the United States. The "birther" movement might not have caught on with the mainstream media (which is totally in the bag for Obama), but 2016 Republican presidential candidate Donald Trump championed it. Speaking on NBC's *Today* show back in 2011, Trump said, "I [previously] thought he was probably born in this country. . . . Right now, I have some real doubts."[3] This is critical because, according to the Constitution, one must be a natural born citizen in order to be qualified for the presidency. The Obama campaign published a short-form copy of the birth certificate on their website, FightTheSmears.com, but it lacked an embossed seal and there were some signs it was produced by a laser printer. Laser printers didn't exist in 1961, when Obama was born.

THE REALITY

To a man who commits his career to the service of his community and then his country, the accusation he isn't even an American could be extraordinarily withering. Before we delve into and debunk the birther claims, President Obama's supporters can find comfort in Margaret Thatcher's reflection on the politics of personal destruction: "I always cheer up immensely if an attack is particularly wounding," she once said, "because I think, well, if they attack one personally, it means they have not a single political argument left."[4] As Donald Trump continues to demonstrate today, personal attacks are often the last resort (and retort!) for someone unequipped with substantive criticism.

And the birther campaign was nothing if it wasn't an attempt to attack Obama personally. One of the primary salesmen of suspicion was Jerome Corsi, once described as a "bizarro all-purpose conspiracy theorist and smear artist."[5] Corsi made a name for himself by adding fuel to the incendiary rumors about John Kerry's service in Vietnam. As the coauthor of one of the leading "swift boater" books, Corsi had a ready-made audience of conspiracy nuts prepared to buy whatever he was selling.

In an episode of Fox News' *Fox & Friends* three months before the 2008 election, host Steve Doocy told Corsi some people think he's trying to "swift boat" the Obama campaign just as he did the Kerry campaign. By this point the Obama camp had posted a copy of its boss's birth certificate on its website but had done little else to dignify the birthers' accusations with a response. Corsi, like a desperate poker player with nothing to lose but a losing hand, doubled down. "The campaign has a false, fake birth certificate posted on their website," he insisted. Incredulous, Doocy asked, "What do you mean they have a false birth certificate . . . couldn't it just be a State of Hawaii–produced duplicate?" Corsi responded, "No, there's been a good analysis of it on the Internet . . . it's a fake document."

Ah, the Internet. That bastion of dispassion. That reliable source of high-quality information and expert analysis. The truth is, as with many things discussed online, there *have* been good analyses of the birth certificate on the Internet alongside many hacky and hysterical analyses. The PolitiFact website has an entire section dedicated to expertly assessing birther claims[6] while a longtime designer of birth certificate printing systems has chosen to spend his retirement gleefully debunking birther conspiracies at his website ObamaConspiracy.org.

One actually authoritative source in this case is Chiyome Fukino, the Hawaiian official who was in charge of state health records when these rumors surfaced in 2008. Fukino recalls that Linda Lingle, the Republican governor of Hawaii (and, incidentally, a McCain supporter), wanted to make a public statement putting these rumors to rest, and so Lingle took Fukino with her to personally inspect the original records. Lingle publicly affirmed the document's validity in 2008. Yet, when the conspiracy theories wouldn't die, she again inspected the document and affirmed its validity in the following year. Two years later, after Donald Trump claimed in a television interview that "nobody has any information" about where the president was born, Fukino became exasperated. "It's kind of ludicrous at this point," she said.[7]

The whole thing would be amusing if it hadn't actually influenced so many people's beliefs. When asked in a poll whether "you believe that Barack Obama was born in the United States of America or not," more Republicans actually responded either "no" or "not sure" than responded "yes."[8] (No word on how many of those polled were aware Hawaii is a U.S. state.) Mark Twain once wrote "the history of our race, and each individual's experience, are sewn thick with evidences that a truth is not hard to kill, and that a lie well told is immortal."[9]

For his part, President Obama eventually developed a sense of serenity and humor amid the personal attacks. Back in 2007, he had reportedly given a "testy" response to a campaign official who, in the hope it would debunk conspiracy theories, asked him to personally sign a birth certificate request form. But by the 2011 White House Correspondents' Dinner, President Obama was in a more cheerful mood. The administration had just fulfilled Donald Trump's request to release the president's long-form birth certificate, and Obama gamely proposed the Donald could now "focus on more important matters like, did we fake the moon landing? What really happened in Roswell? And where are Biggie and Tupac?" With a nod to the insatiable appetite for documentation of his birth, Obama unveiled what he said would be a clip from his "birth video." Reporters were then treated to an excerpt from Disney's *The Lion King*, where Simba, the newborn African lion, is presented to the jungle. He clarified—or at least tried to—by saying, "That was a joke."[10]

—
HE DOESN'T LOVE AMERICA
THE CHARGE

Being born in America isn't a sufficient guarantee that someone will love his country. In the winter of 2015, Rudy Giuliani spoke at a private dinner in Manhattan in support of Wisconsin governor Scott Walker. In remarks that were recorded by *Politico*, the former mayor of New York City stated flatly, "I do not believe, and I know this is a horrible thing to say, but I do not believe that the president loves

America. . . . He wasn't brought up the way you were brought up and I was brought up through love of this country."[11] In the days that followed, Giuliani made the rounds on TV news explaining and defending this charge, accusing the president of "criticizing his country more than other presidents have done."[12] Writing in an op-ed in the *Wall Street Journal*, Giuliani would eventually relent on the mind-reading and heart-reading effort, instead asserting the president lacked "moral clarity" when, according to Giuliani, the president said "that American exceptionalism is no more exceptional than the exceptionalism of any other country."

THE REALITY

Throughout this book, I aim to factually refute conservative criticisms of Barack Obama. It's tricky to factually verify, however, the private feelings of a public person. That said, I think there's an overwhelming amount of circumstantial evidence to reassure readers President Obama does indeed love America. I mean, what's more American than throwing out the first pitch at a baseball game wearing mom jeans?

President Obama speaks interminably about his love for the United States and describes in great detail why he thinks it's exceptional. It's possible Republicans have averted their eyes from these public displays of affection, which offend their backward idea that progressivism and patriotism shouldn't mix. In "hundreds of speeches," President Obama has been unabashed in his love of country, calling the United States "the greatest democratic, economic, and military force for freedom and human dignity the world has ever known," asserting "we will not apologize for our way of life, nor will we waver in its defense," and affirming "I believe in American exceptionalism with every fiber of my being."[13] Pretty unequivocal stuff.

Giuliani's insistence the president spoke of American exceptionalism as "no more exceptional than the exceptionalism of any other country" is just wrong. Giuliani referred to a moment when the president politely said, at a NATO summit in Strasbourg, France, surrounded by European leaders, "I believe in American exceptionalism, just as I suspect that the Brits believe in British exceptionalism and the Greeks believe in Greek exceptionalism."[14] The president's critics glommed onto this somewhat self-evident observation, accusing him of drawing a moral equivalence. They paid less attention to these off-the-cuff words that immediately followed:

I'm enormously proud of my country and its role and history in the world. If you think about the site of this summit and what it means, I don't think America should be embarrassed to see evidence of the sacrifices of our troops, the enormous amount of resources that were put into Europe postwar, and our leadership in crafting an Alliance that ultimately led to the unification of Europe. We should take great pride in that. And if you think of our current situation, the United States remains the largest economy in the world. We have unmatched military capability. And I think that we have a core set of values that are enshrined in our Constitution, in our body of law, in our democratic practices, in our belief in free speech and equality, that, though imperfect, are exceptional.[15]

One fact checker highlighted Giuliani's faulty logic with an analogy tailor-made for the former mayor of New York: "A Yankees fan who admits a Red Sox fan loves his team is not saying the Red Sox are as good as the Yankees."[16]

Conservatives' suspicion of the president's patriotism might have a lot more to do with style rather than with substance. The president is a gifted public speaker, something even many conservatives concede. However, conservatives interpret his skillful use of the English language not as a reflection of clear thinking and passionate advocacy but rather as some kind of verbal sorcery. In this account, plain language reveals while lofty oratory conceals. And after several recent presidents who've self-consciously cultivated a folksy communication style, a president who has a knack for grandiloquence is a curious thing. Sam Leith, the author of a recent book on rhetoric, suggests President Obama's "high style" has led some to regard his patriotism as a put-on, even if the style is consistent with the rhetorical traditions of some of our best presidents. Leith writes, "Rhetoric that declares itself so obviously as rhetoric is vulnerable to attack: it can be made to look self-indulgent, theatrical, and insincere—all charges that have been leveled and continue to be leveled against Obama."[17]

When Mayor Giuliani claimed the president "doesn't love" America, the White House staff understandably resisted the urge to respond. They were smart enough to know that, when presidents negate an argument, they run the risk of unduly amplifying it. When Richard Nixon famously said "I am not a crook," the main thing that stuck in people's memories was the word *crook* and the image of Nixon's scowl. When Bill Clinton looked into the camera and said "I did not have sexual relations with that woman," people remember the president of the United States uttering the phrase "sexual relations." So the White House didn't confront the charges head-on. Instead, spokesman Josh

Earnest told reporters he agreed with Rudy Giuliani on one part of his statement: it was "a horrible thing to say."[18]

REJECTION OF JUDEO-CHRISTIAN VALUES

THE CHARGE

President Obama is not a true Christian and we even have reason to suspect he could be disguising a secret Muslim faith. After all, Obama's father was a Muslim and his stepfather, Lolo Soetoro, with whom he lived when he was young, was Muslim (even if he didn't practice). Regardless of his own personal religious beliefs, President Obama has continuously threatened the Judeo-Christian values that make this nation great. At the beginning of his presidency, while traveling in Turkey, he even said "we do not consider ourselves a Christian nation."[19] Toward the end of his presidency, at the National Prayer Breakfast, President Obama rightly lambasted ISIS and other terrorist groups for debasing the Islamic faith, but then made an awful moral equivalence when he said, "lest we get on our high horse, [remember that] people committed terrible deeds in the name of Christ." Comments like these have earned him the criticism of religious conservatives. In a conference call with evangelical voters in 2012, vice presidential candidate Paul Ryan concluded that President Obama was taking America down a "dangerous path" that compromises our "Judeo-Christian, Western civilization values."[20]

THE REALITY

At a town hall rally in 2008, when John McCain was campaigning against Barack Obama, the McCain supporters were getting anxious. One man said he was "scared" of the prospect of an Obama presidency. "You don't have to be scared," McCain reassured. McCain called on a woman who hauntedly stammered, "I can't trust Obama. I've read about him and he's not, he's not uh—he's an Arab." McCain shook his head and took the microphone back from her. "No, ma'am. He's a decent family man [and] citizen that I just happen to have disagreements with on fundamental issues and that's what this campaign's all about. He's not [an Arab]." The crowd booed.[21]

McCain had a personal reason for sticking up for his political rival. When he campaigned against George W. Bush for the Republican presidential nomination eight years earlier, it was McCain who had been the target of a race-based smear campaign. Before the era of Internet rumors, there were paper flyers and automated phone calls which accused McCain of having an extramarital affair and fathering a dark-skinned daughter out of wedlock.[22] A professor at Bob Jones University, a fundamentalist college which, at the time, had a ban on interracial dating, sent out an e-mail insisting Senator McCain had "chosen to sire children without marriage." The contemptible lie was based on a commendable reality: the McCains had adopted their youngest daughter, Bridget, from an orphanage in Bangladesh. Still, the damage had been done. Karl Rove and the Bush campaign denied involvement in the smear campaign, which was launched right before the South Carolina primary. It effectively stirred the racial prejudices of broad swaths of southern conservatives, and helped Bush defeat McCain in the primaries.

The smear campaign that targeted President Obama commenced even before he ran for the presidency. Shortly after his speech at the Democratic National Convention in 2004, a press release was circulated online claiming that Obama was secretly Muslim. The release was authored by an eccentric fellow named Andy Martin, whom the *New York Times* described as "a prodigious filer of lawsuits . . . [who has] made unsuccessful attempts to win public office for both parties in three states, as well as for president at least twice, in 1988 and 2000."[23] Despite the claim's unreliable source, it spread like wildfire online and, like the smear against McCain, capitalized on the racial prejudice of some and the political ignorance of others.

The idea that Obama, who quotes the Bible like it's going out of style, is a secret Muslim is bonkers. But these days, and among some people, even bonkers ideas can be believable. A political scientist conducted a survey in 2014 and found that, when asked to choose the "deep down" religious beliefs of the president, 54 percent of Republican respondents selected "Muslim."[24] Oddly enough, Obama wasn't the first American president to be the subject of an anti-Islamic smear campaign. In the election of 1800, Thomas Jefferson had been accused of being a Muslim. The *Connecticut Courant* complained nobody could tell "whether Mr. Jefferson believes in the heathen mythology or in the alcoran [Quran]; whether he is a Jew or a Christian; whether he believes in one God, or in many; or in none at all."[25] In Jefferson's case, at least, the criticism was animated by our founding father's unorthodox religious views and not just by *his* silly sounding middle name: Thomas Qaddafi Jefferson. I kid, I kid. Jefferson didn't actually have a middle name (and so was saved the potential for embarrassment).

Clearly, common sense is being replaced by common nonsense.

The bigger problem is that this common nonsense is, in turn, spurring more high-profile nonsense by political leaders trying to pander to it. So we're left with a big old vacuous cycle. As one example, Dick Cheney couldn't bring himself to disabuse his conservative fan base of the idea that Saddam Hussein was involved in 9/11. The government's own investigation conclusively demonstrated there was no link whatsoever between Hussein and the 9/11 attackers. Yet Cheney, aware many Republicans continued to suspect a link, insisted a full decade later simply that we "were never able to confirm" one.[26]

This vacuous cycle has been fueling doubts about Barack Obama's religious beliefs as well. During his campaign for the Republican presidential nomination, Wisconsin governor Scott Walker was asked whether he thinks Obama is a Christian. It was a perfect moment to show some political courage and shed light on dark prejudices, as Senator McCain had done eight years earlier. Instead Walker capitulated to (and kept alive) those prejudices when he responded, "I don't know." His spokeswoman later clarified that "of course the governor thinks the president is a Christian" but complained the press focused too much on "gotcha questions."[27] We've apparently entered an era when questions about a president's religious identity (and national identity) are trick questions.

When the president spoke at the National Prayer Breakfast about how violent people use religions as an excuse for violence, he did not criticize those religions. He wasn't holding Islam accountable for the barbaric interpretation that ISIS uses to justify its ideology, nor did he hold Christianity accountable for the religious wars and racial subjugation that were carried out in its name. Any coolheaded reading of the speech would have understood the president spoke about the bad things people do to religion, not the bad things religions do to people. Yet not every head was so cool. Jim Gilmore, former governor of Virginia, called the remarks "the most offensive I've ever heard a president make in my lifetime" and added President Obama had "offended every believing Christian in the United States. This goes further to the point that Mr. Obama does not believe in America or the values we all share."[28] Perhaps Gilmore's outrage blinded him to the fact that he proved the president's point. By claiming to speak for "every" Christian and invoking religion to de-legitimate a political opponent, he demonstrated how some people still misuse religion as a tool for enmity rather than for empathy. In his speech, the president simply urged us to do the latter.

—

DIVISIVE RACIAL RHETORIC
THE CHARGE

America has come a long way since the civil rights movement fifty years ago. Our schools and our military are integrated, and mixed race marriages are increasingly common. A bevy of black Americans has achieved spectacular success in business, and many others have become popular culture icons. Heck, one even got himself elected president! But since Barack Obama stepped into the Oval Office, race relations in this country have deteriorated. From the public debates that rage around the Trayvon Martin case to the #BlackLivesMatter movement, Americans see the products of Obama's divisive racial politics piped into their living rooms on the nightly news. As a result, according to one Bloomberg Politics poll, a majority of Americans (and nearly half of black Americans) think race relations have actually gotten worse under the first black president.[29] According to one black conservative commentator, President Obama has been the "most racially divisive president" in modern times and has been doing the bidding of race agitators as the head of "the Al Sharpton presidency."[30] Instead of using the language of reconciliation and personal accountability, the president has used a language of victimhood and further fueled racial discord.

THE REALITY

One of the most effective things President Obama has done as America's first black president is abstain from focusing too much attention on issues of race. In doing so, he showed how a minority candidate could attract a majority of voters and, as president, equitably represent the interests of diverse constituencies. Once, when asked to respond to criticism he had not done enough to support black businesses, the president explained how his administration's programs have been targeted at *all* small business owners that have been "least able to get financing through conventional means" after first saying starkly, "I'm not the president of black America. I'm the president of the United States of America."[31] (You've got to admit, that's a pretty badass comeback.)

During his campaign, Obama didn't speak extensively about his painful personal experience with racial prejudice until he was nudged into a wide-ranging speech on the topic when racially tinged comments by his pastor, Jeremiah Wright, stirred up public controversy. In that speech, Barack Obama linked Reverend Wright's remarks with his own white grandmother's use of "racial or ethnic stereotypes that made me cringe." He explained, but did not excuse, the "bitterness and bias that make up the black experience in America."[32] He discussed, but did not display, the sense of anger and feelings of victimization felt by both black and white Americans when it comes to issues of race. It's often said in the recovery movement that the first step is admitting you have a problem. Barack Obama never suggested he could completely heal America's racial wounds, but he did have the clarity and humility to help us admit we had a problem.

Recent polls have indeed shown many Americans believe race relations have gotten worse in the past few years. Fortunately, these beliefs are misguided and have been inflated by a barrage of images of angry protesters in Missouri and spontaneous riots in Maryland. As is their custom, the news media have given more attention to these incendiary incidents than to the more banal, but important, indicators of racial progress. The same thing happened at the dawn of the age of television news. In the 1960s, after Lyndon Johnson promised to expand upon John F. Kennedy's civil rights programs, many black Americans were frustrated with continued discrimination and slow policy responses to peaceful protests. Race riots ensued. The news networks broadcast the most arresting images of these riots into suburban living rooms around the country and famously spurred a "white backlash" as the American people developed an exaggerated sense of the amount of racial discord in the country. These days, B-roll footage of the looting of a CVS building in downtown Baltimore is shown in an endless loop on cable news. If the cameraman were to zoom out, literally or metaphorically, we'd see the majority of Baltimore's black residents just trying to get by and live peaceful and prosperous lives against some pretty daunting odds.

Hardly anybody blamed Kennedy or Johnson for the Watts race riots but Obama hasn't received the same benefit of the doubt. From the moment the voters elected him, some conservatives saw this biracial president as the embodiment not of racial harmony, but of racial tension. Early in his presidency, after an apparent incident of racial profiling involving a Massachusetts police officer and the black Harvard professor Henry Louis Gates, President Obama invited the two men to the White House as a gesture of reconciliation. After Obama made the obvious (but impolitic) observation that the police acted "stupidly" (which he later walked back), conservative commentator Glenn Beck concluded Obama had just revealed his "deep-seated hatred for white people or the white culture" and he believed the president was "a racist."[33] Distasteful as Beck's comments are, they expose some ugly suspicions that infect the thinking of many of Obama's critics.

The truth is, the president frequently calls for personal accountability within the black community and resists feeding into the pathos of victimization. After a federal grand jury acquitted the white police officer who shot Michael Brown, an unarmed black teenager, in Ferguson, Missouri, President Obama knew protests were inevitable. So he made a rare late-night appearance in the White House briefing room and, though acknowledging anger was an understandable response, urged "care and restraint" in making sure protests remain "peaceful."[34] After another unarmed black man, Freddie Gray, died in police custody in Baltimore, when peaceful protests devolved into looting, the president said, "That is not a protest, that is not a statement, it's people—a handful of people taking advantage of the situation for their own purposes, and they need to be treated as criminals."[35] These two messages were likely to have a special salience with the black community having come from a black president.

The president doesn't just *speak* about accountability within the black community. Having grown up with a single mother, he created a federal initiative to promote responsible fatherhood.[36] In the aftermath of the Trayvon Martin shooting, the president launched the My Brother's Keeper program, which marshaled hundreds of millions of dollars from private companies and foundations to "help every boy and young man of color who is willing to do the hard work to get ahead."[37] The initiative has now been spun off as an independent nonprofit, so we can imagine how the president might plan to spend his energy after he leaves office.[38]

In the prologue of this book, I described how Americans began to project their hopes and fears on this hitherto unfamiliar president. This is particularly true when it comes to issues of race. On some level, it was inevitable Barack Obama would disappoint not only supporters who hoped he'd make racial inequality a more prominent theme of his presidency but also detractors who feared he'd make it too prominent. Fortunately, the dim view many Americans have about the state of race relations is uncorroborated by actual indicators of racial progress. After showing how attitudes continue to improve among several variables including belief in equal intelligence across races, disapproval of discrimination, and support for mixed race marriages, Jamelle Bouie of Slate.com demonstrated how America might *seem* more divided amid the Ferguson protests and #BlackLivesMatter movements "because we're more *aware* of our racial shortcomings . . . [but] when it comes to *race relations*, America is better than it's ever been."[39]

PUSHING THE "GAY AGENDA"

THE CHARGE

When it comes to his views on gay rights, the president hasn't been straight with us. As a candidate for the Illinois State Senate in 1996, Barack Obama signed a questionnaire from a Chicago newspaper affirming support for "legalizing same sex marriages." But as a candidate for president, he told Reverend Rick Warren he believed "that marriage is the union between a man and a woman."[40] Finally, in an interview with Robin Roberts of ABC News, President Obama referenced the "evolution" he'd been going through on this issue and affirmed, "I think same-sex couples should be able to get married."[41] The president's flip-flopping on this issue is pure political opportunism. He shifted with the political winds. More troubling than that (after all, most politicians are shifty creatures) is the fact the president has pushed a broader gay rights agenda that contradicts traditional American values.

THE REALITY

Even a casual observer of history will recognize a struggle for equal rights for a disenfranchised group of people is an American tradition. And equality in the eyes of the law is an American value. So even people who disagree with certain pieces of legislation should appreciate the movement for equal rights for gay citizens embodies American values. Disparaging remarks about President Obama's support for a conspiratorial-sounding "gay agenda" have fortunately dissipated in recent years. They're mostly limited to the homophobic corners of the Internet or, in some cases, politicians in some African countries who are sensitive to Western criticism of their antigay laws.[42]

Today there are still people whose religious convictions lead them to consider homosexuality as a lamentable lifestyle choice rather than a fundamental part of one's identity. There are also people whose political ideology leads them to consider such religious convictions a lamentable lifestyle choice rather than a fundamental part of one's identity. This mutual disregard contributes to an impasse that talking heads simplistically characterize as a conflict between LGBT rights and religious liberties. The same news media which shine a spotlight on isolated incidents of invective during otherwise peaceful #BlackLivesMatter protests also aggrandizes the baker or photographer who refuses to serve same-sex couples on their wedding day. (Seriously, how many homophobic bakers can there be out there, sneering at gay people while baking tiny cupcakes with fondant and sprinkles?)

Like business owners who refused to serve black and white customers alongside each other, defending segregation on religious grounds, these religious objections to gay weddings will someday be a relic. Until then, we should realize that, for most Americans, Christian faith and support for gay rights are compatible. After all, most Americans identify as Christian at the same time that most Americans oppose so-called religious freedom laws which would enable businesses to refuse service to gay customers.[43] And according to one recent poll, three in four Americans believe sexual orientation should be a constitutionally protected class, alongside race, gender, and age.[44] Surely that figure includes many people of faith.

In President Obama's case, religious beliefs have alternately fueled his opposition to, and then his support for, marriage equality. When he told Reverend Warren in 2008 he defined marriage as a "union between a man and a woman," Obama explained that "for me as a Christian, it is also a sacred union. God's in the mix."[45] Just two years earlier, Obama had published his book *Audacity of Hope,* which gave a more nuanced insight into how his religious faith informed his position on this issue: "It is my obligation not only as an elected official in a pluralistic society, but also as a Christian, to remain open to the possibility that my unwillingness to support gay marriage is misguided. . . . I must admit that I may have been infected with society's prejudices and predilections and attributed them to God . . . and that in years hence I may be seen as someone who was on the wrong side of history."[46] This proved to be a prophetic reflection indeed.

Obama wasn't alone in coming around on this issue. In 2008, before President Obama's "evolution," the majority of the country opposed same-sex marriage legislation. But by the time he reversed his position in 2012, opposition had weakened, and more Americans supported rather than opposed marriage equality.[47] Almost inevitably, this led to charges the president merely shape-shifted into whichever position proved politically popular. The conservative commentator Andrew Sullivan (who's both openly gay and a practicing Catholic) anticipated this criticism but defended the president's change of position. He observed how the president's experience of discovering his black identity while growing up in an otherwise white family armed him with an intuitive understanding of the experience of people discovering their gay identity amid an otherwise heterosexual family. Responding to the president's about-face on the issue of marriage equality, Sullivan asserts "when you step back a little and assess the record of Obama on gay rights, you see, in fact, that this was not an aberration. It was an inevitable culmination of three years of work. He did this the way he always does: leading from behind and playing the long game."[48]

Sullivan is right. President Obama has accomplished more for the cause of gay rights than any of his predecessors. And I'm not even counting his appearances on *Ellen*! President Obama successfully persuaded Congress to expand the federal hate crimes laws, which had been stalled in the legislature for years, to protect victims who are targeted for their sexual orientation. He directed the Department of Health and Human Services to compel hospitals which received Medicare and Medicaid funds (in other words, most every hospital) to give visitation rights to the partners of LGBT patients. He also directed his Justice Department to stop defending the so-called Defense of Marriage Act, which discriminated against same-sex couples and was more recently struck down by the Supreme Court. President Obama worked with military leadership to overturn "Don't Ask, Don't Tell," effectively telling young Americans who put their lives in harm's way to protect our country that they don't have to conceal who they are. Finally, in discussing his newfound support for same-sex marriage in such a personal way, the president displayed moral leadership that transformed marriage equality from a fringe political issue to a mainstream civil rights cause, one that would find its ultimate protection in the Supreme Court's *Obergefell v. Hodges* decision in the summer of 2015.[49]

In our era of continuous political news and "gotcha" journalism, we tend to prize consistency and penalize flexibility. Of course, nobody wants our political leaders to be fickle. But we also don't live in static times. Our understanding of the world, our understanding of each other, our collective beliefs and our shared values: all of these things are in constant flux and democratically shaped over time. We'll never know for certain whether the president's reversal on the issue of same-sex marriage is confined to his public position or if it extends to his personal beliefs. But at a time when we seem to demand stubborn adherence to prestated political beliefs, it's worth considering a question often attributed to Winston Churchill: "If you don't have the ability to change your mind, are you sure you still have one?" I'm writing this book because I believe we all still have, and retain the ability to change, our minds.

—

PART 2

THE
COUNTRY

—

4

—

THE
ECONOMY
DESTROYER

—

Economics is called the "dismal science" for a reason. Try to host a feisty political debate about the nation's economy and, as soon as the debaters whip out a bunch of economic statistics, eyes will glaze over. "The Obama administration oversaw the creations of millions of jobs, a steep decrease in the unemployment rate, and deficits are way down!" cheers Lefty McSmiley. But Righty Frownberg retorts, "That doesn't account for the labor force participation rate and continued wage stagnation, while the national *debt* is way up!" Snooze. "Now let's compare real weekly earnings to the fluctuations in the consumer price index. . . ." Yawn.

Although wonky economic discussions quickly bore most audiences, when it comes to more personalized reporting on the health of the economy, people perk up. That's because the economy is frequently the single most important issue on the minds of voters during election years. That trend appears to continue in the 2016 contest.[1] And it makes sense. The state of the economy affects everyone, from a millionaire expecting to make a killing from stock dividends to a minimum-wage worker hoping to get a good interest rate on a credit card.

Has President Obama's record on economic issues been "dismal" or dazzling? In this chapter, we pull the curtain back on claims about Obama's tax-hiking, job-killing, budget-crippling, regulation-loving, government-spending, fair-pay-shilling economic policies. By the end of it, we'll have a clearer sense of how much better off we are now than we were eight years ago.

—

JOB-KILLING TAX HIKES

THE CHARGE

By letting President Bush's tax cuts expire, President Obama raised income taxes on hardworking Americans. A lot of people who were hurt by the tax increase were business owners (aka job creators), and so this president created a hostile climate for job creation. When Jeb Bush announced his candidacy for the Republican presidential nomination, it was a hot summer day in Miami. He tore into the president's economic record, claiming the Obama administration is "responsible for the slowest economic recovery ever, the biggest debt increases ever, [and] a massive tax increase on the middle class."[2] Obama's supporters point out the unemployment rate has dropped and the economy continues to add more jobs. But a lot of these aren't good jobs, and barely more than three in every five adult Americans is actively working or looking for a job. This is the lowest level of labor force participation in almost forty years.[3] Obama's economic policies have stymied, not stimulated, job growth.

THE REALITY

It's a true tale often told: when President Obama was sworn in, the economy was in disarray. Incomes had taken a hit, the stock market was avalanching, and the unemployment rate was escalating. Pundits credited Obama's election, at least in part, to the economy's dire straits. In the face of economic despair and the ravages of rampant deregulation, people walked into the voting booth and pulled the lever for financial "hope" and economic policy "change." Did they get it? By almost every measure, the economy has shaken off its slump with the help of Obama administration policies. Let's start with taxes.

Jeb Bush's claim Barack Obama has raised taxes on the middle class is not true.[4] Families that make less than a quarter of a million dollars a year (and individuals who make less than $200,000) have seen their federal income taxes decrease, not increase, under Obama's watch. Federal taxes for middle-class Americans are among the lowest in decades. A tax credit tied to the stimulus package gave $800 back to working couples (or $400 to individuals) in 2009 and 2010. The next two years, middle-class families benefited from a reduction in Social Security payroll taxes.[5] Tax cuts for middle-class families make good economic sense. Those families take that extra money and pay down debt or buy things—as opposed to betting on high-risk hedge funds or hiding it in offshore tax havens—and this improves the overall vitality and liquidity of the economy.

President Obama also cut taxes for small businesses, excluding business investments from some capital gains taxes and winning a tax credit for companies who hire people who'd been unemployed for at least two months.[6] This has helped businesses overcome their post-recession skittishness and continue to grow. But tax cuts aren't the economic panacea Republicans so often claim. Maintaining the world's most powerful military, covering Social Security for an aging population, and providing a humane social safety net for the less fortunate all cost money. The Treasury can get the revenue it needs one of two ways: from taxes (i.e., the pay-as-you-go model) or from borrowing from foreign governments (i.e., the add-it-to-the-national-debt model). This is why the Obama administration let most of the Bush-era tax cuts, which mostly benefited the wealthy and had added about $3 trillion to the national debt,[7] expire.

Republicans who argue Obama hiked taxes on the middle class defend this misleading claim by pointing to new taxes associated with the Obamacare law. Obamacare does set a reasonable limit for the pretax contributions to flexible spending accounts and introduces a modest new tax for indoor tanning salons, but these hardly constitute a "middle class tax hike," as some conservative groups suggest.[8]

Heck, in his State of the Union address in 2015, the president even unveiled a plan to further cut taxes for middle- and low-income families. He proposed offsetting this with some commonsense sources of tax revenue, such as a fee to the country's largest banks when they seek leverage (thereby giving a disincentive to the kind of risky borrowing which precipitated the 2008 crash) or limiting the amount millionaires could contribute to their IRAs to about $3.4 million[9] (since IRAs were designed to help middle-class families save for retirement, not to be a tax shelter for the rich). Of course Congress, which was controlled by Republicans, who were controlled by millionaires, thwarted the plan.

How has President Obama's record been on job creation and economic growth, actually? On the first day of his new job, the economy hemorrhaged about 800,000 jobs per month. It took Obama just one year to steer us from monthly job losses to monthly job gains, and in the following six years, the economy netted more private sector jobs every single month, more than fourteen million of them created in all.[10] Amid the nastiest economic recession in eighty years, the president and his economic advisers charted a course that cut the unemployment rate in half, significantly increased the number of available jobs and the number of business start-ups, and more than doubled corporate profits and stock market valuations.[11]

Republicans hail Ronald Reagan as an economic savior. Compared with Reagan's handling of the economic recession *he* inherited, President Obama has, as Polaris Financial CEO Bob Deitrick notes, "kept unemployment from peaking at as high a level as President Reagan, and promoted people into the workforce faster than President Reagan."[12] And a dollar put into the stock market at the start of the Obama presidency yielded an investor a better return than a dollar invested at the start of the Reagan presidency.[13] Perhaps one day we'll talk about Obama-nomics in reverential tones.

What about the argument that those official employment figures obscure the "hidden" labor force participation rate (which includes people who have stopped searching for work)? Hasn't this figure decreased by 3 percent under Obama? Pointing to a chart by the Bureau of Labor Statistics that tracks this (unhidden!) rate, Deitrick explains "the difference between reported unemployment and all unemployment—including those on the fringe of the workforce—has remained pretty constant since 1994."[14]

What Obama's critics don't tell you is that the labor force participation rate *should* be decreasing, since this figure includes the baby boomers who bow out of the workforce. It would be a *bad* economic sign if older folks postponed their retirements and continued to seek work en masse. Unless you want your grandfather driving for Uber too. Even as the recovery continues, this figure is expected to continue to decrease for the next ten years in light of these demographic trends.[15] As always, the more factors you can include, the more accurate a picture you can achieve of any complex phenomenon. But complexity doesn't always serve cynicism or polarizing political moves.

The recession of 2008 was the worst in generations, and it was global in scale. Fortunately, because of the quick thinking of our political leaders and the resilience of the American people, the American economy recovered faster than almost every European country (Germany is the sole exception).[16] So what do we make of the criticism that Obama's economic policies have choked off job growth? Asked precisely that in an interview on CNBC, Treasury Secretary Jack Lew said plainly, "The facts have proven them wrong."[17]

—
"WALL STREET REFORM" HURTS MAIN STREET BANKS

THE CHARGE

Maybe the president can claim some credit for stabilizing the employment situation in the wake of the crisis. But he took advantage of the recession to push regulatory policies that have tangled small banks and businesses in endless red tape. The president's chief of staff signaled this mentality to a bunch of Wall Street muckety-mucks when he discussed the economy and commented, "You never want a serious crisis to go to waste."[18] So the president, along with the Democratic senator Chris Dodd (D-CT) and the Democratic congressman Barney

Frank (D-MA), parlayed people's fear of more financial instability into the passage of the Dodd-Frank Wall Street Reform and Consumer Protection Act ("Dodd-Frank").

Dodd-Frank has been, frankly, a dudd. It was sold as a way to avoid another "too big to fail" fiasco, in which taxpayers were forced to bail out the big banks. But it has penalized banks if they grow too large or make loans the government doesn't like. Small banks have gone out of business because they can't keep up with the costs of compliance. On the campaign trail, Marco Rubio pointed out "over 40 percent of small and midsize banks that loan money to small businesses have been wiped out since Dodd-Frank has passed." The president of the American Bankers Association recently noted that, since 2008, community banks are shuttering at a rate of one per day.[19] Dodd-Frank was supposed to stabilize the banking sector, but it has only weakened it further.

THE REALITY

In order to understand the urgent need for the Wall Street reform contained in Dodd-Frank, let's take a quick stroll back through the origins of the 2008 financial crisis. Four years after the stock market crash of 1929, which precipitated the Great Depression, Congress passed the Glass-Steagall Act, which told banks that issued home or small business loans they couldn't also place bets on stocks. Large banks which mixed commercial lending and speculative investing were widely believed to have caused the economic instability. In the 1960s, always on the prowl for new revenue streams, banking industry groups began to persuade Congress to start chipping away at Glass-Steagall.[20]

Finally, in 1999, intoxicated by the prosperity of the past decade,

Congress overturned the critical partition between commercial and investment banks. Banks began bundling ordinary home mortgages into collateralized debt obligations (CDOs), which were sold to investors and exchanged on the securities market. Banks now had incentives to hock risky mortgages, because the securities buyers assumed the risk. The credit ratings agencies which were supposed to police all of this committed substantial grade inflation, since the very companies they were rating were the ones paying them.

You know the rest: as the shell game came to an end, home prices tanked, foreclosures skyrocketed, retirement accounts dwindled, credit card interest rates were jacked up, and banks stopped lending. Adding insult to injury, we were told these irresponsible banks were "too big to fail," and so we'd have to bail them out with our tax dollars. The year after we did so, investment bankers were back to making their seven-figure bonuses.[21]

There are a lot of facets to the Dodd-Frank Act, but the most fundamental thing it does is say that taxpayers will never again have to cover the costs of banks that implode. It does this by forcing big banks to keep a certain amount of liquid assets on hand, and have "living wills," aka plans for being quickly dissolved without inciting panic if they fail.[22] To reduce the likelihood that they *do* fail, Dodd-Frank introduced something called the Volcker Rule (named for Paul Volcker, the Reagan-era chairman of the Fed, who promoted it). This rule prohibits commercial banks from running hedge funds or private equity companies on the side, and so it protects ordinary borrowers from the risks associated with these types of "proprietary trading."[23] The Volcker Rule has restored the spirit of the Glass-Steagall Act in a way that suits the modern economy.

So, does Dodd-Frank really destroy small banks, as critics have argued? Many Americans have clearly seen within their own communities that small banks have indeed been disappearing. But economists point out this has less to do with any new regulations than it does with the trend of banking industry consolidation that has been constant since the 1980s. Fact checkers raised an eyebrow at Marco Rubio's claim that "40 percent" of small and medium-size banks had been "wiped out since Dodd-Frank passed." They found the correct figure closer to 14 percent, with most of those banks merging with larger banks, just as they've been doing for decades before Dodd-Frank was law.[24]

The Dodd-Frank Act is less than a decade old and, at the time of this writing, certain provisions are still in the process of being implemented. But the reviews are already, on the whole, positive. The Volcker Rule essentially allows banks to compete with banks and hedge funds to compete with hedge funds, eliminating pressure on commercial banks to wade into risky proprietary trading just to stay successful. As we learned in chapter two, the Consumer Financial Protection Bureau, an upshot of Dodd-Frank, has provided more transparency for people signing loan agreements or reading credit card statements.

And those collateralized debt obligations and other derivatives we discussed before? They're now taking place on derivatives exchanges under the watch of the Securities and Exchange Commission. So if some of them go belly-up, they're isolated and can't cause a ripple effect throughout the entire economy. Though some Republicans gripe that this is just one more way in which the Obama administration's regulatory tentacles have overreached, many in the business community welcome these developments. As Accenture's Steve Culp wrote in *Forbes*, "Firms engaged in derivatives trading typically see significant benefits from Dodd-Frank's push to establish open, transparent derivatives exchanges."[25] When it comes to the chaotic, internationally networked, hypercompetitive financial services industry, the critics have it backward. Rules don't hinder markets from functioning. Rules provide the openness and orderliness that markets need to function.

—

"FAIR PAY" ACT WAS A GIFT TO TRIAL LAWYERS

THE CHARGE

The very first bill Barack Obama signed into law upon assuming the presidency was the Lilly Ledbetter Fair Pay Act of 2009. The law was sold to the American people as a way to ensure women got paid the same as men for doing the same job. But the law was totally unnecessary, since the Equal Pay Act of 1963 had already outlawed pay discrimination based on gender. What Obama really did is give a big payday to trial lawyers, since the law opens the door to frivolous lawsuits against big companies, and fat-cat lawyers are going to get even fatter. If there's no statute of limitations on when a female employee can sue for discriminatory pay, employers are going to be burdened with tedious record keeping and might even decide to hire fewer women altogether! As then-vice presidential nominee Paul Ryan told CBS's morning show, "Lilly Ledbetter was not an equal pay law. It was about opening up the lawsuits and statute of limitations."[26] And Senator Marco Rubio asserted, "Much of this legislation is, in many respects, nothing but an effort to help trial lawyers collect their fees and file lawsuits."[27]

THE REALITY

The Lilly Ledbetter Fair Pay Act was a giveaway to trial lawyers the way that the Voting Rights Act of 1965 was a giveaway to southern poll workers and election inspectors. In other words, yes, of course the expansion and solidification of rights will benefit certain people who are paid to enforce them. Those who truly believe the effort to strengthen the "equal pay for equal work" principle (which has been a Democratic Party priority for decades) is really a kickback for campaign contributions from lawyers have a deeply cynical view of professional politics. Those who don't believe it, but push the narrative anyway, exploit and expand the cynicism of the American people. The only bank accounts President Obama tries to fatten are the bank accounts of women who've endured years of making seventy cents for every dollar their male coworker makes. If lawyers make money by defending these women, good for them. If it's a female lawyer, I hope she's keeping as much of the commission as her male counterpart.

Critics are right to point out the Equal Pay Act of 1963 had already outlawed pay discrimination. What they fail to mention is that women who filed a lawsuit to enforce these rights had to do so within 180 days of receiving their first unfairly low paycheck (i.e., from the time the "discriminatory decision" was made). Lilly Ledbetter had worked at a Goodyear Tire factory in Alabama for nineteen years. She had been paid less than her male counterparts for the entire time she worked there. Unaware of the salaries of her colleagues until close to her retirement, her 180 days were well up and so, under the 1963 law, she'd lost the opportunity to enforce her rights. Or so said the 5–4 majority ruling of the Supreme Court.

In explaining the majority ruling, Justice Alito said employers must be protected from "stale claims" or "tardy lawsuits." Justice Ginsburg, on the other hand, criticized this as a "cramped interpretation of the law" and argued for an interpretation in which the 180-day statute of limitations would be reset every time a discriminatory paycheck was issued. Her argument provided the impetus for Democrats to act. George Miller, the Democratic chairman of the House Education and Labor Committee, put it this way: "A key provision of the legislation will make it clear that discrimination occurs not just when the decision to discriminate is made, but also when someone becomes subject to that discriminatory decision, and when they are affected by that discriminatory decision, including each time they are issued a discriminatory paycheck."[28]

To those of you who think this might all be much ado about not very much (after all, how many of us know women who are suing their employer over pay discrimination?), consider that in the year and a half between the Supreme Court issuing its decision in *Ledbetter v. Goodyear Tire and Rubber Co.* and the president signing the Lilly Ledbetter Fair Pay Act into law, judges in more than three hundred federal cases cited the *Ledbetter* decision.[29] A lot of those plaintiffs were presumably told their equal rights had expired. But no longer. Perhaps more important than the ability to broadly enforce the right to equal pay is the catalytic effect the law will have in getting companies to make sure their managers are setting salaries based solely on factors related to merits and markets. As opposed to paying people based on their ability to open big glass pickle jars or bottle up their emotions for years at a time.

More than five years after the law was established, "the median woman working full-time all year earned 78 percent of what the median man working full-time all year earned."[30] This is similar to the pay gap that existed before the law. Conservatives cite this statistic as evidence the new law hasn't been effective, and liberals cite it as evidence that the president needs to do more and help pass the Paycheck Fairness Act, which would make wages more transparent and prevent retaliation against employees who inquire about possible discrimination.[31]

The reality is that it's easily conceivable discrimination has decreased in the wake of the new law, and yet the wage gap stubbornly persists, perpetuated mostly by cultural and structural factors such as the tendency of mothers (more than fathers) to let child rearing interrupt their career progression. But these longer-term cultural explanations only go so far. Researchers recently discovered that, in the year after they graduate from college, female applicants could expect to make just 82 percent of their male peers for work in the same industries.[32]

The pay gap costs the average woman $431,000 over a forty-year career.[33] It's a more complicated and vexing problem than the straightforward issue of discrimination, which contributes to it. But the part of the gap that's caused by discrimination will continue to be closed as employers and employees—and their trial lawyers—become more vigilant of the right to equal pay.

THE NATIONAL DEBT AND DEBT CEILING KEEP RISING

THE CHARGE

On President Obama's watch, the national debt doubled from about $10 trillion to about $20 trillion. Republicans have tried to prevent this mounting debt by threatening to vote against lifting the "debt ceiling." The debt ceiling is basically the U.S. government's credit limit, and Congress has the right and responsibility to establish it. Yet each time Republicans in Congress tried to negotiate to keep the debt ceiling where it is, effectively shutting down the government's spending spree, they were harshly criticized by Obama's lackeys in the liberal "lamestream" media. By jacking up our national debt to an eye-popping $20 trillion is saddling the next generation with a devastating burden.

THE REALITY

Some people like to think President Obama has taken the American economy into an episode of *Shop 'til You Drop*. The truth is, the national debt is an accumulation of all the annual budget shortfalls (i.e., deficits) we've incurred. While the president has managed to ensure these deficits have shrunk year after year (as we saw in chapter two), large chunks of the federal budget are untouchable. More than 40 percent of the budget goes to Medicare, Medicaid, and Social Security payments and most of the remaining budget is committed to defense spending.[34] But the president has control over the remaining budget, right? Wrong. As it has demonstrated so theatrically in its debt ceiling "showdowns" and "standoffs" over the past five years, Congress has the "power of the purse." They are the ones who set the federal budget and pass laws that make new taxpayer-funded outlays. So while the White House can try to influence Congress by building public support for new programs and new laws, Congress is ultimately responsible for every federal dollar that gets spent. Think of all that power! And with great power comes great responsibility, or so Spider-Man was told. How did Congress handle that responsibility? It threw tantrums in 2011, 2013, and 2015, threatening to freeze the debt ceiling and let the United States go into default, unless Democrats agreed to a budget which overturned its existing laws—e.g., defunding Obamacare, slashing Social Security payments, or cutting environmental rules.

For his part, President Obama responded like a clearheaded father whose tween needed to learn a little responsibility with his allowance. He pushed for the "Pay As You Go Act of 2010" that said Congress could only authorize new spending if that spending were balanced by new revenue streams. The law is predicated on the basic principle of budget neutrality and it was modeled on a similar law that is credited for the budget surpluses we enjoyed in the 1990s.[35] The president tried to get our country back to living within its means, so it's a head-scratcher that the law passed with a party line vote, with all sixty Democratic senators supporting it and all forty Republican senators, supposedly representing the party of "fiscal responsibility," opposing it.[36]

In the fall of 2013, budget brinksmanship returned to the headlines. Anti-Obamacare fervor was at its height as Republicans were in the midst of a last-ditch effort to scrap President Obama's signature domestic achievement. They said they would not raise the debt limit unless Obamacare were defunded or repealed. As anyone who ever watched a 1980s action movie knows, America has a long-standing policy of not negotiating with hostage takers. The Obama administration extended this philosophy to dealing with Republican lawmakers who took the budget hostage in a desperate attempt to refight the legislative negotiations they had lost.

Two years earlier, such threats of a default had led Standard & Poor's to downgrade the country's credit rating for the first time in history.[37] This time Republicans would follow through on their threats. The government was shut down for just over two weeks: hundreds of thousands of government employees were furloughed, national parks were closed to tourists and surrendered hundreds of millions of dollars in revenue, scientific research was suspended, health and environmental inspections came to a halt, and 120,000 fewer private sector jobs were created that October.[38]

In a perfect symbol of the childishness of the "showdown and shutdown" two-step, Senator Cruz's filibuster in protest of Obamacare consisted of a reading, on the Senate floor, of Dr. Seuss's famous book *Green Eggs and Ham.* Cruz must not have been reading closely enough to see the irony of his literary choice. As his Senate colleague Claire McCaskill pointed out, the story is about a grumpy and stubborn little boy who avowed he did not like green eggs and ham. Yet, when he tries eating them, he finds out he likes them after all. The point of the story, McCaskill gleefully pointed out, is "that you can't knock things [such as Obamacare] till you try it."[39]

The worst damage didn't come from the costs of the government shutdown, however substantial. It came from the threats to the country's "full faith and credit," which gets jeopardized when politicians threaten to default on our debt. President Reagan would have been startled and embarrassed by the tactics of today's Republicans. He wrote in a letter to his Republican Senate colleagues back in 1983:

> The full consequences of a default—or even the serious prospect of default—by the United States are impossible to predict and awesome to contemplate. Denigration of the full faith and credit of the United States would have substantial effects on the domestic financial markets and the value of the dollar in exchange markets. The Nation can ill afford to allow such a result.[40]

Some Republicans are slowly learning they can't take the creditworthiness of our country hostage as they pursue political goals. As budget negotiations proceeded in 2015, Senator Mitch McConnell affirmed "we won't default on the budget." But McConnell was also reported to have been "drawing up a list of agenda items that he apparently want[ed] to squeeze out of Democrats in exchange for an increase to the debt limit."[41] This was interpreted within the Beltway as either a weak bluff in the direction of the White House or a genuflection in the direction of the Tea Party wing of his party. After all, those guys had largely pushed aside John Boehner as speaker of the house after he'd committed the heinous crime of pursuing budget compromises with the White House. But Americans largely want their leaders to have the capacity for compromise,[42] and so there's reason to hope politicians will eventually get beyond this zero-sum mentality.

One way to ensure we stop holding ourselves hostage to these perennial budget battles would be to get rid of the debt ceiling completely. Most countries don't have one and opt instead to detail borrowing and spending in any new legislation (just as the "Pay As You Go Act" mandates). Our debt ceiling was created in 1939 and has been raised about a hundred times since then, and mostly without fanfare. It started being used as a political weapon only in the 1980s.[43] And in a recent study, 84 percent of economists agreed "a separate debt ceiling that has to be increased periodically creates unneeded uncertainty and can potentially lead to worse fiscal outcomes."[44]

How bad is a national debt of $20 trillion anyway? Look at it this way. Our country's annual GDP is roughly equivalent to its national debt. Let's say your family's income is about $60,000 (around the national "per capita GDP") and its total debt is the same. This debt breaks down into $35,000 in student loans, a $20,000 car loan, and $5,000 in credit card debt. (We'll leave aside mortgages because they're material investments that can appreciate.) Assuming you have good economic stability, your income continues to steadily increase each year, and you maintain a solid credit score, you're probably not freaking out. Debt is okay if it tracks with economic growth and represents smart investments, such as an individual getting a college degree that helps him get a good job or a country making Social Security payments that keep seniors financially solvent and economically active.

Now, some economists might argue with this analogy. A country isn't a family, but I use this example just to give a sense of proportion. As the Nobel Prize-winning economist Paul Krugman observes, recognizing one distinction between families and countries should free us further from our debt panics. Krugman writes, "An indebted family owes money to other people; the world economy as a whole owes money to itself. And while it's true countries can borrow from other countries, America has actually been borrowing less from abroad since 2008 than it did before."[45] Krugman suggests debt can be bad if it's a source of instability, but single-minded attempts to reduce debt can be worse if they deprive us of smart investments or spur deflation.

There's no question the next president will need to work with Congress to tackle entitlement spending and tax policy in creative ways. If Congress is sincere about wanting to shrink the national debt, and not just using the debt ceiling as a stone on which it can grind its partisan ax, it's going to have to couple its "power of the purse" with a "responsibility of the revenue," even if power is more exciting than responsibility.

POVERTY AND ECONOMIC INEQUALITY UP

THE CHARGE

Halfway into President Obama's second term, the United States celebrated an anniversary: fifty years had passed since President Lyndon Johnson had declared war on poverty. After nearly $20 trillion in tax dollars spent on federal programs to help the poor, the percentage of the population living in poverty has barely decreased since the days of LBJ (from about 17 percent then to about 15 percent today).[46]

For all of the president's talk about supporting the middle class and helping disadvantaged populations, the poverty problem has actually gotten worse under his watch. As Jeb Bush said in one of the Republican primary debates, "Six million more people are living in poverty than the day that Barack Obama got elected president."[47] Even while the private sector adds new jobs and the economy, as a whole, recovers, the poor have been left behind. Adjusting for inflation, the wealthy make about 3 percent more today than they did in 1999 while the income of the poorest tenth of Americans has dropped more than 16 percent.[48] Meanwhile, the president is preoccupied with trying to hike up the minimum wage. But the wage is already higher than it's ever been. Raising it further would kill jobs, as employers won't be able to afford to pay as many workers.

THE REALITY

It's true the thorny problems of poverty and income inequality have persisted under President Obama. However, they have persisted despite, not because of, the president's policies. As you can imagine, when President Obama took the baton from President Bush, the recession had already put the poverty rate on the upswing. That trend line continued upward through the first year of the Obama presidency, but then plateaued and has since dipped down a bit.

What prevented the poverty rate from climbing higher? For starters, the economic stimulus. Though it had been intended mostly as a way to boost the overall economy and not target the poor specifically, the Center on Budget and Policy Priorities found that, without the stimulus, another six million Americans would be living in poverty today.[49] Even low-income people who weren't directly helped by the new jobs that came from the stimulus saw their living conditions improve as the earned income tax credit, food stamps, and unemployment insurance became more available. (And the rate of insurance among people making less than $36,000 a year jumped by about 10 percent in just two years, thanks to Obamacare.)[50] Incidentally, the government's formula for determining the poverty rate is tragicomically outmoded. It doesn't figure in these benefits (or Medicaid, or income taxes) and is pegged to the "minimum food diet" in 1963, back when Americans spent 25 percent of their budget on food rather than the 6 percent we spend on it today.[51] (So think about that the next time you complain about the price of mangos or almond butter!)

Even using this antiquated measure, the inconvenient truth for Jeb Bush is that, as of 2015, the percentage of Americans living in poverty has increased a mere 0.2 percent under Obama while it increased 3 percent during his brother's presidency.[52] Republicans like to chide Obama for not solving the poverty problem. Democrats have even criticized the president for not pushing for an even larger stimulus and for cutting back on food stamp funding in 2014. But the truth is, according to Danielle Kurtzleben, an NPR reporter who analyzed this issue in depth, "Obama's recession-era policies made life better for America's poor and prevented poverty from growing even more than it did."[53]

There is one way President Obama and members of Congress could swiftly lift working Americans out of poverty and without involving another government program. And yes, that is by elevating the minimum wage. An American worker paid the federal minimum wage of $7.25 who works forty hours a week makes less than $15,000 a year, well below the poverty line. And $7.25 may be the highest the minimum wage has ever been, but when we adjust for inflation, that figure represents *a decrease* from the $10.77 (in today's dollars) a minimum wage worker made back in 1968.[54] By raising it to $10.10, as the president and congressional Democrats want to do, the full-time minimum wage worker would now make just over $20,000 and land on the other side of the poverty line.[55] As the president often insists, "In the richest nation on earth, nobody who works full-time should have to live in poverty."[56]

The fight to raise the minimum wage stems not only from a sense of moral obligation, but also from an economic imperative. According to a report by Goldman Sachs: (1) an increase in the minimum wage would "ripple" through the economy, with employers calibrating other wages upward based on the new baseline, and (2) the job losses based on the higher costs of labor, which Republicans constantly discuss, would be negligible.[57] One analysis found that, in the wake of the recession, states which increased their minimum wage experienced faster job growth than those that didn't.[58] Conservative economic orthodoxy just hasn't been supported by a look at that stubborn variable called "reality." A bump in the minimum wage isn't about fattening the wallets of kids flipping burgers on weekends, as the popular stereotype would suggest. According to the Economic Policy Institute, of the people who'd be affected by the wage hike, over 88 percent are at least twenty years old, and the average minimum wage worker earns about half of his or her family's total income.[59]

More than anything, an increase in the minimum wage would provide an incentive to find honest work. After all, what's the point of looking for a job if the available jobs pay poverty wages? And, conversely, why should taxpayers be in a position to have to subsidize the groceries of people who work full-time but still have to rely on food stamps? More income for the working poor would alleviate wage stagnation, channel $35 billion in new wages into the economy, and reduce demand for government assistance. It's that simple.

An increase in buying power of minimum-wage workers (aka consumers) is one of the reasons most small business owners support increasing the minimum wage to $10.10, according to one small business advocacy organization.[60] Another reason is small business owners, most of whom pay higher than the minimum wage, often compete with big chains that undercut them on labor costs. Two other recent polls of business owners also found majority support for a $10.10 minimum wage and revealed employers think higher wages will reduce employee turnover and help them increase productivity.[61] Both of these polls included more Republicans than Democrats.

Finally, a majority of the American people supports a $10.10 minimum wage.[62] People are bored with abstract economic philosophies that tell them an increase in baseline wages will distort market logic. They know a professional caregiver or a dishwasher or a construction worker should be able to provide for the basic needs of his or her family. The president has already used his executive authority to make sure people working for government contractors received the $10.10 minimum wage. So the lives of the dishwasher who works on a military base and the construction worker at a federal building site will improve a bit. But this reaches just a small fraction of American workers. Why would Republicans block a modest minimum wage increase when most Americans and most small business owners want it? Maybe it's because the big box retailers and fast-food chains behind the U.S. Chamber of Commerce, and others in the Republican donor base, don't approve. Maybe it's because they have a sincere—but misguided—sense of what's required for economic growth. Or maybe because, if the poverty rate suddenly dropped, they'd have one less issue for which to criticize Barack Obama. But as you keep turning the pages, you'll see they've got plenty of other issues.

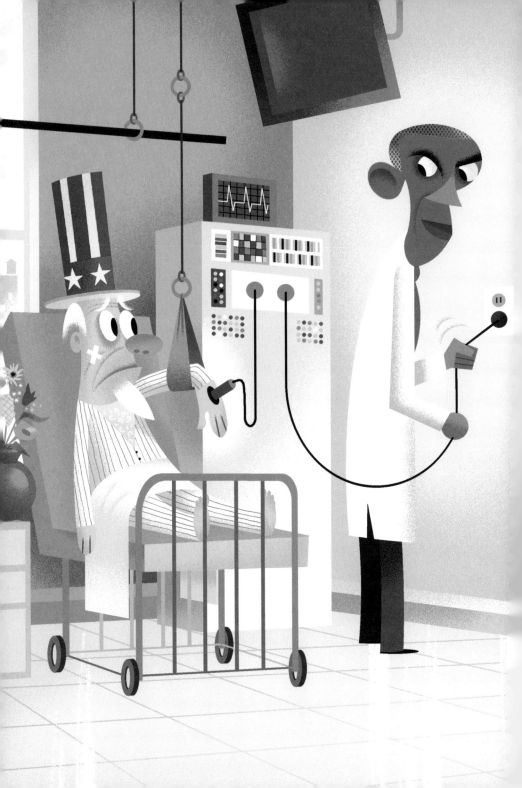

5

—

THE
HEALTH CARE
USURPER

—

I f there is a signature domestic policy triumph that has come to define Barack Obama's presidency, it is probably the Affordable Care Act—aka "Obamacare." In recent decades, the United States has spent more money per person on health care than any other industrialized nation, and yet all we've had to show for it are some of the worst health outcomes.[1] And while most every other developed country granted some form of universal health care,[2] about one in five American adults was uninsured when Barack Obama was elected.[3] Politicians of every stripe could diagnose the problem; it's the prescription they couldn't seem to agree on.

Health care is a sprawling industry, so sprawling it's hard to describe succinctly. It accounts for one-sixth of the economy. It encompasses everything from insurance and pharmaceutical companies to hospitals and community health clinics. So it's no wonder any attempt to reform the health care sector would inevitably raise the specter of "big government" interference. But as you'll see throughout this chapter, Obamacare doesn't quite *transform* the American health care system. It *expands access to the existing system*. Still, Republicans perceive Obamacare as a government intervention (which it was) into an otherwise free market (which it was not—more on this shortly), and they are seemingly allergic to things that smell like government intervention. So they've tried desperately to destroy or deter the law, voting more than sixty times to repeal, defund, or modify Obama's eponymous legislation—which wasn't even eponymous until conservatives started getting mad about it.[4]

When he debated President Obama during the 2012 reelection campaign, Mitt Romney called out government programs he'd like to have cut. "Obamacare is on my list," he said but, realizing the term had been used as a pejorative by Republican critics, quickly added, "I apologize, Mr. President. I use that term with all respect." The president responded, "I like it!" A few moments later, while talking about the dangers of repealing the law, Obama gamely mused, "I have become fond of this term, 'Obamacare.'"[5] A year earlier, he had decided to own the term, saying, "I have no problem with people saying 'Obama cares.' I do care. If the other side wants to be the folks who don't care? That's fine with me."[6] The president knew then what we know now: the health care reform he championed would be one of the most enduring and successful aspects of his legacy.

OBAMACARE IS SOCIALIZED HEALTH CARE

THE CHARGE

In launching a monumental government takeover of the health care sector, President Obama has essentially socialized America's medical system. There are plenty of legitimate complaints one can make about insurance and pharmaceutical companies, but the reality is the free markets of health insurance and medicine have led to the creation of lifesaving pharmaceutical drugs and the world's best medical treatment. Compare that with Britain's National Health Service (NHS), which faces bankruptcy, or even the old Soviet system, where doctors and nurses were state employees and the government dictated all medical treatments. Obamacare was inspired by these miserable failures of state-run health care systems, and Democrats who continue to support it, in the words of Rush Limbaugh, "fund the relentless drive toward socialized medicine."[7]

THE REALITY

A number of Democrats wanted to create a "single payer" model of health care. In this scheme, every American would be eligible for Medicare and the government could more forcefully haggle over the prices it paid to hospitals and pharmaceutical companies on behalf of the public. Barack Obama expressed some early support for this model, but knowing it was a nonstarter with Republicans, he committed to developing a compromise plan. We could fill an entire book debating the merits of single payer—which conservatives characterize as "socialized medicine" and liberals tout as "Medicare for all"—but that would be pointless, since Obamacare is a significant departure from that model. Obamacare is instead a simultaneous expansion of the free market and the existing social safety net programs. More people became eligible for Medicaid and government subsidies at the same time that a flood of customers was directed toward the private insurance market. New customers led to new demand, which led to growth, innovation, and competition within the health insurance industry. This reality flies in the face of the critics who try to portray the law as socialized medicine. In the words of Chief Justice John Roberts, in the Supreme Court ruling that upheld Obamacare, "Congress passed the Affordable Care Act to improve health insurance markets, not to destroy them."[8]

Has Obamacare lived up to that objective? Has it improved health insurance markets? Even though private health insurance plans offered under the federal exchange aren't as profitable (because of increased competition), insurance companies are posting record earnings and profits, and higher stock prices, as a result of the new customer base that Obamacare delivers.[9] Pharmaceutical companies have also benefited. Millions more insured Americans means millions more potential customers. Even accounting for new drug rebates that Obamacare offers patients, the industry is expected to yield between "$10 billion and $35 billion in additional profits over the next decade" and grow by a third in the U.S. market alone within just eight years.[10] This comes at a time when the patents on some of the biggest and most profitable blockbuster drugs are about to expire. So Obamacare actually helps the industry bounce back and further invest in its research pipeline. Of course Obamacare was passed to improve the health of its citizens, not the health of big companies. But the revenue figures and growth data illustrate how the private health care marketplace has been thriving—not threatened—as a result of Obamacare.

Medical providers—doctors, hospitals and health clinics—have also benefited from an influx of patients. In the wake of the Obamacare law, hospitals began hiring new employees at a rate unseen for roughly twenty-five years.[11] Some providers have complained, yes, about snags in processing reimbursements, but those frustrations have been around as long as Medicare and private insurance. And doctors—who know something about health care—are happy to see the number of insured Americans climb higher, since people with insurance are more likely to seek treatment for their illnesses.

Did Obamacare introduce new rules and regulations that make the health care market less "free"? It certainly places new requirements on insurance companies. Young adults can now stay on their parents' insurance policies until they're twenty-six years old (no more borrowing expired Z-Paks from your roommate!). Insurance companies can't cancel coverage when someone gets sick. They must also spend at least 80 percent of the revenue they get from premiums on medical care and quality improvements, and they must cover certain preventive services such as cancer screening.[12] But because these rules apply equally to all insurance companies, they don't hamper competition.

The idea that health care in America represented a true free market before the age of Obamacare is something of a fiction. The health care market was obscured at two levels: (1) when hospitals set outrageously inflated prices because they deal with insurance companies rather than their customers, and (2) when insurance companies sell their plans not directly to customers, but to the customers' employers. We've all heard about hospital price gouging. A 10,000 percent markup on a pill of Tylenol was one famous example chronicled in Steven Brill's cover story for *Time* magazine.[13] In the introduction to that article, *Time* managing editor Richard Stengel observed, "It's a $5.8 trillion market, but it's not a free one. Hospitals and health care providers offer services at prices that very often bear little relationship to costs. They charge what they want to and mostly—because it's a life-and-death issue—we have to pay."

Americans receive their health insurance plans from their employers, and so there's not a ton of shopping around or transparent pricing. An historical footnote for people who like this model but despise all government intervention: the trend of employers offering private health insurance started, in fact, with another government intervention—the creation of wage controls during World War II. Intending to curb inflation during wartime, the Roosevelt administration set limits on salary increases, which led employers to offer health coverage to entice new recruits.[14] Health benefits are great, though how many of us can honestly say we give close scrutiny to our employer-provided health insurance plans? My personal method is to pick whichever one has the word *platinum* or *star* or *preferred* in it. Most of us don't pay close attention, even though employers can be attracted to group plans which don't always align with the interests of individual employees. Contrast this with the Obamacare exchanges, which require insurers to list plan details in clear language and directly compete with one another for customers. From this vantage point, Obamacare's individual marketplace gets closer to a real "free market" than the employer-brokered model so many of us are used to.

If Obamacare really isn't socialized medicine, but rather an expansion of both private and public insurance, why do the president's critics like to call it that? Republicans have tried to characterize Democratic health care proposals as "socialized" ever since President Harry Truman proposed a national health insurance plan in the 1940s. In attacking Truman's plan, Senator Robert Taft of Ohio played upon the emerging Communist scare and "suggested that compulsory health insurance . . . came right out of the Soviet constitution."[15] When President Kennedy revived the dream of a public health care plan, critics said it "opens the way for a form of socialized medicine."[16] A few years later, as Lyndon Johnson was getting Medicare passed in 1965, the American Medical Association lobbied hard against it "on the ground it would be a step toward socialized medicine."[17] More recently, conservative critics have hurled the "socialist" epithet at the health care proposals of Bill Clinton, Al Gore, and John Kerry. We all know conservatism is characterized by a resistance to change. We can see here how conservatives' resistance to change extends to their choice of insults. In their criticism of the various Democratic health care plans, Republicans have suffered from a deficiency of originality that appears quite chronic.

PEOPLE JUST AREN'T INTO OBAMACARE

THE CHARGE

Americans were so eager for Obamacare that, on the first day it became available, it attracted . . . just six customers! That's right. According to internal notes taken at a meeting of the Centers for Medicare & Medicaid Services, just a half a dozen Americans were ready, willing, and able to enroll in Obamacare during its big debut on October 1, 2013. By the end of the second day, just about 250 people had signed up.[18] The trickle of customers in the early days of Obamacare wasn't just a result of the technical failures of the website—it was a sign of the American public's total lack of interest in actually getting Obamacare for themselves and their families. While more people have inevitably signed up since then, the enrollment numbers are unimpressive, millions remain uninsured, and President Obama's dream of "universal health care" will continue to be unfulfilled.

THE REALITY

A few months before Obamacare began enrolling new insurance customers, Ted Cruz made a dark prophecy. The junior senator from Texas, who'd recently rodeo'ed into the Capitol on the bucking bull of Tea Party outrage, warned President Obama's "strategy is to get as many Americans as possible hooked on the subsidies, addicted to the sugar. If we get to January 1, this thing is here forever."[19] According to Cruz's logic, the American people were about to get a dose of affordable health care and, like a bunch of flu shot junkies, were never going to want to give it up. And he was right. Americans are slowly but steadily getting "hooked" on Obamacare just like they got hooked on Social Security in 1935, just like they got hooked on the right to a free public defender in 1963, and just like they got hooked on the right to same-sex marriage in 2015. When provided with new sources of security and new freedoms, most people are loath to give them back.

Before correcting the record on enrollment numbers, we might want to clear up a basic misperception of Obamacare, one that many smart people still hold on to. Obamacare is not a form of health insurance. Technically, one can't "sign up for Obamacare." Instead, Obamacare is the law that creates new requirements—and makes need-based subsidies available—for private insurers, and expands eligibility for public insurance like Medicare, Medicaid, and CHIP. So when we measure the law's success, we have to look at the increase in the rate of insurance overall (and satisfaction with that new insurance). The amount of consumer activity on the Healthcare.gov exchange is just one part of that increase.

As soon as we look at the bigger picture, we find good news: the epidemic of uninsurance is abating appreciably. For the past fifty years, the CDC has conducted surveys to track the percentage of Americans who are uninsured. In the summer of 2015, for the first time ever, the CDC reported this percentage fell to single digits.[20] Within just two years of the advent of Obamacare, the rate of Americans living without insurance was halved from about 18 percent[21] to about 9 percent. Before Obamacare rolled out, more than forty-seven million Americans were uninsured.[22] Six years later, twenty million of them have gained coverage, and more get covered every day.[23]

In many counties—from Kentucky to Colorado and from Nevada to New Mexico—the uninsurance rate dropped by half within a year.[24] Millions of people under the age of twenty-six gained coverage by staying on their parents' insurance plans. And by the fall of 2015, more than fifteen million people had signed up for health care in the individual marketplace or through the expansion of Medicaid.[25] Nearly forty million senior citizens have taken advantage of free preventive services introduced by Obamacare. And thanks to Obamacare, Americans who have some type of preexisting health condition—as many as 129 million of us—are now protected from coverage denials or reduced benefits when the time comes to change our insurance provider.[26] With so many millions of Americans able to access affordable health care, the burden to hospitals and taxpayers represented by uninsured patients who can't pay their medical bills has been eased.

The work is not yet complete, and there are still millions more Americans who lack health insurance. One of the quickest ways of closing this "coverage gap" would be for every state to accept Medicaid expansion. The Obamacare law originally required all states to make Medicaid available to everyone making up to 138 percent of the federal poverty level (so, roughly $33,000 for a family of four). But the Supreme Court ruled individual states get to decide whether they would implement this Medicaid expansion. Even though the federal government would absorb the vast majority of the costs, many Republican governors refuse to expand Medicaid because it's part of a law they don't like. They effectively deprive thousands of their low-income residents access to health insurance—footed largely by wealthy taxpayers in New York and Los Angeles—so they can settle a political score. If these holdout states were to allow Medicaid expansion, more than four million more of their residents would gain insurance.[27] And hospitals and medical providers in those states would benefit from the revenue associated with these newly insured patients—revenue on which they currently lose out.[28]

We might ask if Obamacare is even unpopular with citizens—not Republican politicians. In 2013, as the public was bombarded with negative news stories about the flawed rollout of Healthcare.gov, more Americans had an unfavorable impression of the law than a favorable one. But this initial unpopularity has begun to reverse.[29] One of the central paradoxes of Obamacare's popularity has been that the most well known provisions of the law are the least popular (e.g., the individual mandate) and the least-known provisions are the most popular (e.g., the existence of exchanges or small business tax credits).[30]

This conclusion, from the Kaiser Family Foundation, led the *Washington Post* to explain how "media coverage focuses on what's going wrong rather than what's going right or what hasn't happened yet. That doesn't represent a conspiracy or a bias. It's natural to the news business, where controversial, hard questions are more interesting than settled, smooth processes."[31] So back when the news reported Obamacare was "unpopular," it could have been more precise—though less concise—and reported that "as it was understood, Obamacare was unpopular." Put even more precisely and less concisely: "as it is grossly misunderstood, resulting from the news media's preoccupation with exploiting political drama over explaining policy substance, Obamacare was unpopular." To paraphrase a golden oldie, to know, know, know Obamacare is to love, love, love Obamacare.

And who knows Obamacare better than people who purchased health insurance plans or received Medicaid coverage as part of it?

Nearly 90 percent of these people report being satisfied with their new health insurance. This includes 74 percent of newly insured Republicans.[32] As Obamacare continues to match people up with private and public insurance plans, and creates millions more happy (and healthy!) customers, the American public gets accustomed—if not downright "addicted"—to Obamacare. In an ironic twist, one of those happy customers just might just be Ted Cruz. One day after Cruz announced his presidential candidacy swearing to repeal "every word of Obamacare," CNN's Dana Bash asked him how he planned to procure health insurance for his family, now that his wife was taking a leave from her job at Goldman Sachs. Cruz responded, "We'll be getting new health insurance and we'll presumably do it through my job with the Senate, and so we'll be on the federal [Obamacare] exchange with millions of others on the federal [Obamacare] exchange." When Bash asked him whether he'd take the subsidy offered to people who work on Capitol Hill, Cruz criticized the subsidy but said, "I believe we should follow the text of the law."[33] Take a bite, Senator. I think you're going to like that sweet, sweet "sugar."

PEOPLE KICKED OFF EXISTING INSURANCE & COSTS UP

THE CHARGE

A year after the rollout of Obamacare, Speaker John Boehner told reporters more people had lost insurance than gained it under the new law. Boehner said, "When you look at the 6 million Americans who have lost their policies and some—they claim 4.2 million people who have signed up . . . that would indicate to me a net loss of people with health insurance."[34] Republicans have since acknowledged the overall growth in the rate of insured. But when President Obama declared "if you like your health care plan, you can keep it," he misled millions who had their plans yanked out from under them. We all heard the stories of people who had received cancellation notices from their insurance companies. But it's not just the people who lost their insurance who had a rude awakening—the costs of coverage have increased as a result of this disastrous new law. Whether people get their coverage through work or on the Obamacare exchanges, their insurance premiums continue to skyrocket!

THE REALITY

It's unclear exactly how many people actually received cancellation notices. Boehner's claim of "6 million" canceled plans is higher than most estimates but is within the range of possibility. But about half of those plans were restored through 2016 by an administrative fix by the

White House, and in the vast majority of the remaining cases, people were able to acquire new policies or, in many cases, found better and less expensive plans on the Obamacare exchanges.[35]

At first, the administration bid good riddance to "cut-rate" or "subpar" health insurance plans that Obamacare was designed to overhaul. But while millions of families quietly benefited from new health insurance plans they could finally afford, the news media again shined a spotlight on what went wrong rather than what went right. The administration was suddenly confronted with anecdotes like that of Deborah Persico, the Obamacare supporter who was kicked off her insurance. Ms. Persico told *PBS NewsHour* she had to pay $5,000 more per year for a new plan even though the only new benefits of that plan—maternity care and pediatric services—were useless to her at fifty-eight years old.[36] Ms. Persico's case was uncommon and hardly representative of most people's experience with the Obamacare law. But as reporters continued to ferret out rare examples of people who "liked" their plan, but were not in fact able to "keep" it, the president apologized. Though emphasizing the "majority of folks will end up being better off, of course," the president admitted "we weren't as clear as we needed to be in terms of the changes that were taking place."[37]

There was one aspect of Obamacare about which the president was quite clear: the new law would "bend the cost curve." The costs of health care had been getting out of control. The typical American's health-related expenses had increased, on average, more than 8 percent each year since 1970.[38] In the fourteen years leading up to Obamacare's implementation, premiums had tripled while wages had increased merely 50 percent.[39]

On the campaign trail, Barack Obama told the gathered crowds his health care plan would "lower premiums by up to $2,500 for a typ-ical family per year."[40] As premiums continued to rise while Obama was in office, conservative pundits fixated on this claim. What they don't mention is that the Obama campaign had immediately released a memo clarifying the $2,500 would not necessarily come directly out of premiums, but from an *overall reduction* in health care costs per family.[41] After he was elected, and trying to hash out the Obamacare law through compromises among doctors, insurers, and labor unions, the president reaffirmed the spirit of his campaign pledge, saying "comprehensive reform . . . could save families $2,500 in the coming years—$2,500 per family."[42]

Even with this newer formulation, many thought he was overly optimistic. After all, health care spending had shot up relentlessly for the past several decades. So it surprises many that, at least by one measurement, the savings have actually become a reality. Right before Obamacare passed, in January of 2009, health spending was estimated to ring in at 19.3 percent of the GDP in 2016. But a few years later, based on new figures coming out of the Obamacare rollout, the projection for 2016 was decreased by a percentage point, to 18.3 percent. As the Harvard researcher who'd worked on Obamacare pointed out, "One percent of GDP turns out to be—surprise—$2,470 for a family of four given expected GDP that year . . . or basically $2,500."[43]

People who get their insurance from their employer had seen their premiums increase by about 8 percent a year between 2000 and 2010. By 2015, the annual increase had been chopped in half to roughly 4 percent a year. The amount of those premiums paid by the employee (rather than the employer) have decreased even more substantially. And the infamous "cost curve" continues to bend as the Congressional Budget Office has repeatedly revised the estimates of Obamacare's costs downward.[44] What about people getting health insurance on the Obamacare exchange? They too pay lower premiums than the CBO initially projected, since they opt for plans with higher deductibles.[45] Here's where the Obamacare bashers will point out deductibles have risen, even if premium growth has slowed. They ignore three crucial things: (1) the rate of rising deductibles is consistent with the pre-Obamacare rate,[46] (2) many people who get insurance through work partially offset these increases with pretax health savings accounts while those who buy insurance on the individual market have *freely chosen* low-premium, high-deductible plans, and (3) from a macroeconomic perspective, when people spend their own money in deductible costs, they tend to avoid unnecessary treatments and medical providers become more price-sensitive. Both of these drive overall health care costs down.

Nobody can predict the future fluctuations in health care spending with perfect certainty. And the numbers aren't always clear indicators of success or failure. For example, the Kaiser Family Foundation points out overall spending on health care is likely to continue increasing (albeit more gradually than in recent years), but the reason for that is a positive one: as many more people get insured, they're able to pay for necessary medical treatment.[47] So now you have the antidote to the contagious deceptions about the costs of Obamacare. So far, the Affordable Care Act has lived up to every word of its name, including the first.

BOTCHED HEALTHCARE.GOV SITE

THE CHARGE

We all remember that hideous unveiling of Healthcare.gov, home of the federal Obamacare exchange. Even Kathleen Sebelius, the secretary of Health and Human Services, admitted the rollout was "terribly flawed" and that her agency's timeline was "flat-out wrong" shortly after she resigned. As much as the Obama administration would like us to believe the problems were just some technological snafus, the real issue goes to the crux of why the federal government was poorly equipped to manage a project like this. The Obama administration employees who doled out hundreds of millions of dollars in government contracts were poorly qualified and undertrained.[48] Now, we're hearing the cost of the websites has climbed to $5 billion. How does any organization—even one as famously inept as the federal government— end up spending $5 billion to build *any* website, let alone one that doesn't work? An inspector general report from the Centers for Medicare & Medicaid Services details the lapses in oversight—the report is a veritable blooper reel of shoddy government work.[49] As Senator Mitch McConnell said at the time, "God only knows how much money they've spent and it's a failure . . . You know, the government simply isn't going to be able to get this job done correctly."[50]

THE REALITY

There might be some things only God knows, about which we mortals are totally ignorant. The cost of building Healthcare.gov is not one of them. Contrary to the hastily reported—and widely parroted—$5 billion figure, the actual cost to taxpayers was far less. Even Glenn Beck's conservative news outlet, *The Blaze,* displayed a rare moment of fact-checking clarity when it reported an early estimate of a $600 million cost "includ[ed] all of the [main Obamacare website contractor's] contracts for a Health and Human Services Department program over the last seven years, covering 114 transactions."[51] In the month of the infamous rollout, the Sunlight Foundation, a government watchdog group, put forward an estimate of $70 million.[52] When the *Washington Post* checked the math of both administration officials and critics, it put the range between $70 million and $150 million.[53] Other fact-checkers show how later estimates that escalated into the multi-billion-dollar range were pulling in all sorts of costs unrelated to the website, such as: staffing telephone hotlines, helping insurers join the exchanges, and hiring "navigators" who help people throughout the country sign up.[54] In any case, the $5 billion figure was a bloated and bogus number that was all-too-frantically seized upon by right-wingers who were desperately looking for a harbinger of Obamacare's demise.

Critics who deride the Obamacare website as "good enough for government work" are missing the most useful moral of the story. As the administration scrambled to rehabilitate the faulty website, it reimagined the nature of "government work." Todd Park, the country's chief technology officer, enlisted Jini Kim, formerly of Google, to help put together a "Healthcare.gov ad hoc team," a sort of swat team of the geekiest minds from Silicon Valley. It was the autumn of 2013, as the website was flailing, when Kim got to work. She called her old colleagues from Google and the tech start-up world and asked, "Are you ready to skip Thanksgiving, skip Christmas, and skip New Year's?"

The recruits worked around the clock, ultimately developing a simplified and scalable log-in system and a significantly improved site.[55]

Within a year, the website offered a more streamlined experience. Before, customers had to make their way through seventy-six pages on their computer screen, thwarted by technological glitches along the way. After the relaunch, most customers could breeze through just sixteen pages, with a modern design and sleek user-experience.[56] After working with clunky government contractors who'd become comfortable and complacent, the Obama administration tried—and succeeded with—a new approach that attracted top talent through an implicit promise to contribute to a project of national importance. To be sure, the Healthcare.gov turnaround was likely, for those involved in it, a tedious and painstaking story of incremental improvement over the course of eighty-hour workweeks while hunched over laptops in the unsexy conference rooms of drab federal office buildings. But for us outside observers, the turnaround is nothing short of a redemption story in which a handful of the country's brightest young people revamped an online portal that helps millions of others secure affordable health insurance for themselves and their families. I envision a *Lifetime* movie coming out called *Health Care. Dot. Love.*

When the botched rollout of Healthcare.gov made headlines and gave fodder to President Obama's critics, Nancy Pelosi went onto ABC's *This Week*. She was straight up about the website's problems but urged some perspective: "This has to be fixed, but what doesn't have to be fixed is the fact that tens of millions of more people will have access to affordable, quality health care."[57] In other words, let's not let the temporary and rectifiable problems of a website overshadow the enduring and inviolable solutions of the law of which the website is a part.

AMERICA CAN'T AFFORD "AFFORDABLE" CARE

THE CHARGE

President Obama passed his health care law at a time of economic crisis. Americans were worried about many things, from their job security to the value of their homes. However, for the majority of Americans who already had health insurance, expanding health care to the uninsured wasn't a priority. Even if we grant that it's a good that more people have health insurance, the price tag of Obamacare was estimated to be $1.35 trillion over the next ten years! Our country is already more than $18 trillion in debt, so it's delusional to think we can afford more government-sponsored stuff when, as a country, we're already struggling to pay our bills. As has been reported, if you divide that trillion-dollar price tag by the twenty-seven million people who are likely to gain insurance, Obamacare ends up costing about $50,000 per person who gets covered!

THE REALITY

The $50,000 figure, like the $5 billion website figure in the previous section, is wildly misleading. It was taken from disparate estimates contained in a lengthy Congressional Budget Office report and slapped together by the *Daily Mail*, a British tabloid, before being swiftly circulated among right-wing news outlets. But as Joe Antos, a health policy analyst at the American Enterprise Institute (a conservative think tank that frequently criticizes Obamacare), points out, "you can't divide a 10-year spending number by the average number of people who are newly insured. That's not the way it works."[58] Antos is critical of the law but is also critical of people who unscrupulously touted this figure. "[The] two numbers don't relate to each other. . . . [and] good arithmetic doesn't count when it's based on bad logic."[59] After all, the cost estimate of Obamacare extends well beyond simple coverage for the uninsured and includes subsidies for people changing insurance, tax credits for small businesses, and upgrades to Medicaid coverage. To put Obamacare's price tag in perspective, the country's total health care spending in 2013 alone rang in at $2.9 trillion—about three times as much as Obamacare will cost over the course of an entire decade.[60]

The sensational article in the *Daily Mail* that pulled this "stunning figure" from the "bombshell budget report"[61] neglected to mention the $1.35 trillion estimate of Obamacare's cost actually represented a 7 percent *reduction* from the projection the CBO had published nine months earlier. And just two months after *that* report, the CBO reduced the projected costs of Obamacare another 10 percent, down to $1.207 trillion.[62] These projections continue to decrease because premiums are rising more slowly than anticipated and companies are not canceling health coverage to the extent some economists had expected.[63] Still, a trillion-dollar health care reform remains a pricey proposition . . . at least until we shift our focus from the cost side of the ledger to the savings side.

We discussed, in chapter two, how President Obama had actually decreased the deficit every year of his presidency. Part of that deficit reduction actually comes from Obamacare itself. According to the administration, Obamacare reduces the deficit by more than $200 billion within the first decade and by more than $1 trillion in the second decade.[64] It does this by lowering health care's overall costs (and, by extension, the amount the government spends on it) and by providing incentives for competent—rather than costly—care. It also does this by rooting out fraud and abuse. Since President Obama took office, penalties for fraud have become more severe and the number of people who are charged with criminal fraud has increased by 75 percent, saving billions of dollars for taxpayers each year.[65]

Republicans weren't having any of it. Not surprisingly, they distrusted the administration's estimates and weren't able to reconcile them with a worldview dictated by supply-side economic doctrine. So Mike Enzi, an Obamacare critic and the Republican chairman of the Senate Budget Committee, had an idea. President George W. Bush's economic adviser Keith Hall had just taken over the Congressional Budget Office. The CBO is a nonpartisan agency, but Hall had been handpicked by the Republican majorities in the House and Senate. Senator Enzi likely thought that, with Hall at the helm, maybe the CBO would validate Republicans' claim Obamacare would drive the deficit up, not down. So he requested a report that would detail the impact that repealing Obamacare would have on the deficit.

Enzi had another trick up his sleeve: he wanted the CBO, which typically did "static scoring" (i.e., assessing just the provisions of the law) to also do "dynamic scoring" (i.e., including in its assessment how the law influences other parts of the economy). Enzi hoped the CBO report would help him make the case for repeal. But he was in for a surprise. The report came back, and either way the CBO sliced it, repealing Obamacare would *increase* the deficit over the next decade. With the newfangled dynamic scoring, the increase was estimated at $137 billion and, with the traditional static scoring, the increase would be $353 billion.[66] So Obama's estimate that the health care law will save $200 billion to the deficit within the first decade landed right between these goalposts.

According to the report, the money the government might save by ditching the insurance subsidies would be outweighed by the higher prices the government would have to pay if Medicare reverted to its older, more expensive, pay rates.

Finally, let's not forget the human costs of repeal. The same CBO report found that repealing Obamacare would add twenty-four million Americans to the ranks of the uninsured. It's easy to get bogged down in numbers, and for our eyes to glaze over at the mention of billions of dollars and millions of individuals. When dealing with such large-scale data, there's a level of abstraction that's unavoidable. We began this section by debunking the $50,000 figure, the supposed cost to taxpayers per Obamacare enrollee. However, there's another 50,000 figure that *does* stand up to scrutiny. It's the decrease in the number of preventable deaths between 2010 and 2013 that is largely attributable to a program called Partnership for Patients.[67] That program gets hospitals across the country, together with doctors, nurses, and public officials, to collaborate on finding ways to minimize "hospital-acquired conditions" and reduce hospital readmission. It was created by the Obamacare law. People with health insurance are also less likely to die from treatable illnesses. A 2014 study in the *Annals of Internal Medicine* looked at the outcomes of health care reform in Massachusetts, upon which Obamacare was partly modeled. The study found that, for every 830 people who became newly insured, one person avoided a premature death.[68] If you extrapolate this number to the tens of millions of people who have gained—and continue to gain—

health insurance, it's an inescapable conclusion that Obamacare is saving thousands of lives.

Politicians will keep vilifying one another over health care legislation, industry analysts will keep speculating about the fluctuations of premiums and deductibles, and most of us who get insured through our employer will keep paying scant attention to it all. In the meantime, millions more are signing up for health insurance which they can finally afford. And, for so many of our fellow Americans, this law has become a matter of death and life.

6

—

THE
PLANET
"HEALER"

—

fter a hard-fought primary campaign in 2008, when it became clear he had secured his party's presidential nomination over Hillary Clinton, Barack Obama gave a rousing victory speech in Saint Paul, Minnesota. As he headed into the peroration, his voice reaching a crescendo so it could be heard over the audience's cheers, Obama exclaimed, "If we are willing to work for it, and fight for it, and believe in it, then I am absolutely certain that generations from now, we will be able to look back and tell our children that . . . this was the moment when the rise of the oceans began to slow and our planet began to heal."[1] In the same breath, Obama repeated his "this was the moment" trope to call for extending health care, helping people find jobs, and restoring America's global reputation. But it was the environmental imagery that caught the eyes of skeptical Republicans. To them, Obama's words weren't inspirational or even aspirational. They were messianic mumbo jumbo meant to stir up and sucker a gullible public.

After all, many of Obama's critics maintain a position on environmental issues that looks like willful ignorance at best, and cynical denial at worst. And to those who deny common scientific knowledge, "the rise of the oceans" couldn't possibly be a literal description of an actual problem. So it must just be the flowery figurative language of a false prophet. Four years later, Mitt Romney accepted his party's nomination at a Republican Convention delayed by a hurricane, a destructive climatic event now occurring with greater frequency than ever before. So it was a bit ironic when he chided, in his acceptance speech, "President Obama promised to begin to slow the rise of the oceans and to heal the planet. My promise is to help you and your family."[2] As if your family didn't need a habitable planet to call home.

Republicans aren't just detaching from the empirical reality of climate change—they're also increasingly detaching from its political reality. When Pope Francis called for policies that would mitigate climate change, Jeb Bush responded, "I think religion ought to be about making us better as people, less about things [that] end up getting into the political realm."[3] (Because Republicans *never* use their religious faith as a rationale for political positions, right?) Yet a recent poll found twice as many voters in the crucial swing states of Colorado, Iowa, and Virginia agree with Pope Francis and fully understand that climate change is caused by human activity.[4] Let's hope Republicans will at least start to pay attention to the changes within, at least, the *political* climate.

When Republicans are asked about global warming or climate change, in recent days their regular refrain has been: "I am not a scientist." But this is baffling to everyone, scientists included. Republicans have no problem advocating for tax cuts even though they are not economists, or calling for military intervention even though they are not generals. But when it comes to environmental policy, their lack of expertise suddenly paralyzes them. After hearing the Republican leaders of the House and Senate using the "I am not a scientist" line to obstruct his climate agenda, President Obama said, "I'm not a scientist, either. But you know what—I know a lot of really good scientists at NASA, and NOAA, and at our major universities."[5] These scientists report climate change is the most urgent environmental issue of our time. But if environmental issues aren't your bag, then let's follow President Obama's lead and heed the economists who tell us climate change will likely harm the global economy[6] and military generals who tell us it threatens our national security.[7]

THE SOLYNDRA BOONDOGGLE

THE CHARGE

Renewable energy is fine. It'd be great if Americans were conscientious consumers of our natural resources. But when the government gets involved, political patronage and waste result. The Obama administration gave away billions of taxpayer dollars to help green energy companies, many of which are backed by Democratic donors. And if this political patronage wasn't bad enough, one of the biggest recipients of this government largesse, Solyndra, went belly-up just two and a half years after receiving a $535 million loan guarantee. Hello, inane big government program; good-bye, everyone's money.

THE REALITY

The federal government has long played an active role in supporting new energy sources. In the late 1800s, the federal government heavily subsidized the American coal industry. After World War II, the government kick-started the nuclear energy sector. Even today, the government supports oil and gas companies with billions of dollars in subsidies and tax breaks. So it's in this tradition that the Obama administration has set out to support clean energy companies, identifying them as the great economic and environmental promise of this sector's future. After all, traditions often contain important ideas—and even liberals know this!

There's no question entrepreneurs and investors in the clean energy sector donate heavily to Democratic candidates, including President Obama, just as oil industry executives donate more heavily to Republicans. But this presents a classic conundrum of campaign finance: do donors give money to politicians because they support their policies or do politicians enact policies because those policies support their donors? Republicans who criticize the president for giving kickbacks to the clean energy sector ignore the fact that President Obama supported energy independence—and respected the scientific method—long before he became president.

They also ignore the fact that the Department of Energy lending program which funded Solyndra was created by an Act of Congress in 2005, years before President Obama took office. When the Bush administration announced the loan program, it publicized sixteen applicants it had vetted and invited to apply.[8] Solyndra was one of the sixteen. Even after Solyndra's demise, the DOE loan program continues to do well. Having allocated $33 billion of the $40 billion under its authority, it now expects to reap $5 billion in profit. So taxpayers are actually making out on the clean energy investment program which funded Solyndra, even if that one start-up failed spectacularly.

This accounting is hardly important, however, when compared to the urgent need to combat climate change. The Department of Defense argues climate change poses an "immediate risk" to the United States because it exacerbates international water and energy insecurity. Rear Admiral David Titley declared climate change was a "contributing factor" to political instability globally. Right on cue, ISIS began amassing numbers and marching on its murderous rampage, its growth now demonstrated by one study to have been catalyzed by climate-change-induced drought in Syria.[9] By increasing solar energy production tenfold, tripling wind-generated power, and overseeing the U.S. ascension into the number one oil and gas producer in the world, President Obama has pursued an "all of the above" energy strategy that has made our country less dependent now on foreign oil than at any time in the past twenty years, and well positioned it to discover ways to deliver clean and affordable energy sources in the future.

Whatever happened to Solyndra's lavish facility in Fremont, California, that we heard so much about in the news? In a tale of renewal within the renewables, it is now inhabited by SolarCity, a leading manufacturer and installer of rooftop solar power.[10] SolarCity's chairman is Tesla Motors CEO Elon Musk, who donates to both Democrats and Republicans.

—

"CASH FOR CLUNKERS" WAS A LEMON

THE CHARGE

What is a president to do when the American auto industry breaks down in the midst of a recession? Should he aggressively promote American-made cars in American trade deals, and champion them with American consumers? Should he let the free market do what it does best and shake out less competitive models? Or should he exploit the situation to promote environmentally friendly hybrid cars? Not only did this president give a colossal taxpayer-funded bailout to car companies but, in a multi-billion-dollar redistribution scheme, he took money from some taxpayers and gave it to others—specifically, to those who were willing to trade in their older cars for new models that guzzled less gas. The problem is, people with old cars would have bought new cars eventually anyway. And this government handout went to the people who didn't need it: a report from the left-leaning Brookings Institution found Cash for Clunkers program participants were more likely to be educated, affluent, and white than people who bought a car in the same year without the voucher program.[11]

President Obama also promised there would be environmental benefits. But that same Brookings report also found "total emissions reduction was not substantial because only about half a percent of all vehicles in the United States were the new, more energy efficient" vehicles. At a cost of $3 billion, the Cash for Clunkers program was another unnecessary and inefficient government program. With the economy in tatters, the president decided to become the Car Salesman-in-Chief, hocking coupons backed by our tax dollars so rich people could buy Japanese hybrids. Jim DeMint, the Republican senator from South Carolina, summed it up best when he said, "I just think this is a great example of the stupidity coming out of Washington right now."[12]

THE REALITY

There are two ways to attack the Cash for Clunkers program: you can say it didn't work as an economic stimulus or that its environmental impact was minimal. Let's look at each of these objections in turn, with as much patience as we can muster for their poor engineering.

First, the critics who say this was a redistribution of money are right—but only in part. It wasn't as if the $3 billion went into some new bureaucracy or government trust fund. It was circulated directly back into the economy through the vouchers. And it wasn't a redistribution of wealth from the rich to the poor, or from the poor to the rich, but a redistribution from economically *unproductive* uses to economically *productive* uses. This is true of any tax credit. It might be true that a lot of white-collar folks took advantage of the program, but remember that the goal of Cash for Clunkers wasn't created to benefit a certain class of people, but to jump-start the auto industry. If we don't think about its purpose, we're not really addressing the thing at all.

Did it accomplish this goal? The answer, according to Paul Taylor, the chief economist at the National Automobile Dealers Association, is a resounding yes. Taylor points to the roughly 700,000 cars that were purchased in the Cash for Clunkers program, which injected over $18 billion in retail sales. He estimates about 40 percent of the vehicles were bought by people who would, in fact, *not* have bought a new car otherwise.[13] Moody's was even more optimistic, suggesting about 60 percent of program participants only purchased a new car because of the voucher.[14] The turnaround in sales figures was accompanied by cascading economic activity, such as a flurry in dealership advertising and increased overtime pay for salespeople.[15] Not to mention more people likely building up the courage to go out and spend money on a first date without the shameful prospect of showing up in a jalopy. Ford Motor Company reported Cash for Clunkers helped prompt a 33 percent increase in production over the previous year.[16] A top sales analyst at General Motors said, "We clearly see a strengthening and a recovery."[17]

It's true Ford and GM weren't the only car companies to benefit and that Japanese companies also profited quite nicely. But this criticism overlooks the globally interconnected nature of automobile manufacturing. According to one report, "The Toyota Corolla was the most popular new vehicle purchased under the program. The Honda Civic, Toyota Camry and Ford Focus held the next three top spots. *All four are built in the United States.*"[18] More than half of the cars sold as part of Cash for Clunkers were built in the United States,[19] and the program created or saved at least forty-two thousand American jobs.[20] And it had a really catchy name—that's got to count for something, right? A lesser president might have called it "Money for Rusty Automobiles," or might have been tripped up by the classic cliché and called it "Turn Your Lemons into Lemonade."

And even when you account for the fact that people drive new cars more frequently and for longer distances than clunkers, as critics are eager to point out, the swap of 700,000 gas guzzlers for more-fuel-efficient cars is still estimated to have decreased our gas consumption by 140 million gallons per year. This translates to about $500 million a year that new car owners put back in their wallets. Energy policy blogger Joe Romm did the math and pointed out, "The $3 billion program 'pays for itself' in oil savings in 6 years. And most of that oil savings is money that would have left the country, so it is a (small) secondary stimulus."[21]

Was the environmental impact as minuscule as critics claim? With more than 200 million cars on the road in the United States, the removal of fewer than a million gas guzzlers seems to make a mere dent. But given how much pollution comes out of our country's exhaust pipes, that dent starts to seem much more significant, something more like a big ol' chunk. Seven hundred thousand fewer junk heaps on the road could translate to about five billion pounds of carbon emissions per year.[22] And the results in fuel efficiency beat expectations: a typical clunker traded in got 15.8 mpg, while a typical car bought with the program got 24.9 mpg.[23] That's a 10 mpg difference, when the program only required a 4 mpg upgrade to qualify. Another key environmental benefit was psychological. American buyers have traditionally been skeptical of newer hybrids and fuel-efficient models, but Cash for Clunkers helped reassure them by increasing their prevalence on the road.[24]

But all this is almost insignificant compared to what the Obama administration did with the Corporate Average Fuel Economy (CAFE) standards. These were lifted to 54.5 mpg by 2025. This means that, within the next decade, the average car will get nearly four times as many miles to the gallon as the clunkers that were traded in. For decades, the auto industry had been lobbying hard against such fuel standards, effectively thwarting presidential leadership on this issue. But the Obama administration succeeded where other presidents had failed.[25] Part of the president's strength in negotiating these environmentally friendly fuel standards came from the goodwill generated from the auto industry bailout and the Cash for Clunkers program. In the president's words, the increase in fuel standards was the "single most important step we've ever taken as a nation to reduce our dependence on foreign oil."[26] A cleaner car industry, a more energy-independent America: that's a part of President Obama's legacy that will surely get some mileage.

THE INEFFECTIVE
"CLEAN POWER PLAN"

THE CHARGE

Obama's Environmental Protection Agency foists a "Clean Power Plan" upon the states, leading to aggressive and burdensome emissions reduction targets. Overall, the plan would reduce annual carbon pollution by 30 percent from 2005 levels by the year 2030. Reducing pollution is fine, but we can't jeopardize people's jobs or hike up their utility bills. Marco Rubio suggested in one of the Republican Party debates that the Obama administration's environmental position makes "America a harder place to create jobs in order to pursue policies that will do absolutely nothing, nothing to change our climate . . . America is not a planet. And we are not even the largest carbon producer anymore: China is. And they're drilling a hole and digging anywhere in the world that they can get a hold of."[27]

THE REALITY

Senator Rubio is right about two things. America is not, in fact, a planet. And China is indeed the largest carbon "producer" (or, if you prefer, "emitter" or "polluter"). But let's look at what he's implying. Does the fact that we are not a planet really mean we can't do anything about a problem of planetary proportions? America is also not an ocean, but we can do something about water pollution. America is not a penitentiary, but we can do something about prison reform. Time and again, our country has shown itself capable of tackling problems of all shapes and sizes, from the global to the local. Rubio was also correct that China's rapid economic development has led it to overtake the United States as the world's worst polluter. Is that a reason for the United States to give up on the global environment and let China—and every other country rapidly installing streetlights and air conditioners—build the cheapest and dirtiest coal-fired power plants possible, contaminating the air we share? Or is that a reason for the United States to lead by example, and by diplomatic pressure, to help shape international standards?

President Obama chose to do the latter. By pledging to reduce America's carbon pollution, Obama was able to persuade President Xi Jinping to make China's first ever commitment to begin reducing its carbon emissions. This reduction will begin in 2030. Given China's pace of industrialization, it's impressive Obama persuaded the country to aggressively invest in clean energy at all. In fifteen years, China will produce more energy from "zero emissions" sources like solar and nuclear than from the many coal-fired power plants it's operating today.[28]

How does China intend to achieve this? In a grand irony, the Communist country has announced a market-driven cap-and-trade program to rein in its emissions[29] while our capitalist country has resorted to a centralized bureaucratic solution. This is because, to President Obama's deep frustration, congressional Republicans rejected a market-based cap-and-trade solution. Paul Bledsoe, who worked on climate issues in Bill Clinton's White House, observed, "Communist China has the opportunity to create a far more economically efficient emissions reduction effort than the command and control regulations which the supposedly free market U.S. has adopted."[30] Regardless of the method, the specter of the world's two biggest polluters pumping the brakes on carbon pollution simultaneously will continue to inspire (and pressure) other nations to act.

In any case, if China is able to peak its emissions five years before its deadline, as some experts predict, and the United States continues to reduce its emissions on pace, the world could stay within 3.6 degrees Fahrenheit of preindustrial levels. This is a temperature scientists tell us is critical for averting some of the worst consequences of climate change.[31] So no, America is not itself a planet, but its leadership can do—and is doing—something to preserve and protect the planet to which it's affixed.

People who criticize the Clean Power Plan for attacking the coal industry or burdening states are not reading the plan very closely. The plan mandates coal-related emissions be cut by 30 percent from 2005 levels by 2030. Nobody's been building new coal-fired power plants anyway and, as it is, about 15 percent of the country's coal plants are already slated for retirement. Existing environmental regulation and market trends have seen to it that coal emissions are already down 20 percent from the 2005 level, moving us more than halfway to the national target. And, in order to ease their transition, states that are in the heart of coal country—Kentucky, West Virginia, and Indiana—have been given state-specific targets that are some of the most lenient in the country.[32] As industry analysts have pointed out, coal's real enemy has been the success of natural gas in the marketplace, not the federal government.[33] Oh, and also, children who have been really nice all year long.

Republican governors who try to characterize this plan as big centralized government impinging upon states' autonomy are being disingenuous. Throughout his tenure, President Obama has set ambitious but feasible national goals, letting the states experiment and innovate to achieve them in a way that best serves them. (We saw this in previous chapters with Obamacare's state-run insurance exchanges, education reform's call for interstate collaboration on academic standards, and granting management of welfare subsidies to the states.) The Obama administration has embraced the idea that states are the "laboratories of democracy," as articulated by Supreme Court Justice Louis Brandeis.[34] The same is true of the Clean Power Plan. Gina McCarthy, the head of the EPA, has pointed out states can "customize plans to meet their goals in ways that make sense for their communities, businesses, and utilities." They might choose to "run their more efficient plants more often, switch to cleaner fuels, use more renewable energy, and take advantage of emissions trading and energy efficiency options."[35] But ultimately the choice is theirs.

The Clean Power Plan is predominantly about environmental stewardship. But there are economic and health payoffs too. Contrary to the claims that the cost of electricity will go up, the average family will save $85 per year on their energy bill by 2030 as a result of this pollution reduction plan.[36] How can that be true, if complying with new environmental standards requires the power companies to make expensive investments in renewable energy? As one study showed, even if the price per watt of electricity sees a *minor increase,* the improvements in energy efficiency results in a more *significant decrease* in prices for customers.[37] The White House also sees benefits for public health, estimating that, by 2030, American children will suffer from ninety thousand fewer asthma attacks each year. That's what happens when kids breathe cleaner air.[38]

Republicans continue to think addressing climate change is a losing political strategy. As Mitt Romney said, from the beginning of the chapter, he'd rather "help you and your family" while Obama is busy trying to "heal the planet." But those Republicans would be hard-pressed to find more concrete ways of helping families than reducing electric bills and improving public health. They might want to position themselves as the "realists" opposed to the hippy tree-hugging "idealists" who have come to characterize the environmentalist stereotype. But as long as they continue to ignore the overwhelming evidence of climate change, and keep tripping on a mind-altering political ideology, their understanding of our environment will remain helplessly hallucinatory.

—
KEYSTONE XL PIPELINE — VETOING JOBS

THE CHARGE

This president constantly says he will help American workers find good jobs and get Congress to invest in infrastructure projects. But going into the second half of his second term—the so-called fourth quarter of his presidency—President Obama was given the opportunity to make progress on both of those goals. Congress had just approved the Keystone XL Pipeline project, which would bring 830,000 barrels of oil every day from western Canada to refineries in Texas. As Republican senator Joni Ernst said in her 2015 State of the Union response, "The President's own State Department has said Keystone's construction could support thousands of jobs and pump billions into our economy, and do it with minimal environmental impact."[39] So what did the president do? Having previously expressed ambivalence about the project, he ultimately caved in to pressure from environmental groups and vetoed the bill!

THE REALITY

It might come as a surprise to some that the Keystone Pipeline *already exists* and has delivered oil to the United States since 2010. The new proposed "Keystone XL" project was, in fact, a shortcut across the existing pipeline which would cut across Montana, South Dakota, and Nebraska with a thirty-six-inch-wide pipe instead of the current, thirty-inch pipe.[40] The company that would run, and profit from, the XL project isn't even American—it's the Canadian energy giant Trans-Canada. Yes, oil companies in Houston are hungry for a new supply of petroleum from suppliers up north. But many American landowners don't quite like being told a foreign oil company can use eminent domain law to build an oil pipeline across their property. In fact, a coalition of Nebraska landowners recently made some progress in the courts asserting their land rights against TransCanada.[41]

Did Obama's State Department actually find that the Keystone XL project would have "minimal environmental impact" as Senator Ernst claimed? It depends on how we define "minimal." The State Department's report found that, regardless of whether the new pipeline was built, the U.S. would continue to import oil from Canada using existing railroad infrastructure. It predicted the project "is unlikely to significantly impact the rate of extraction in the oil sands, or the continued demand for heavy crude oil at refineries in the United States."[42] Presumably Senator Ernst picked up what this part of the report put down. But her conclusion ignores a ton of other findings by State and other agencies. In response to the State Department's report, the EPA sent back a letter showing how a recent drop in oil prices would in fact spur more demand and increase the rate of extraction in the oil sands.[43] They showed how this demand would produce 27.4 million metric tons of carbon pollution every year, akin to building eight new coal-fired power plants.[44] Environmental groups think the EPA's numbers are too conservative, and their forecasts are more than six times higher ("equivalent to the tailpipe emissions from . . . more cars than are currently registered on the entire West Coast . . . plus Florida, Michigan, and New York"[45]).

Why are environmentalists so focused on obscure oil sands in western Canada to begin with, when we're fracking and drilling all over the United States? It's an interesting question, with an answer that ought to make us cheer for the president's veto of the Keystone XL Project. The nonpartisan Congressional Research Service analyzed a trove of scientific research on "bitumen," the type of petroleum that's found in these oil sands. Bitumen is a particularly filthy form of petroleum, which is, in the words of the Canadian oil industry, as "hard as a hockey puck." It must be heated up or diluted so it can flow through pipelines. And when it's processed and used as fuel, it throws off roughly double the greenhouse gas pollution of regular oil and gas.[46] If windmills and solar panels are inherently clean, like housecats, bitumen is a comparative dung beetle of energy sources.

What about the thousands of jobs which the State Department

report claimed the Keystone XL project could have created? What Republicans don't like to specify is that pretty much all of those jobs would be temporary construction gigs. They'd last a year or two and then disappear as soon as the pipeline was built. According to the report, "Once the proposed project enters service, operations would require approximately fifty total employees in the United States; thirty-five permanent employees and fifteen temporary contractors."[47] Just imagine a post-Keystone XL conversation: "Honey, I'm home!" . . ."What are you doing home?" . . . "We built the pipeline. It's done." . . . "Oh, that's it? I thought it was a job, like a job-job." . . . "Nope, it was a temp thing." . . . "Are you sure you didn't do anything wrong? I saw on TV there were all these new jobs." . . . "You can't believe everything you see on TV!"

Conservative pundits tout the "good jobs" the project will create. Now that we know a paltry thirty-five of them will be created, I think it's fair to wonder whose interests these pipeline supporters are looking out for. Maybe it's the energy consumers' interests. Just a thought. After all, those pundits predict gas prices will drop if the pipeline is built. But that State Department report which Obama's critics are so fond of citing also concluded that because refineries in Texas will continue to get a steady supply of Canadian, Venezuelan, and Middle Eastern oil without the pipeline, the project would have "little impact on the prices that U.S. consumers pay for refined products such as gasoline."[48]

So let's review. The Keystone XL Pipeline, which Obama vetoed and for which Republicans mourn, would have: trampled upon the property rights of landowners, spewed significantly more carbon pollution into our atmosphere, excavated one of the world's most pristine ecosystems to get at one of the world's dirtiest fuel sources, created thirty-five full-time jobs, and kept gas prices the same. The proper eulogy for this failed project—which would have added over a thousand miles of pipeline and slurped out hundreds of millions of barrels of bitumen every year—is also a concise description of it: "So long, sucker."

ABANDONING TRADITIONAL ENERGY SOURCES

THE CHARGE

President Obama touts an "all-of-the-above" energy policy that, he claims, encourages the use of all energy sources at our disposal. But when the BP spill occurred in 2010, the president overreacted, placing a moratorium on deep-water drilling which burdened American oil companies. The president can give all the lip service he wants to supporting a diverse array of American energy, but it's clear America's oil and gas companies have been hurt by the preferential treatment Obama gives to renewable energy companies.

THE REALITY

It was April 2010, and workers on the Deepwater Horizon drilling rig were hard at work in the middle of the Gulf of Mexico, on a platform a mile above the ocean floor. The bright blue sky was above them and the dark water below. Suddenly, a burst of natural gas broke through the rig's poorly made concrete core and shot an explosion high into the air. The rig was set ablaze, the structural components were ruptured, and, two days later, the man-made island collapsed, sinking into the Gulf.[49] In all, eleven workers died and seventeen more were injured.

The death and destruction was horrific, and in a very real way, it would continue for months. The underwater canyon hemorrhaged oil from April until September, frustrating efforts to plug the well. Over a thousand miles of coastline in Alabama, Mississippi, and Florida saw oil and tar balls wash ashore over the summer, and tourism came to a halt. The commercial fishing industry was devastated, as was a national treasure of a marine ecosystem. In the end, the BP spill was "by far the world's largest accidental release of oil into marine waters."[50]

It quickly became clear the kind of safety inspections that would have prevented the explosion weren't conducted with nearly enough frequency and that shoddily made "blowout preventers" like the one in the BP spill were too commonly used. The cheap concrete mixture which led to the busted core was responsible for another BP accident two years earlier.[51] A six-month moratorium on deepwater drilling by the secretary of the interior was a commonsense response designed to restore basic safety to working conditions on deepwater rigs and protect our oceans from another spill. Predictably, Republican critics blasted the moratorium for its economic impact, while environmental groups claimed it didn't last long enough.[52] When all the hyperventilating subsided, the Obama administration had reduced the risks of another deepwater spill, and oil and gas companies were doing just fine.

As a matter of fact, oil and gas companies have been doing better than fine under President Obama. At the same time the president has vigorously encouraged and incentivized renewable energy sources, he has worked with energy companies to increase production domestically. Under his watch, the United States has surpassed Russia as the world's largest producer of petroleum and natural gas.[53] As American companies produce more and American citizens consume less, we steadily wean ourselves off of our dependence on foreign oil. In fact, today we're less reliant on foreign oil—including imports from countries with dismal human rights records and simmering anti-American sentiment—than at any time in the past forty years.[54] This new independence is not only good for American energy producers, but it also frees up the United States to manage foreign relations based more on political, and less on economic, interests.

The people who argue the federal government's incentive programs for clean energy companies somehow interfere in a free market and disadvantage oil and gas companies ignore the fact that tax breaks for fossil fuel exploration have doubled to more than $5 billion while Obama has been president.[55] The president has tried to phase out those tax breaks. These are corporations, after all, whose recent profits would make them blush . . . that is, if corporations were people. Complaints over incentives for renewable energy companies while oil and gas companies enjoy tax breaks are a little like complaints about scholarships for the middle-class valedictorian. Why should she get the leg up on the dull kid of investment bankers who stash their wealth in offshore tax shelters?

Criticism of the president's all-of-the-above strategy hasn't come from just the right, though. A few environmentalists have scolded the president for not intervening in the fracking boom,[56] and for allow-ing permits for drilling off the coast of Alaska (before canceling lease sales because of lack of interest).[57] But this opposition underscores the fact that the president has been a pragmatist when it comes to the environment. His priorities balance our environmental imperatives with our economic interests. As the president said in his 2014 State of the Union address, "Taken together, our energy policy is creating jobs and leading to a cleaner, safer planet. . . . But we have to act with more urgency—because a changing climate is already harming western communities struggling with drought, and coastal cities dealing with floods."[58]

The next president must adopt this sense of urgency if we want future generations to inherit a planet which resembles the one we've come to know and love. If we continue to use scientific knowledge to serve political interests, rather than the other way around, our collective ignorance will have been willful. If we continue to fool ourselves into thinking climate change doesn't exist, sooner or later, perhaps it will be we who won't. President Obama has done more than any president to help us avert such an eventuality, seeking to conserve our planet while conservatives—ironically named in this case—pollute our political environment and neglect our natural environment with all of their hot air.

7
—
THE
FREEDOM
WRECKER
—

U p until this point, the anti-Obama attacks we've defused or debunked have come overwhelmingly from conservatives. When it comes to the president's record on protecting the freedoms Americans hold dear, the president has taken incoming attacks from both the right and the left. This makes sense, when you consider the divergent ideas of freedom held by most partisans. When hardcore conservatives hear the word *liberty,* they might think of school prayer, gun rights, and freedom from high taxes or too many regulations. When staunch progressives hear it, they think of freedom from government surveillance, reproductive freedom, whistle-blowing, and press freedom, and the ability to vote without unnecessary obstacles.

Each side has its martyrs. Kim Davis, the Kentucky county clerk who was jailed after refusing to grant marriage licenses to same-sex couples, has come to embody an idea of "religious freedom" held by some conservatives. Edward Snowden, the contractor for the National Security Agency who leaked troves of classified state secrets to British and American newspapers, has become a symbol of the "hacktivist" conscience for some liberals. And each side has interest groups—from the National Rifle Association to the American Civil Liberties Union—that advocate for the freedoms it cares most deeply about.

So let us now look at the criticisms hurled at the Obama administration from both sides. We'll start with conservative complaints that the president infringes on our constitutionally protected gun ownership rights and blocks "voucher" programs which promote school choice. Then we'll respond to liberal criticisms: Did the president really allow the NSA to spy with impunity on American citizens, authorize expanded drone strikes with dubious legal authority, and snub our traditions of press freedom, siccing his Justice Department on reporters and whistle-blowers? Read on, and all shall be revealed!

—

TAKING AIM AT AMERICA'S GUN RIGHTS

THE CHARGE

Every time a mass shooting has occurred during his presidency, Barack Obama has stepped up to the microphone to help the country mourn. However, his remarks too swiftly shift from appropriate expressions of grief to opportunistic expressions of grievance. The president has admitted he has tried to get Congress to pass restrictions on gun rights and that his failure to do so is an issue on which he feels the "most frustrated and most stymied."[1] Obama has politicized national tragedies as a way to pursue gun control legislation. But after a dozen mass shootings and a dozen speeches, he still hasn't been able to build public support for new gun laws. That's because Americans know what Obama really thinks about people who "cling to guns and religion," and they know new gun laws wouldn't prevent mass shootings as much they'd put our Second Amendment rights in the crosshairs.

THE REALITY

Let's start by acknowledging there are limits to all rights, including those guaranteed by the Second Amendment. Just as First Amendment's protection of press freedom doesn't allow NBC to broadcast pornographic films during daytime television and its protection of freedom of speech doesn't allow you to incite violence or panic in a crowd, there are reasonable limits to what the Second Amendment grants.

Let's look at what the amendment actually says: "A well-regulated militia, being necessary to the security of a free state, the right of the people to keep and bear arms, shall not be infringed." Now let's make a wild speculation that this premise—i.e., that a citizen militia is necessary to our national security—doesn't make much sense in a modern context. This isn't a blasphemous argument. After all, the framers also got it wrong that slaves counted as "three-fifths of all other Persons." The possession of the world's strongest modern military sort of makes it pointless to have a militia of gun-toting private citizens (sporting felt hats cocked on three sides, if they're really into it). And one doesn't need to be a syllogistically sophisticated expert in propositional logic to know that, if a premise is moot, the conclusion can't be taken for granted. I'm sure more than a few of the founding fathers roll over in their graves every time they hear a Republican politician defending a right to sell semiautomatics without background checks by citing the document they wrote with quill pens.

But even as we accept the Second Amendment in an era of modern weaponry, no reasonable person thinks the right to bear arms is infinite or absolute. Even the most avid gun enthusiast is likely to support restrictions on the private ownership of tanks, the open carry of flamethrowers, and the purchase and sale of drone-mounted machine guns. So where does rhetoric end and reasonableness begin?

Fortunately, there is broad bipartisan support for commonsense gun laws. As of late 2015, nearly 80 percent of Americans support laws which would prevent gun sales to people with mental illness, 70 percent of us endorse a federal database to track gun sales, and nearly 60 percent support banning assault weapons.[2] So why can't Obama get such laws passed?

The political calculus of gun safety legislation is tricky. Republican strategist and NRA board member Grover Norquist summed it up best back in 2000 when he said, "It is an issue where intensity trumps preference."[3] The majority might support reasonable gun laws, but they don't care as much about the issue as the minority who oppose such laws. The latter are what pundits call "single-issue voters." In hotly contested rural congressional districts in Ohio, Pennsylvania, and Colorado, the pro-gun voting bloc can make a critical difference. Often, it's 5 percent of voters who side with the Democratic candidate on every other issue but defect when they start to think their guns are going to be taken away. Norquist concluded, "Like moths to a flame, the Democrats keep coming back to guns. It is my favorite issue in the world."

Following the mass shooting at a community college in Oregon in the fall of 2015, President Obama was exasperated. He understood a small minority of gun owners who took their direction from the NRA wielded an outsized influence on the gun control debate. He understood most gun owners supported commonsense legislation and so he urged gun owners to ask whether their interests were being faithfully represented by organizations like the NRA. He then asked supporters of gun safety laws to, themselves, become single-issue voters. "Here's what you need to do: you have to make sure that anybody that you are voting for is on the right side of this issue," Obama said. If candidates oppose commonsense gun laws, he continued, "Even if they're great on other stuff, you've got to vote against them."[4]

Anticipating the criticism he'd receive for "politicizing" another mass killing, the president said bluntly, "Well, this is something we should politicize. It is relevant to our common life together, to the body politic." Pointing out that Congress acts to pass safety measures when we learn our mines or roads or communities are unsafe, but is seemingly paralyzed when it comes to guns, Obama concluded, "This is a political choice that we make to allow this to happen every few months in America. We collectively are answerable to those families who lose their loved ones because of our inaction."[5] A couple months later, after a married couple who had been inspired by ISIS shot and killed fourteen people in San Bernardino, Democrats tried to pass a bill outlawing anyone on the FBI's terrorist watch list from purchasing a gun. In a show of how polarized the issue had become, and how terrified Republicans were of being portrayed as "antigun," every Republican senator except one voted against the bill. Frustrated and flustered, the next month, President Obama announced modest executive actions that would broaden the definition of *gun seller* to people who sold guns online and in gun shows, and implored the Republican Congress who, after every mass shooting, had conveniently put the blame on mental health issues to "put [their] money where [their] mouth is" and fund mental health treatment. And as he recounted the children, including those at Sandy Hook Elementary, who'd been deprived of their Constitutional rights by gun violence, the president shed a tear. "Every time I think about those kids it gets me mad. And, by the way, it happens on the streets of Chicago every day." For the president, this was personal.

One question remains: Why is all of this so important if, as Obama's critics suggest, gun laws don't correspond with the number of gun deaths? The thing is, they do. In general, states with more gun laws have the fewest gun deaths. In Connecticut, for example, the passage of a handgun purchase permit law was followed by a drop in the number of murders there. When a similar law was repealed in Missouri, murders increased.[6] There's no question gun laws are only part of the solution. We should improve mental health monitoring, be careful to avoid a culture in which shooters receive the fame they seek, and invest in first responder training. But enacting laws which help keep guns out of the hands of maladjusted young men who might commit a copycat killing is a necessary first step.

In late 2015, Malcolm Gladwell wrote an article for the *New Yorker* on young men who commit heinous acts of gun violence. They invariably have access to websites where they learn about mass killers who they come to idolize. And they have access to guns. Gladwell concluded, "The problem is not that there is an endless supply of deeply disturbed young men who are willing to contemplate horrific acts. It's worse. It's that young men no longer need to be deeply disturbed to contemplate horrific acts."[7] A violent subculture, in which insecure kids celebrate infamous killers, has found space to fester online. Off-line, these kids have the weapons of their dark dreams at their fingertips. We're fooling ourselves if we think that's not a part of the problem.

—

BLOCKING SCHOOL CHOICE AND VOUCHERS

THE CHARGE

America's educational system is losing its competitive edge. Among industrialized countries, American students scored below average in math and are falling behind in science and reading as well.[8] Kids in the United States lag behind Russia; in fact, they're placed right between the Slovak Republic and Lithuania in rankings by the Organisation for Economic Co-operation and Development's Program for International Student Assessment. We need to make American education more competitive internationally . . . but how? Increased competition among schools here at home might work. More than half of the states in the union have tried out some kind of school voucher program, in which families receive a tax-subsidized voucher that allows them to choose the best school for their kids. Families get the freedom to choose among public and private schools. Schools compete with one another for students, which improves standards across the board. It's a no-brainer. But President Obama and his Education secretary, Arne

Duncan, have criticized the school choice movement and obstructed the voucher program in the only place where the federal government has direct jurisdiction over education: Washington, D.C.

Obama and his cronies in the teachers' unions think taxpayer-funded vouchers are okay when it comes to purchasing private insurance on Obamacare exchanges, but not when it comes to picking a school for their kids.[9] If these teachers' unions cared as much about the kids who fall through the cracks of our failing public education system as they did about protecting their job security, they'd stop trying to thwart school choice.

THE REALITY

Republican politicians love to pit public school teachers against students, as if the interests of these two groups were somehow at odds. But anyone who knows a teacher knows that a teacher's proudest professional accomplishment is seeing students succeed. On the flip side, students (and parents) want teachers to be paid well and have good working conditions so they can focus more on educating kids and less on bureaucratic issues.

I should disclose that my mother has been a music teacher at a public middle school in a small town in New England for well over thirty years. She, like most teachers I know, could care less about the politics of this issue. But I asked her what she'd think if her salary increases were tied to how well her chorus sang at the annual holiday concert, or whether she should get paid more than the music teacher in the neighboring town that has slightly fewer kids. She thought both ideas were preposterous.

This is personal—and anecdotal—evidence, but competition isn't—and shouldn't be—the motivating force behind education. Competition is terrific in business. It makes financial markets more efficient, and it improves the quality and affordability of commodities. But education is not, in its essence, a market or a commodity. Quality and accountability are important, but they can't be easily quantified the way a stock price or a box score can be. This is partly because education and information are not scarce goods. When a product gains market share, another product necessarily loses it. When a baseball team ascends through the rankings, another inevitably descends. But the success of one student or school doesn't fundamentally come at the expense of the success of another.

That means rankings of academic performance are based on hopelessly faulty formulas which ignore important parts of the educational experience: we can't really trust the numbers we have because numbers aren't useful here. As the American sociologist William Bruce Cameron once wrote, "Not everything that counts can be counted, and not everything that can be counted counts."[10] Will the college ranked thirtieth by *U.S. News & World Report* really provide your daughter or son a better education than the college ranked thirty-fifth? Don't be so sure. And what do those international rankings, which conservatives use as a rationale for overhauling our system of public education, really show us? A Harvard professor who *does* use the language of competitiveness has described the results this way: "Other countries that were behind us, like Italy and Portugal, are now catching up. . . . The problem is not that we're slowing down. The problem is that the other runners are getting faster."[11] Republicans who cite these rankings as evidence that public education is deteriorating might need to, themselves, get educated on how to interpret data. In the end, our obsession with national rankings and superficial indicators of school quality likely stems more from a kind of "status anxiety"[12] than from anything else.

Even if we can all agree that there's plenty of room for improvement in public education, we're left with the question of whether school vouchers are the solution. The topic came up in a prime-time television interview between Fox News's Bill O'Reilly and President Obama in 2014. O'Reilly suggested to the president that vouchers could be a "way to level the playing field."

The president responded, "Actually—every study that's been done on school vouchers, Bill, says that it has very limited impact, if any."

"Try it," O'Reilly insisted. To which the president swiftly pointed out, "It has been tried, it's been tried in Milwaukee, it's been tried right here in DC." O'Reilly suggested, "And it worked here."

But the president swatted away O'Reilly's claim. "No, actually it didn't. When you end up taking a look at it, it didn't actually make that much of a difference . . . I've taken a look at it. As a general proposition, vouchers [have] not significantly improved the performance of kids that are in these poorest communities."[13]

The president is right that voucher programs have not demonstrated any comparative advantage over traditional public schools. They don't improve learning outcomes, and school competition and school "choice" have not turned out to be the panacea for which their proponents had hoped. So what have experiments with vouchers given us? They've diverted tax dollars away from the public schools that need them badly and given them to private and religious schools that are unaccountable to the public and can pick and choose the students they want to serve. Moreover, since public education is often locally funded and managed, it drives cooperation within communities. For most kids, school pride is a form of hometown pride. (Especially for that kid in the hawk costume at the foot of the bleachers!) A voucher system could easily disrupt civic traditions which have flourished in every corner of the country for hundreds of years.

And then there are the obvious abuses. A few years ago, in Louisiana, Republican governor Bobby Jindal implemented a voucher program that would use tax dollars to cover the private school tuition of a number of lucky applicants. The thing is, the private schools that coveted the voucher money were mostly Christian schools that integrated biblical teachings throughout the curriculum. While the well-respected Dunham School in Baton Rouge said it would take only four voucher students, the New Living Word School—"which has a top-ranked basketball team but no library [and] students spend most of the day watching TVs in bare-bones classrooms"—was willing to take 314 students. Upperroom Bible Church Academy, a "bunker-like building with no windows or playground" sought $1.8 million in state funding by opening 214 slots. Eternity Christian Academy has "first- through eighth-grade students [who] sit in cubicles for much of the day and move at their own pace through Christian workbooks" and was willing to take 135 voucher students.[14] But when some Republican lawmakers learned the Islamic School of Greater New Orleans had applied for 38 vouchers, they were "spooked"—at least one of those Republican lawmakers "mistakenly assumed 'religious' meant 'Christian.'"[15]

Fortunately, Louisiana's supreme court ruled Governor Jindal's vouchers unconstitutional. By a ruling of 6–1, the court decided public funds couldn't be siphoned into "nonpublic schools or other nonpublic course providers according to the clear, specific and unambiguous language of the [state's] constitution."[16]

But the problem of vouchers hasn't gone away. Zack Kopplin, a nineteen-year-old student from Louisiana, was so embarrassed by his home state's promotion of vouchers that he drew up a report identifying more than three hundred schools throughout the country which receive taxpayer dollars and teach creationism as a scientific fact and evolution as "a mistaken belief" or a "flawed theory."[17] Tennessee recently came close to passing a voucher law that would have funded religious schools until an Islamophobic lawmaker threatened to block the law unless it prohibited Muslim schools from receiving money.[18] Tennessee's governor ultimately gave up on the law in response.[19]

The founders of our republic were deeply committed to providing and maintaining a strong public education system. Thomas Jefferson once wrote "a system of general instruction, which shall reach every description of our citizens, from the richest to the poorest, as it was the earliest, so will it be the latest, of all the public concerns in which I shall permit myself to take an interest."[20] Some lawmakers would like to privatize this "public concern," to turn students into customers and schools into commodities, to supplant the spirit of enrichment with the logic of competition. Eventually, they'll learn.

—

SPYING ON AMERICANS
THE CHARGE

As a senator, back in 2005, Barack Obama criticized a version of the reauthorization of the Patriot Act, which gave the government expanded power to investigate terrorism, because it failed to protect Americans' civil liberties. Just a few years later, as president of the United States, Obama sang a different tune. When Edward Snowden, a contractor working with the National Security Agency, leaked evidence of the agency's widespread surveillance of Americans, the president quickly defended the NSA. The Snowden revelations showed how the Obama administration actually expanded the NSA's warrantless surveillance of international Internet traffic. Conveniently enough, when Obama was president, he had a higher tolerance for the federal government snooping on Americans than when he was a senator.

THE REALITY

When Edward Snowden leaked state secrets to journalists, some praised him as a hero and others pilloried him as a traitor. Neither label quite fits. His motives might have been sincere. His decision to hand over a trove of classified material—given the scale, he couldn't have reviewed all the material before making it public—to the press might have been conscience-driven. But even Snowden fans will acknowledge that we can't allow every individual entrusted with high-level security clearance to e-mail a reporter with classified information whenever he or she objects to a policy. Doing so would sorely jeopardize America's intelligence operation and the national security objectives they support.

And even Snowden foes will acknowledge the scope of government surveillance of ordinary citizens that he revealed was breathtaking and downright creepy. After nearly a year of awkward conversations with the American people, the administration called for new restrictions on, and oversight of, intelligence-gathering activities.[21] So it's fair to say that Snowden's leak spurred public discussion about the breadth of these surveillance programs, and exerted political pressure on the White House to moderate them.

In a closely watched speech at the Justice Department, President Obama struck a sober tone in explaining how his administration would balance the imperatives of national security and the traditions of privacy. Criticizing the sensational media coverage of these leaks as having "shed more heat than light," the president reminded the American people that our country has "real enemies and threats" and that our intelligence agencies need to retain the ability to "penetrate" communication networks and "intercept" terrorist activities or malware that tries to damage our electric grid or stock exchange. At the same time, as a former professor of Constitutional law, this president could give clear voice to the concerns of civil libertarians. He said:

> *Given the unique power of the state, it is not enough for leaders to say: trust us, we won't abuse the data we collect. For history has too many examples when that trust has been breached. Our system of government is built on the premise that our liberty cannot depend on the good intentions of those in power; it depends on the law to constrain those in power.*[22]

The truth is, liberals actually aren't as opposed to these intelligence programs as you might think.

In a poll conducted in the summer of 2015, two years after the Snowden leaks, nearly two-thirds of Democrats (and an even higher percentage of Republicans) expressed a desire to see Congress "renew the law enabling the government to collect data on the public's telephone calls in bulk."[23] If Snowden publicly shamed the NSA, why aren't all the privacy-loving, civil-liberties-minded Democrats up in arms?

In fact, there is a liberal case to be made for the NSA metadata collection program. The lefty pundit Bill Scher notes liberals "are not libertarians or anarchists" and that they "believe in a proper use of government to maximize the common good, including public safety." Scher goes on to argue the NSA program that was exposed "has not produced any substantive infringement on personal freedom."[24] He has a point. After all, the NSA might be collecting bulk data into enormous data files, but there are laws which prevent them from intrusively or unduly surveilling that data. (It's not as if they're systematically reading the content of our e-mails and text messages.)

Compare this with the abuses by intelligence community in the 1950s through the 1970s. The NSA eavesdropped on all of the telegrams coming into and out of the United States.[25] The CIA spied on antiwar protesters and civil rights protestors.[26] And the FBI bugged Martin Luther King Jr.'s hotel rooms and sent him threatening recordings of his indiscretions, even including an anonymous letter encouraging him to commit suicide.[27] One could argue this track record of extrajudicial harassment should make Americans distrustful of any clandestine agencies which purport to serve the common good. But a more optimistic take is that these agencies have likely learned from these spectacular breaches of the public trust and that presidents, including this one, have likely constrained these practices in light of past abuses.

The question remains: Has the NSA bulk surveillance program been effective? If we're going to let the NSA officials collect metadata about our electronic communications, they better be tripping up some terrorists while they do it! Trying to get a solid answer to this question is thorny because so much of the evidence that might support the government's case is, well, classified. A report by the New America Foundation found instances—including a citizen's plot to bomb the NYC subway—in which the government exaggerated the success of the NSA program. But it also found "additional plots that the government has not publicly claimed as NSA successes, but in which court records and public reporting suggest the NSA had a role."[28] Nobody is asking the American people to simply "trust" America's spy agencies. The president made that clear in the quote about civil liberties above. But it's important that his administration's intelligence professionals who are paid to *not trust,* and to be suspicious, are given all (and only) the latitude they need to keep the rest of us safe.

—

DRONE WARFARE SUSPENDS HABEAS CORPUS

THE CHARGE

You can argue all you want that the collection of metadata, such as the timestamps of phone records and the location of people in an e-mail exchange, isn't as intrusive as actually monitoring the content of that communication. But as the former NSA and CIA director Michael Hayden frankly admitted in a debate at Johns Hopkins in 2014, "We kill people based on metadata."[29] Of course he referred to overseas drone strikes and, of course, most all of these strikes are targeted at foreign terrorists. But not all of them. Obama famously ordered the drone strike on the New Mexico–born cleric Anwar al-Awlaki in Yemen in 2011. His sixteen-year-old son, who was killed a month later by another U.S. drone strike, had been born in Colorado. No doubt these were bad guys who threatened America's national security, but as American citizens, they had the right to know, and object to, the charges brought against them in front of a judge, a principle known as habeas corpus.[30]

Senator Rand Paul insisted these terrorist suspects should have been tried for treason in American courts, even in absentia. "That's something that separates us from the rest of the world, is that we adjudicate things by taking it to an independent body who is not politically motivated or elected," Paul said.[31] Moreover, by relying on "signals intelligence" (i.e., interception of electronic communication, including metadata) more than "human intelligence" (gathered from sources on the ground), the drone program isn't as precise as many of its defenders claim.[32] Unidentifiable civilians are too often killed. But as long as they're "military age males," they're categorized as "enemies killed in action." Perhaps the most troubling thing is the secrecy of the program. Tom Junod, a journalist who coined Obama's tenure as the "Lethal Presidency," concludes that, by and large, the American people, and most of their representatives in Congress, "have no idea what crimes those killed in their name are supposed to have committed, and have been told that they are not entitled to know."[33]

THE REALITY

In the fall of 2009, soldiers on a military base in Texas were undergoing medical checkups and training exercises, readying themselves to deploy to Afghanistan. As they prepared to leave their families and friends behind to go and fight in an increasingly forgotten war, that war abruptly descended on them. An army psychiatrist stationed at Fort Hood, who had become radicalized and decided to "switch sides," fitted a high-capacity handgun with laser sights and began a shooting spree. After firing more than two hundred shots, he had killed thirteen people and wounded thirty-two others.[34] In the year leading up to the massacre, the shooter had been corresponding over e-mail with Anwar al-Awlaki.[35] While al-Awlaki refused to say whether he urged this army psychiatrist to carry out the shooting, he praised him as a "hero" on his website and claimed his actions were the only way a true Muslim could justify serving in the U.S. military.[36]

Senator Paul might be standing on principle when he claims al-Awlaki, as an American citizen, is legally entitled to face trial. Yet, far from being oblivious to the legal issues involved, Obama's Justice Department carefully considered the targeted killing of al-Awlaki in Yemen by drones. This is evident in an internal memo obtained by NBC News's Michael Isikoff. According to that document, "senior operational leaders" of "Al-Qaida or an associated force" are deemed acceptable targets even if they're U.S. citizens. The memo grapples with international legal issues, national laws, and previous executive orders banning assassinations. It concludes "a lethal operation conducted against a U.S. citizen whose conduct poses an imminent threat of violent attack against the United States would be a legitimate act of national self-defense."[37]

It's unclear whether al-Awlaki directly incited the massacre at Fort Hood, but it's crystal clear he was a terrorist operative committed to killing Americans. One expert on these topics compared Obama's dilemma to that of a police officer dealing with a hostage taker. The police officer would shoot and kill the suspect if there were the chance to do so. In a nod to the limits of habeas corpus, the expert explained that the officer "will do so without judicial pre-approval when the threat to the lives of the hostages is adequately serious and when there are no available alternatives."[38]

What about the civilian casualties that drone attacks incur? There are many legitimate arguments to be made about the ethics of drone warfare in general, but on the issue of civilian deaths (what's antiseptically referred to as "collateral damage") independent analysts tell us that drones are *better* than conventional warfare. In four studies of drone attacks within Pakistan, the proportion of civilian deaths was estimated at 4 percent, 6 percent, 17 percent, and 20 percent, respectively. Tragic though these deaths are, compare these numbers with a case of Pakistani ground troops chasing after militants, in which civilians represented 46 percent of the dead. And an Israeli human rights group found that, when Israel conducts targeted rocket strikes on Hamas militants, 41 percent of the deaths are civilians.[39] And yet, statistics and proportions don't tell the full story. Aside from our Arab and Pakistani partners' indiscriminate bombing raids (similar to the "carpet bombing" Ted Cruz has so recklessly called for), they're also known to commit gruesome acts of torture, execute detainees, and "use scorched earth tactics against militant groups."[40] These horrors abate when drone pilots take over.

Drones are not a perfect weapon of war. Given their technical imperfections, and the human imperfections of their pilots, they will periodically hit the wrong target. They will periodically breed resentment among foreign publics as the specter of anonymous, airborne killings introduces new anxieties to living in a war zone. And they will continue to raise new questions about the empirical observations and ethical obligations of our war fighters. Though they're not a perfect weapon, they are an important one in our arsenal of counterterrorism. When used selectively and surgically, they can be tremendously effective in targeting people who are determined to kill Americans. Even Senator Bernie Sanders, the liberal Democratic presidential candidate, has recognized their effectiveness and affirmed that the drone program would continue if he were president.[41] The trick is making sure the drone program continues to be piloted by another president who, like Obama, is conscientious of the values that both support and constrain its legitimate use.

—

ASSAULTS ON FREEDOM OF THE PRESS

THE CHARGE

When he was on the campaign trail, Barack Obama promised us the "most transparent administration in history." To his credit, Obama did implement a few new open-government initiatives. He made the White House visitors' log and all federal rules and laws publicly visible online, he revived a program by President Clinton that made federal agencies think twice before classifying documents, and he established a "presumption of disclosure" in handling Freedom of Information Act requests. But the Obama administration has been chillingly retrogressive with its dealings with the press and its sources whenever they shine a spotlight on government wrongdoing. This administration has prosecuted more leakers under the 1917 Espionage Act than every other administration combined, prompting a leading national security reporter to characterize it as "the most closed, control freak administration I've ever covered."[42] In 2015, international press freedom groups scolded the United States, citing the "judicial harassment" of *New York Times* reporter James Risen, who had refused to name his source for national security secrets in his book *State of War*. We were the ones who *invented* freedom of the press, and Obama has shamefully trampled on that legacy!

THE REALITY

Our country does pride itself on a long tradition of, and robust legal protections for, an independent and adversarial press. Reporters have a Constitutional right to pursue confidential sources and publish their discoveries (assuming it doesn't pose a clear and present danger to America's national security). But that doesn't mean employees of the government have the right to share state secrets with reporters at their whim.

Journalists who claim this administration prosecuted "more leakers than every other administration combined" often fail to mention that the prosecution total for all previous administrations amounts to . . . just three cases. It's easy to imagine how there could be more leakers doling out state secrets to journalists in our era of political polarization, encrypted file sharing, and easy e-mail correspondence.

After all, one of two scenarios is possible. On one hand, the Obama administration could be overzealously attacking journalists and vio-lating the sanctity of press freedom in order to exact retribution for stories which have embarrassed the administration. On the other hand, there could be significantly more national-security-related leaks and the potential for future leaks could be so high that the admin-istration's actions might just be a proportionate response—a sincere and restrained effort to protect information that shouldn't be public.

If you look at President Obama's public statements, it's clear he's committed to the principles of press freedom even when—or especially when—he's the target of the press's criticism. Speaking in the White House's Roosevelt Room on World Press Freedom Day, the president said, "Journalists give all of us as citizens the chance to know the truth about our countries, ourselves, our governments. . . . That makes us better, it makes us stronger, it gives voice to the voiceless, it exposes injustice, and holds leaders like me accountable."[43] In a more frank ex-change with Bill O'Reilly, the president was asked whether he thought Fox News had been treating his administration unfairly. "Absolutely. Of course you have, Bill. But I like you anyway . . . if you want to be president of the United States, then you know that you're going to be the subject of criticism."[44] These days, we all know a thin-skinned politician who regularly grumbles about the media treating him "un-fairly" and seems deeply insecure over press scrutiny (hint: his sur-name rhymes with "Grump"), but President Obama is not he.

Let's look at the case of James Risen, the *New York Times* reporter who refused to disclose his source of classified information in his book *State of War*. It's one of the higher-profile leak cases. It began before President Obama even assumed office, as Risen's book was published in 2006. In 2015, a federal court reviewed the evidence that a former

CIA officer named Jeffrey Sterling had been Risen's secret source and convicted him of nine counts of unauthorized disclosure of defense information. More than a decade earlier, Sterling had been involved in a clandestine operation that enlisted a Russian engineer working for the CIA to disseminate flawed nuclear designs in an effort to mislead the Iranian government. He leaked his story to Risen reportedly because he wanted to get revenge on the CIA after being fired.[45] Iran's nuclear program was, and remains, one of America's most grave national security threats. The public disclosure of covert activities like these likely threatened sensitive diplomatic activities. Former secretary of state Condoleezza Rice testified the mission that Sterling leaked "was one of the few options available to the U.S. as it sought to stop Iran's nuclear program." He was sentenced to three and a half years, and rightfully so.

How did Risen turn out? Was he "judicially harassed," as Reporters Without Borders suggested? Not exactly. In order to put together the best case against Sterling, prosecutors tried to get Risen to testify about the identity of his source. With obedience to the journalistic tradition of protecting the confidentiality of sources at all costs, Risen refused to do so. Responding to Risen's case, a federal appeals court ruled that, even with the First Amendment, the government can compel journalists to testify about the criminal wrongdoing of their sources.[46] The Supreme Court rejected an appeal by Risen. In the end, the government was able to build its case against Sterling using circumstantial evidence which showed regular contact between Risen and Sterling by phone and e-mail. The Justice Department had the right to force Risen to testify against his source, and it would have made its case stronger if it did so. However, Attorney General Holder set out to re-write the Justice Department's rules so journalists wouldn't face jail time in cases like these. When Risen took the stand and affirmed he would not name his source, prosecutors startled many by not prying further. They had been ordered by the attorney general himself not to ask follow-ups that would put Risen in contempt of court and, potentially, jail.[47]

President Obama's administration has vigorously pursued disgruntled intelligence agents and double-crossing security contractors who divulge state secrets. At the same time, press freedom groups have stepped up their calls for a federal shield law, which would grant journalists protection from being forced to testify against such sources. But they're not the only ones. The White House has actually led the advocacy for such a shield law.[48] After all, as Obama's comments to Bill O'Reilly and Attorney General Holder's eleventh-hour intervention with James Risen show, this administration appreciates the important role of the free press, even when that appreciation isn't reciprocated. In this country, media organizations have positioned themselves as independent and adversarial toward the government for centuries. They might not always support or even respect this president, as is their custom, but this president has always supported and respected them.

—

PART 3
THE
WORLD

—

8
—
THE
BUNGLER
OF FOREIGN
POLICY
—

If there's a part of President Obama's record as president that conservatives most love to hate, it's his foreign policy. The narrative goes something like this: we're living in dangerous times. The scourge of Islamic terrorism is clear and present. While ISIS amasses territory and wages jihad against Western Civilization, the president and his advisers are preoccupied with making sure we use the phrase "violent extremism" rather than "Islamic terrorism." This is because he's more determined to protect the feelings of our enemies than to protect the lives of Americans. Despite the threats facing our country, Obama's international outlook remains recklessly disengaged and hopelessly optimistic. Or so say the right-wing radio talk show hosts, who read the right-wing blogs that, in turn, cite their right-wing sources.

In the summer of 2015, Mitt Romney gathered Republican donors from across the country for a three-day retreat that would include six of the party's presidential candidates. Romney had prepared a PowerPoint presentation that mocked everything from the president's "Middle East apology tour" to Hillary Clinton's peripatetic travel schedule as secretary of state (or "Secretary of Schlep," according to Romney). "With all that bad news, is it not true that arguably President Obama is the worst foreign policy president in history?"

Romney asked. "I think he is."[1] Yikes. Those were some harsh and unsportsmanlike words on the part of the president's defeated rival.

It wasn't always thus. Once upon a time, Republicans and Democrats would duke it out over domestic politics while they generally presented a united front to the rest of the world on foreign policy. The presidential campaign of 1948 was the first campaign after the United States emerged victorious from World War II, and the first in which it had distinguished itself as the "leader of the free world." The cold war had just begun, and the Democratic president, Harry Truman, was a vulnerable reelection candidate, with an approval rating sagging at around 39 percent.[2] One of the most influential Republicans at the time was Arthur Vandenberg, a senator from Michigan who chaired the Senate Foreign Relations Committee. Vandenberg staunchly opposed Truman and even ran briefly for the Republican presidential nomination so that he could unseat him. But when it came to foreign policy, Vandenberg was more circumspect in his criticism of the president. On the campaign trail, he repeatedly used a line which would become famous for its bipartisan spirit: "We must stop politics at the water's edge."[3]

After Truman won reelection, Vandenberg, as a member of

the loyal opposition, continued to lock horns with the president on domestic policy. But on foreign policy, the Republican senator urged his colleagues to seek compromise and unity with the administration. The successful passage of his Vandenberg Resolution paved the way for bipartisan cooperation on international security agreements, eventually leading to the Truman Doctrine, the Marshall Plan, and the creation of NATO. America's global leadership was at its strongest.

Sixty years later, the Republican Party is an altogether new animal, and that spirit of cooperation has evaporated. Republicans are now ambivalent about the role America should play in the world after a military misadventure in Iraq proved intractable and unpopular. And so the party leaders complain when President Obama pursues decisive intervention and they complain when he shows judicious restraint. The only consistent thing about the right's position on Obama's foreign policy is that it appears aimed less at America's enemies and more at America's president. When it comes to national defense and international diplomacy, the Republican Party of America's "Greatest Generation" sought common ground while their grandkids excavate a mutually isolating chasm. This is the dark backdrop against which our chapter takes place.

LIBYA: THE QADDAFI OUSTER

THE CHARGE

Nobody disputes Libyan dictator Muammar el-Qaddafi was a bad guy. So it was impressive to see that, as the wave of democratic protests (now called the "Arab Spring") washed over the Middle East, ordinary citizens in Libya began to revolt against him. A real political revolution seemed possible. That is, until the Obama administration got involved. Prodded by a trio of hawkish female advisers—Hillary Clinton, Susan Rice, and Samantha Power—Obama authorized hundreds of NATO airstrikes but no ground forces. Ultimately, the bombing campaigns hit a road down which Qaddafi's motorcade drove, which allowed rebels to capture and kill the dictator.

But even with his human rights abuses, the Qaddafi regime had been a source of stability in the region. So when NATO forces abruptly withdrew from Libya, chaos ensued—predictably. Today Libya is a lawless war zone. ISIS gains ground there, beheading and stoning people for "un-Islamic" behavior. So it took some gall for Obama's secretary of state then, Hillary Clinton, in a Democratic primary debate, to call America's intervention in Libya "smart power at its best."

THE REALITY

The uprisings against Qaddafi in early 2011 put a democratic dream on display. The eccentric dictator had been in power since he took over the country in a coup in 1969. His bevy of attractive female bodyguards and the state-owned industries that made his friends and family rich came to serve as symbols of Qaddafi's bizarre, dysfunctional government. As did the 1980s terrorist attacks at a Berlin nightclub and on a PanAm flight, which Qaddafi authorized. In 2011, emboldened by democracy movements in Tunisia and Egypt, ordinary Libyans staged protests that, within a week, became an armed rebellion against the strongman. But, without initial support from the West, they were overpowered. Qaddafi's militias "employed ruthless force against the rebels and indiscriminately opened fire on civilians, in full view of international journalists."[4] Libyan rebels pleaded with democratic countries in Europe and North America to help them before they were fully subdued.

Despite the humanitarian horror, the White House carefully weighed the costs and benefits of intervention. People were clear-eyed about how Qaddafi's demise would leave a power vacuum. Tony Blinken, one of the president's top national security advisers, recalls, "From Day One, one of the big questions that the president engaged with was, 'Well, what happens if the end result is that Qaddafi's gone?' . . . What comes next? Is that better, worse, or the same?"[5] A robust two-week long debate inside the White House took place, and ultimately the humanitarian case for intervention won out. Advocates for intervention included such diverse voices as the head of Human Rights Watch, the governments of Britain and France, the Arab League, and neoconservatives like Paul Wolfowitz, who was one of forty right-wingers that signed a letter urging President Obama to protect Libyan civilians and help them overthrow Qaddafi.[6] It's a bit baffling as to why many of these right-wingers then criticized the president for taking the very political action that they had urged him to take.

The rationale for intervention also sprung up from a foreign policy principle called "the responsibility to protect" (or "R2P"), which the UN member states unanimously adopted in 2005.[7] This principle encourages the international community to decisively intervene when innocent civilians are massacred. It was born just a few years after Samantha Power, then a Harvard professor, wrote in her Pulitzer Prize–winning book, *A Problem from Hell: America and the Age of Genocide,* about America's failure to respond swiftly to humanitarian crises in the past. Power wrote:

> *Time and again the U.S. government would be reluctant to cast aside its neutrality and formally denounce a fellow state for its atrocities. Time and again, though U.S. officials would learn that huge numbers of civilians were being slaughtered, the impact of this knowledge would be blunted by their uncertainty about the facts and their rationalization that a firmer U.S. stand would make little difference.*[8]

Less than a decade after writing these words, Power was a senior White House official with the ear of the president. She was in a unique position to help enforce the international norms which her research helped inspire. When President Obama spoke to the American people about the fighter pilots sent into Libyan airspace, he invoked our crucial role as an "advocate for human freedom" while acknowledging that R2P isn't an absolutist principle. "Given the costs and risks of intervention," he said, "we must always measure our interests against the need for action."[9] In Libya, the president pointed out, we had the "unique ability" to act.

Critics aren't wrong to point out regime change in Libya (like regime change anywhere) gives rise to instability. And the road to democracy hasn't been without its potholes. Rival parliaments have left competing politicians scrambling for power and, at the time of this writing, the United Nations is helping to negotiate power-sharing agreements, and facilitate meetings to draft a new Libyan constitution. But one thing critics can't contest is that America's military support of a popular uprising led to the defeat of a tyrant who had directed terrorist attacks which claimed American lives. President Obama decided to act only after America's European and Arab allies had asked for our leadership and after conservative hawks and liberal humanitarians advocated for intervention. And, for the first time in sixty years, Libya hosted democratic elections. The majority of Libyans voted for moderate leaders.

The picture on the ground in Libya certainly isn't a rosy one. The economy is stagnant as oil output is just around 15 percent of capacity,[10] and crime and political tension are considerable. ISIS and Al Qaeda have even fought each other in small cities on the outskirts of the country. But with the Qaddafi regime out of power and the majority of Libyans wanting peace and prosperity, the prospects for a democratic Libya have not been higher.

THE BENGHAZI ATTACKS . . . ON CLINTON

THE CHARGE

After Qaddafi's demise, Libya was a tinderbox. A year later, on the night of September 11, 2012, an American consulate in the Libyan city of Benghazi was attacked and four Americans, including ambassador Chris Stevens, were killed. Because it was an election year and President Obama didn't want it to appear that Al Qaeda was resurgent, his administration told the American people the Benghazi attacks were the result of a spontaneous protest inspired by an anti-Islamic YouTube video rather than a preplanned terrorist attack. The administration says it relied on analysis from the CIA, but Jonathan Karl of ABC News obtained twelve different versions of the CIA's talking points, showing the State Department had removed references to Al Qaeda.[11]

As secretary of state, Hillary Clinton told the public the attacks were caused by the videos while privately e-mailing her daughter, Chelsea, the attacks had come from "an Al Qaeda–like group." This came out in an eleven-hour public testimony by Clinton in front of the House of Representatives' Select Committee on Benghazi. Clinton gave an impressive performance, but she didn't adequately explain why our diplomatic security in Benghazi was so shoddy, why the administration didn't send in a special operations team to rescue our guys, or why she said one thing publicly and another privately. Marco Rubio remarked, "The mainstream media is going around saying it was the greatest week in Hillary Clinton's campaign. It was the week she got exposed as a liar."[12]

THE REALITY

It's commonplace for the CIA and the State Department to go back and forth on talking points, like the ones drafted in the immediate aftermath of Benghazi, which get written for members of Congress and the media. Victoria Nuland, the State Department spokeswoman who apparently removed references to Al Qaeda, had served in the Foreign Service for thirty years and worked for both Republican and Democratic administrations. An objective observer might recognize the likelihood she cut references to Al Qaeda not because she was pre-occupied with the reputation and reelection of Obama but because she didn't want to unduly alarm the American people when the CIA didn't have solid evidence of Al Qaeda's direct involvement. She wondered, according to another e-mail leaked to the press, why they would want Congress to "start making assertions to the media [about the Al Qaeda connection] that we ourselves are not making because we don't want to prejudice the investigation?"[13] But for people interested in attacking Obama, lack of evidence would be evidence of a scandal.

As it turned out, the intelligence community's analysis that there had been a spontaneous protest in Benghazi, which was based on nearly two dozen reports from the media and intelligence sources, proved wrong. Michael Morell, the deputy director of the CIA, testified he didn't detect the inaccuracy of these reports until he received an e-mail from the Libya station chief three days after the attack, and the CIA changed its assessment a week later after they gathered eyewitness accounts.[14] The morning after he claimed Hillary Clinton was "exposed as a liar," Rubio told CNN it was "not accurate" that the CIA changed its assessment and "there was never a single shred of evidence presented to anyone that this was spontaneous. And . . . the CIA . . . understood that."[15] I don't want to stoop to calling Rubio a "liar," but this is certainly is a flat-out falsehood from someone who should (and might just) know so.

After all, the Senate Intelligence Committee conducted a bipartisan investigation into the Benghazi attacks. Did it detect an inappropriate cover-up by the State Department? Nope. Instead, it concluded CIA analysts "inaccurately referred to the presence of a protest" and that "the [intelligence community] took too long to correct these erroneous reports, which caused confusion and influenced the public statements."[16] And can you guess who was a member of the Senate Intelligence Committee? Marco Rubio! But that was merely one committee investigation. There were six—six!—other investigations into Benghazi, mostly conducted by a Republican-led Congress before they even created the Select Committee on Benghazi.[17] What did those investigations yield? After thirteen hearings, twenty-five thousand pages of documents, and fifty briefings, there's been no evidence of wrongdoing.[18] Compare that with just one investigation into the Boston Marathon bombing and only two investigations into terrorist attacks of September 11, 2001.

One of those myriad investigations, spearheaded by the Republican-controlled House Intelligence Committee over the course of two years, debunked some of the more querulous assertions behind conservative conspiracy theories and affirmed "there was no intelligence failure, no delay in sending a CIA rescue team, no missed opportunity for a military rescue, and no evidence the CIA was covertly shipping arms from Libya to Syria."[19] Ambassador Thomas Pickering, a decorated diplomat who started his career working alongside Henry Kissinger in the Nixon administration and who served as George Bush Sr.'s ambassador to the UN, cochaired another investigation into the attacks. He concluded "the notion of quote, cover up, has all the elements of Pulitzer Prize fiction attached to it."[20] And Bob Gates, George W. Bush's secretary of defense, told CBS's *Face the Nation* program, "Frankly, had I been in the job at the time, I think my decisions would have been just as theirs were." Gates responded to the idea, put forward by Obama's critics, that we could have sent special forces into Benghazi without fully understanding the environment by saying, "It's a sort of cartoonish impression of military capabilities and military forces."[21]

Why was our diplomatic facility so inadequately protected, then? There was, after all, a lot of Republican hand-wringing about the lack of security at the facility. Some of the criticism of the State Department's processing of security requests is justifiable, and some of the investigations yielded recommendations which Secretary Clinton proactively pursued. But in one House Intelligence Committee hearing Democratic Congressman Gary Ackerman could no longer stomach the hypocrisy. "If you want to know who is responsible in this town, buy yourself a mirror," he told his colleagues. The Obama administration had "requested for worldwide security $440 million more than you guys wanted to provide. A quarter of a billion dollars in security upgrades that you refused to make in this committee. And then you have the audacity to come here and say why wasn't the protection of these people provided for?"[22] In short, congressional Republicans blocked requests for more diplomatic security and then wondered why our diplomatic security was left wanting.

But why did Hillary Clinton tell her daughter in a private e-mail the attacks came from an "Al Qaeda–like group"—and tell the Egyptian prime minister something similar on the phone—but then tell the public they were the result of a video? Clinton told the Select Committee she was more willing to share incomplete and unconfirmed information in private exchanges than she'd be comfortable doing in public. As she said in her testimony, "When I was speaking to the Egyptian prime minister or in the other two examples you showed, we had been told by Ansar al-Sharia that they took credit for it. It wasn't until about twenty-four or more hours later, that they retracted taking credit for it."[23] In light of this reversal, I'd say it's a good thing Obama's secretary of state has higher standards of confirmation for sharing information with the world.

As for whether Clinton blamed the attack on the video, people who watched closely noticed it wasn't as simple as that. Amid uncertainty about the cause of the attack in Benghazi and with forty anti-American protests taking place around the world in response to that video, it's easy to imagine the nation's top diplomat would want to take any opportunity to publicly distance the United States from that video and make it clear we would not tolerate those who used it as a pretext to attack our diplomatic facilities. As the *Washington Post*'s fact-checker points out, "Looking at Clinton's public statements, it is clear she was very careful to keep the attacks separate from the video; the two incidents do not appear in the same sentence."[24]

In the summer of 2014, American special forces captured Ahmed Abu Khattala, who is widely suspected to be one of the masterminds of the attack. It was a moment of justice for the families of the Americans killed in Benghazi, and for diplomats around the world. Republicans were too busy prosecuting Hillary Clinton to take a breather and congratulate our president and our military for this capture. Does Abu Khattala represent an Al Qaeda syndicate, proving the administration's decision to remove Al Qaeda from the talking points was political? Hardly. He's described as "a local, small-time Islamic militant" with "no known connections to international terrorist groups" who even reportedly told the fighters he led that the assault was in response to the anti-Islamic video. Yet Republicans continue to insist that video was nothing more than a red herring meant to protect Obama's reputation.[25] This whole episode shows Republicans know a thing or two about red herrings.

We still don't know all the motivations of the people who attacked the American embassy in Libya. But some light has been shed on the motivations of people who attacked Hillary Clinton in its aftermath. Republican congressman Kevin McCarthy was about to be named speaker of the house until he told Sean Hannity "everybody thought Hillary Clinton was unbeatable, right? But we put together a Benghazi special committee, a select committee. What are her numbers today? Her numbers are dropping."[26] How did McCarthy's Republican colleagues respond to this rare moment of candor? The Select Committee's chairman, Trey Gowdy, had advice for him and any other Republican who might want to air the political motivations of Gowdy's committee: "Shut up talking about things that you don't know anything about."[27] And yet it's unclear whether Gowdy and his Republican colleagues on the committee "know anything about" what happened on that tragic night in Benghazi.

—
THE BERGDAHL SWAP
THE CHARGE

The American soldier Bowe Bergdahl deserted his unit in Afghanistan and was captured by the Taliban, who held him for five years. Despite the fact that Sergeant Bergdahl willingly abandoned his post, President Obama thought it would be a good idea to swap five senior Taliban fighters being held at Guantanamo Bay for him. But as Ted Cruz pointed out, the "U.S. has had the policy for decades of not negotiating with terrorists" and the release of Taliban leaders is "very disturbing."[28] Dick Cheney similarly said Obama was guilty of "negotiating with terrorists" and that there is a "distinct possibility" these five will "launch strikes or attacks against Americans."[29] Donald Trump put it more bluntly, as Donald Trump is wont to do: "We get a no-good traitor, and they get the five people that they wanted for years, and those people are now back on the battlefield trying to kill us."[30] In other words, if you're going to negotiate with terrorists, you'd better know "the art of the deal." And this president apparently doesn't!

THE REALITY

Any American who answers the country's call for military service, puts on its uniform, and fights in our volunteer army receives a special obligation from his or her commander in chief. As the Code of Conduct for members of the armed forces tells service members, "If you are unfortunate enough to become a prisoner of war . . . the government will use every practical means to contact, support, and gain release for you and for all other prisoners of war."[31]

Bowe Bergdahl was not captured by terrorists. According to the government's definition, *terrorism* targets "noncombatants," not soldiers. This is more than a technical quibble. Obama is criticized for sending a dangerous message to "terrorists." In actuality, his critics send a dangerous message to our troops (and to young people thinking of enlisting) when they suggest the government shouldn't bend over backward to retrieve every prisoner of war regardless of their alleged misdeeds.[32]

As with many of the president's actions, there is an extensive precedent—conservatives aren't the only ones who abide by tradition. Any time the United States has fought in a war, it has conducted prisoner exchanges in order to bring home our POWs. We released redcoats during the Revolutionary War and Nazis during World War II. Donald Trump might think a swap of five bad guys for one American might be a terrible, horrible, no good, very bad deal. But as the military historian Paul Springer pointed out, we released about ten prisoners for every one we got back at the end of the Korean War. By Vietnam, the ratio was about forty to one.[33]

We have to ask too whether these Taliban prisoners are the dangerous, cold-blooded terrorists capable of doing serious harm to Americans. Or were they just standard-issue Taliban adversaries? (Let's remember to distinguish between Al Qaeda, which was our real enemy in Afghanistan, and the Taliban, which was the ruling political network there.) According to the nonprofit Afghanistan Analysts Network, only one of the five "faces accusations of explicit war crimes," while one led an agency that conducted torture (though "torture has always been carried out by Afghan intelligence . . . this has been no bar to close cooperation" with the United States), and "there is no or little evidence of criminal wrongdoing" against the other three. Four out of five of the men reportedly surrendered "in return for promised safe passage home" shortly after the United States entered Afghanistan or were detained after they "reached out to the new administration in Kabul."[34] The State Department acknowledged that, even without the transfer, the five detainees were "unlikely" to be prosecuted. So, with the administration trying to close Guantanamo Bay, they would likely have been transferred anyway, and in the words of one spokeswoman, "We should get something for them."[35] In that sense, the swap was a good deal, maybe even the best one President Obama could have made.

And even if these were bad and dangerous guys, cable news reports that the so-called Taliban Five would reengage with their "old terror networks" were overblown. And Donald Trump's claim that they "are now back on the battlefield trying to kill us" is dopey hype. As State Department spokeswoman Marie Harf attested in the summer of 2015, "All five men are subject to a travel ban and none have left Qatar. None of the individuals has engaged in physical violence. Many actions have been taken to restrict their activities . . . none of the five have returned to the battlefield."[36] Can we ever be 100 percent sure every prisoner we release will abstain from anti-American agitation for the rest of his life? Unfortunately not. But the principle of keeping faith with those who serve in our military, no matter how imperfect they are, should override a need for absolute certainty.

Some critics of the Bergdahl swap point to a law stating that the secretary of defense has to notify Congress at least thirty days before transferring out Guantanamo prisoners. But congressional notification isn't required when a soldier's life is in danger.[37] Indeed, after Bergdahl was released, the White House took the video that the Taliban had previously provided to prove Bergdahl was alive and showed it to dozens of members of Congress. As they left the briefing, several senators said Bergdahl appeared to be emotionally and physically deteriorating. Senator Mark Kirk, a Republican, said, "It did not look good . . . I would definitely think that it would have had an emotional impact on the president when he saw it."[38]

By all accounts, Bowe Bergdahl wasn't a model soldier. But he had answered his country's call of duty and, as such, there was a strong bipartisan agreement that the president should bring him home. Republican Senator Kelly Ayotte, from New Hampshire, had urged the Obama administration to "do all it can to find Sergeant Bowe Bergdahl and bring him home safely."[39] Until the administration did just that. Then she told her home state newspaper President Obama's decision "sets a precedent that could encourage our enemies to capture more Americans in order to gain concessions from our government."[40] To be clear, Senator Ayotte, we're talking about a man who was held captive, not a guy you invited to a party but then realized you didn't want there.

When asked by CNN's Anderson Cooper whether he would support a prisoner swap for Bowe Bergdahl's release, John McCain, a former POW himself, replied, "I would be inclined to support such a thing depending on a lot of the details. . . . I would support ways of bringing him home, and if exchange was one of them, I think that would be something I think we should seriously consider."[41] Yet after the president did bring him home through a prisoner exchange, McCain played his "depending on the details" card and criticized the swap, saying, "It is disturbing that these individuals would have the ability to reenter the fight."[42] (It's now probably pretty awkward when McCain bumps into Bergdahl at POW events!) Not to be outdone, former Republican congressman Allen West went from accusing the president of neglect before the swap—"Have there been any actions? Any time, attention, or even mention [of Bergdahl] from the commander in chief?"—to saying that the president should be impeached because of it.[43]

If any doubt remains about the way in which partisan politics has stained the public conversation around the rescue of one of America's highest-profile prisoners of war, let's consider the platoon mates of Bowe Bergdahl. Sergeant Bergdahl wouldn't have been popular among the soldiers on whom he walked out. They would go on to serve as character assassins in the court of public opinion as they took to the cable news circuit. If you watched them being interviewed, and it seemed like they were trying to publicly shame their commander in chief as much as their platoon mate, you might be interested to learn the PR guy who volunteered to work for them pro bono, and to get them on television, was the former foreign policy spokesman for Mitt Romney and a President George W. Bush appointee.[44] I'm sure he kept his partisan views about the president to himself.

—

SYRIA: RED LINES AND REFUGEES

THE CHARGE

The Arab Spring protests of 2011 destabilized many parts of the Middle East, but the people who have suffered the most have probably been the Syrians. Syrian president Bashar al-Assad has played the Obama administration like a fiddle while he violently oppresses his people. Horrified at the atrocities committed by the Assad regime, some Americans called for the U.S. military to intervene. President Obama even said, in August of 2012, that the United States would draw a "red line" if Assad were to use chemical weapons on his own people. As if Obama were tempting fate, that's exactly what Assad did. Syrian children were gassed to death by their own government. And what did President Obama do? He blinked. One year after President Obama's "red line" warning, the Assad government attacked a rebel-held suburb of Damascus with sarin gas, killing a thousand adults and more than four hundred children.[45] Obama and Secretary of State Kerry settled on a "diplomatic solution" that left Assad in power and moderate rebels unprotected.

As if things weren't bad enough, ISIS stepped into the power vacuum Obama's weakness created, fighting both the Assad regime and the rebels, and established its radical Islamic caliphate. And, in order to protect his ally Assad, Russian president Vladimir Putin has started bombing ISIS targets and anti-Assad rebels. A once proud country has become a hell on earth, and refugees flee in record numbers. While the international community should be sympathetic to their plight, Obama's proposal to let ten thousand Syrian refugees into the United States in 2016 is as reckless as his treatment of the situation in Syria four years ago. As Marco Rubio told ABC News, "We won't be able to take more refugees. . . . It's not that we don't want to—it's that we can't. Because there's no way to background check someone that's coming from Syria."[46]

THE REALITY

When protests broke out in opposition to President Bashar al-Assad in 2011, the Russian- and Iranian-backed dictator, who'd inherited the government from his father, retaliated with stunning brutality. And, yes, a year after the president made a comment about a "red line," the

Syrian military distributed gas masks to its troops and proceeded to launch rockets filled with sarin gas into eleven rebel-held neighborhoods.

But what if Obama never promised to punish Syria based on the use of gas? What if the "red line" predated the situation in Syria? Republicans in Congress fixated on the president's "red line" phrase, which was part of a longer response to a reporter, "We have been very clear to the Assad regime . . . that a red line for us is we start seeing a whole bunch of chemical weapons moving around or being utilized. That would change my calculus." Because it was an unscripted response which reportedly caught his foreign policy staffers by surprise, Republicans thought it must have been a gaffe.

But a red line against the use of chemical weapons has been in place for nearly a century. After the world saw the horrors of their use in World War I, it began to develop the chemical weapons convention, an international treaty signed by 95 percent of the nations on the globe. Critics will retort that we haven't consistently punished countries which use chemical weapons. For example, President Reagan sat on the sidelines when Saddam Hussein gassed the Kurds in northern Iraq after the first Gulf War. But those critics—especially Republicans in Congress—will have no ready response when their attention is drawn to the Syria Accountability Act, passed *by Congress* during George W. Bush's presidency, which says Syria's chemical weapons "threaten the security of the Middle East and the United States national security interests."[47] It seems Republicans are only staunchly opposed to Syria's use of chemical weapons until it's clear Obama is also staunchly opposed to Syria's use of chemical weapons. Then they oppose his opposition.

Take Ted Cruz. After it became clear Assad had used chemical weapons on his own people, he encouraged the president to respond. He insisted "bullies and tyrants don't respect weakness." (Instigating comedian Jon Stewart to respond, "Oh right, we have to bomb Syria because we're in seventh grade!")[48] Here's the thing: the president actually agreed with Senator Cruz and was having his military commanders draw up plans for an airstrike on Syrian targets which would "deter" Assad from using chemical weapons again, "degrade" his ability to do so, and to "make clear to the world that we will not tolerate their use."[49] In an address to the American people, the president acknowledged the country was war-weary after a decade in the Middle East and skeptical about getting involved in another country's civil war. But he insisted that a finite mission consisting of a limited set of airstrikes—with no boots on the ground—was a proportionate response to the humanitarian horrors of the Assad regime and would send a strong message that the United States doesn't tolerate chemical weapons.

In other words, he didn't blink at all. He vowed to follow through on the threat of force underpinning his "red line" reasoning. And, to demonstrate unity and get the support from the people's representatives, he asked Congress for authorization. What did Congress do? A mere week after Ted Cruz had chided the president into being more assertive, on the day before the president addressed the country, laying out the rationale for airstrikes, Cruz penned an op-ed for the *Washington Post* entitled "Why I'll Vote No on Syria Strike."[50] Other Republicans who had previously supported a more assertive response similarly shifted their position when public opinion polls told them the American people were wary of a strike.[51]

Republicans who were "for the strikes before they were against them" could have either helped the president explain the rationale for a strike to the American people or opposed it substantively. Instead they decided to razz John Kerry who, in trying to assure Americans that this wouldn't become another Iraq or Afghanistan, had rather artlessly said the military action would be "unbelievably small," like a "pinprick." The president clarified Kerry's remark when he told NBC "the United States does not do pinpricks. Our military is the greatest the world has ever known. And when we take even limited strikes, it has an impact on a country like Syria."[52] But it was too late. Republicans had changed the conversation from a serious argument about the merits of intervention in a humanitarian crisis that, according to a law passed by Congress, threatened America's national security interests, into a childish argument over semantics. While they mocked Kerry's description, they failed to notice the Syrian deputy prime minister, in an interview on Lebanese television, mocking them, enjoying America's "muddled" position on airstrikes and delighting in our having "abandoned" the rebel fighters.[53]

Kerry might have had the last laugh, though. As Congress equivocated on supporting the president's use of military force, the administration's constant and credible threat of force helped lead to a diplomatic solution on the chemical weapons issue. When reporters asked Secretary Kerry whether there was a scenario under which Syria might avert airstrikes, Kerry responded, "Sure, he could turn over every bit of his weapons to the international community within the next week, without delay.... But he isn't about to."[54] It's possible the remarks were a spontaneous and accidental ultimatum rather than a deliberate and diplomatic bit of telegraphy. But in any case, within six weeks, a diplomatic solution was negotiated, Syria's chemical weapons were surrendered, and international inspectors verified that Syria's capacity to make chemical weapons had been destroyed.[55]

As the Syrian civil war continues, the United States will need to do its part to be a safe haven for refugees fleeing the devastation. Much of the opposition to President Obama's plan to welcome 10,000 refugees in 2016 emerged after the attacks in Paris in November of 2015, as anxiety about international terrorism grew. But even then, America's envoy on the coalition to defeat ISIS, General John Allen, expressed confidence we could defend against the possibility of terrorists infiltrating groups of refugees.[56] By the time the Paris attacks took place, there were roughly four million refugees, with half of them fleeing to Turkey, and Germany taking in about 800,000 in 2015 alone.[57] By contrast, when the Paris attacks took place, the United States had admitted merely 2,000 Syrian refugees in the previous four years.[58] Efforts by Republican presidential candidates to ban Syrian refugees are criticized by some Christian groups, who are among the biggest advocates for refugee resettlement.[59] Some Americans are too petrified of being attacked to welcome more of the "homeless, tempest-tost" foreigners and "lift [our] lamp beside the golden door," to quote Emma Lazarus's poem at the base of the Statue of Liberty. Their paranoid positions on the refugee crisis represent a small victory for the terrorists and a small defeat for American values. But the war isn't over yet.

ISIS AS AN
"OBAMA CREATION"

THE CHARGE

When George Bush handed over the keys to the Situation Room to Barack Obama, Iraq was stable. But when Barack Obama withdrew our troops in 2011, he left an opening for ISIS to invade. As Vice President Cheney said, "There was no stay-behind agreement, no advisers left in Iraq, and the vacuum that was created is what led, ultimately, to the rise in ISIS."[60] President Obama did not just pave the way for ISIS in Iraq, but he also gave them the conditions to enter Syria as well. According to Rudy Giuliani, if President Obama had "set up a no-fly zone in Syria" and "worked with the Syrian legitimate rebels . . . ISIS would never have emerged." The conclusion is inarguable: as Giuliani flatly stated, "ISIS is an Obama creation."[61]

THE REALITY

The idea that ISIS was "created" by any U.S. president is outrageous and more than a little obscene. The conditions which led to the creation of ISIS, and the Sunni extremism of which ISIS is a part, are complicated and don't lend themselves to super-simplified finger-pointing. But one of those conditions was a strategy pursued right after American forces toppled the Hussein regime. It was called "de-Baathification." To make a long story short, America's Coalition Provisional Authority, headed up by Paul Bremer, put out a decree in 2003 expelling all members of Saddam Hussein's political party, the Baath Party. This wasn't a particularly good move. Bremer insisted Hussein's political opinions were the problem and they needed to be extinguished along with Hussein himself.

According to one analyst, however, the expulsion of the Baath Party created the kind of climate that led to the expulsion of people who had had no active role in it, including "university teachers or grade school teachers, not simply people who had some kind of tie to the senior structure."[62] Almost overnight, nearly fifty thousand Baathists—mostly Sunnis—were driven underground. Most experts now realize the de-Baathification strategy was championed by Iraqis in exile because they wanted America to neutralize their political rivals. American bureaucrats who parachuted in without much local knowledge effectively, and unwittingly, picked sides in a local political spat which would come back to haunt them.

From that moment, the oppression of the once-powerful Sunni minority (Baathists and others) by the Shiite majority continued under Iraq's Shiite prime minister Nouri al-Maliki. President Bush's own national security adviser, Stephen Hadley, sounded the alarm that Maliki's government blocked aid deliveries to Sunni citizens and dismissed Sunni military commanders. President Bush continued to coach Maliki on leadership skills in regularly scheduled video conference meetings while the political factionalism persisted. Many Sunnis began to doubt that the United States and its Western allies were committed to seeking a truly inclusive government, and the Sunnis' simmering anti-American sentiment came to a boil. The tyranny of the Shiite majority was on full display when, the day after American troops withdrew from Iraq, Prime Minister Maliki publicly accused his Sunni vice president, with scant evidence, of leading death squads. An

Iraqi court eventually found him guilty and sentenced him to death, further jeopardizing any political cooperation between the sects.

All this is to say, the modern roots of the Sunni extremism that are embodied by ISIS and Al Qaeda are more complex than the sound bites would suggest and often trip up American politicians. In a hearing of the Senate Foreign Relations Committee, Senator Marco Rubio displayed his own confusion of the issue when he proposed to John Kerry one theory as to why Obama hasn't cleaned ISIS's clock. Rubio said, "I believe that much of our strategy with regards to ISIS is being driven by a desire not to upset Iran so that they don't walk away from the negotiating table on the [nuclear weapons] deal that you're working on."[63] Apparently, Rubio thought Shiite-led Iran, which is a sworn enemy of Sunni-led ISIS, would resent rather than welcome American airstrikes. Rubio presumably hadn't seen the news that Iranian officials had publicly called on the international community to help them fight ISIS.[64] Rubio continued, "Tell me why I'm wrong." Kerry, the former chairman of that committee, told him. He succinctly explained to the junior senator, "Because the facts completely contradict that. . . . They want us to destroy ISIS; they want to destroy ISIS . . . ISIS is a threat to them; it's a threat to the region."[65] After dropping that truth bomb, Kerry dropped the mic and then strutted out of the meeting. Well, he didn't, but he could have.

People who say President Obama shouldn't have pulled American forces out of Iraq in 2011 seem to forget a sizable majority of American people wanted him to do just that. After nearly a decade of war, which had cost the lives of 4,500 American service members[66] and more than $2 trillion of taxpayer money,[67] which had traumatized Iraqi civilians and reenergized anti-American extremism, which was waged on a false premise about some mythical "weapons of mass destruction," and which had done little to nothing to further America's national interests, Americans were spent. They elected Barack Obama, in part, on the campaign promise that on "my first day in office, I would give the military a new mission: ending this war."[68]

Critics like Jeb Bush, who claim the president could have signed an agreement to leave ten thousand forces in Iraq, are just wrong. Jeb's brother left President Obama with a "Status of Forces" agreement between the United States and Iraq which called for full troop removal by 2011. Nothing in that agreement mentioned the possibility of leaving residual troops behind.[69] Even if Obama had wanted to leave ten thousand troops behind—and he reportedly considered it[70]—Iraq's parliament insisted on the ability to prosecute American soldiers if they broke Iraqi laws. This was a deal breaker for our military commanders. In the end, Iraq's parliament resisted the idea of a lingering American presence even more than the American people did. Iraq finally had democratic institutions which represented the will of the Iraqi people. For President Obama to undermine those institutions, and that collective will, would have erased the war's only silver lining. By focusing on making the world safe for democracy, we had less ability to make democracy safe for the world.

The American military has actively fought ISIS since August 2014. The president outlined a war plan that includes six planks: expanding the bombing campaign in Iraq; training and equipping the Iraqi army and Kurdish troops; begin bombing Syrian targets; training and arming the Syrian rebels; getting Arab and European allies to counter ISIS's influence; and abstaining from a ground war.[71] The coalition has conducted more than eight thousand airstrikes in Iraq and Syria and killed approximately twenty thousand ISIS fighters.[72] The president has the authority to fight terrorist groups like ISIS under a post-9/11 law called the Authorization for the Use of Military Force (AUMF). But he's asked Congress to pass a new AUMF, specific to the fight against ISIS, to signal to American service members, our allies, and our adversaries that the United States is unified in its commitment to defeat ISIS. How did Congress respond? The speaker of the house, John Boehner, objected because the president's request hadn't called for *enough* authority complaining that it "calls for less authority than he has today"—and actually asked the president's military advisers to start over from scratch.[73] Boehner knows many Democratic representatives have constituents who are wary of open-ended military engagements in the Middle East and that he can hurt them politically by forcing them to vote for authorizing a broader military engagement than is necessary. When asked to show support for the troops, Congressional Republicans took the opportunity to show opposition to the president. President Obama neither created, nor gets much help in destroying, ISIS. If, like Rip Van Winkle, Arthur Vandenberg, that Truman-era Republican who thought that politics should stop at the water's edge, awoke today, he would be stunned and saddened to see how most of the members of his party are behaving.

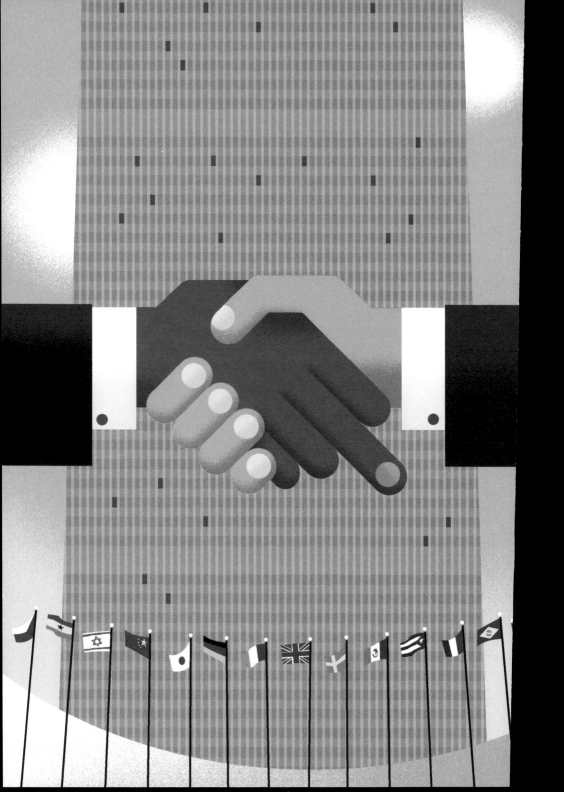

9
—
THE
ALIENATOR
OF ALLIES
—

The way the Republicans see it, the United States was the envy of the whole wide world until Barack Obama came along. We were a beacon of freedom and a symbol of strength. We were the planet's star quarterback and homecoming king. We were popular. That is, until Barack Obama proceeded to ruin our reputation. The scrawny, nerdy new kid in charge didn't even know who our friends and enemies were. He apologized to the kids we'd humiliated and told our buddies they shouldn't take our friendship for granted. Ted Cruz complained "in the Obama/Clinton foreign policy, all members of the international community are equal . . . and should be dealt with respectfully and with empathy." But for Cruz and the Republicans, that's a disastrous outlook. They reckon "our friends no longer trust us, and our enemies no longer fear us."[1]

It would be an interesting criticism if it weren't absolutely false. Despite the adolescent insecurities of Obama's critics, the United States is doing quite well in the international popularity contest. In fact, before Obama took office, global attitudes toward the United States had tanked. Mistaken war in Iraq and global economic collapse had stained the image of American authority worldwide. But today, after embarking on a foreign policy that's more cooperative than combative, and after painstakingly steering the economy back onto the right track, America has regained the admiration of its allies. Republicans have failed to notice. Former Pennsylvania senator Rick Santorum claimed the "only two countries that we have a better relationship with now than when Barack Obama came into office are Cuba and Iran." In point of fact, "the U.S. is viewed more favorably overseas now than it was before Obama took office."[2]

In 2008, the last year of Bush's presidency, only half of British citizens had a favorable opinion of the United States and 16 percent of them had confidence in the American president's leadership. Fast-forward to 2015: about two-thirds of Brits reported a favorable opinion and 76 percent have confidence in our president. In the same period, the French people's confidence in our president jumped from 13 percent to 83 percent (and favorability toward the United States from 42 percent to 73 percent), while the Germans' confidence in our president went from 14 percent to 73 percent (and favorability toward the United States from 31 percent to 50 percent).[3] America's reputation has similarly rebounded with the vast majority of foreign publics surveyed, including the Japanese, Mexicans, Italians, and Poles. Republicans need to relax. Getting all worked up and self-conscious about what the other countries think about us just isn't cool. And, thanks to Barack Obama, we're finally cool again.

— SNOOPING ON GERMANY

THE CHARGE

We learned, among the eye-popping revelations of Edward Snowden's dump of secret documents, that President Obama's intelligence agencies had tapped the cell phone of German chancellor Angela Merkel. In fact, sixty-nine phone numbers of senior German officials were reportedly targeted.[4] So furious was Merkel that she kicked out the CIA station chief in Berlin, saying "spying on allies . . . is a waste of energy."[5] She'd previously said, "Spying between friends . . . that's just not done."[6] How did President Obama respond? He admitted to spying and said America needed to rebuild trust with our European ally. But then he asked the German people to "give us the benefit of the doubt" and to stop "assuming the worst."[7] As a result of our president's penchant for snooping on friendly nations, and the arrogance with which he does so, the German people actually have more admiration for Edward Snowden than for Barack Obama.[8]

THE REALITY

Angela Merkel and Barack Obama are kindred political spirits. The former physicist and the former law professor share a wonky, logic-driven leadership style. Also, as a woman and a black man, both come from groups underrepresented in their countries' national politics. Their aides report a strong bond between them has developed over the course of Obama's tenure. In his first term, President Obama honored Merkel with the Presidential Medal of Freedom. After the ceremony, James Taylor sweetly serenaded the chancellor with a rendition of "You've Got a Friend" as the White House pastry chef served apple strudel (of course). A year before Snowden's disclosures, world leaders were at a meeting of the Group of Eight (G8) industrialized countries at Camp David. As the meeting broke up and other leaders departed Washington, Obama asked Merkel to stay behind, and as the sun set, the two of them concocted a plan to help save Greece's faltering economy.[9]

Since the leaders of these proud and powerful countries had developed such a strong relationship, it should be surprising to learn that we were spying on our ally, right? Actually no. Friendly countries spy on one another all the time, and have been doing so for centuries. In the sixteenth century, Spain's King Philip II teamed up with the pope to attack Britain with the Spanish Armada. Yet throughout their alliance, the Spanish king's aides and the Vatican snooped on one another to make sure each was fully committed to their joint effort. After World War I, as the Allies began to negotiate the Paris Peace Conference, aides to President Woodrow Wilson hired the cryptologist Herbert Yardley to tap into the planning sessions of our fellow victors. And, in the 1980s, the Israeli government bought state secrets from an American analyst, Jonathan Pollard (who now resides in a North Carolina prison, where he is serving a life sentence for espionage).

At the time of the Merkel business, national security expert Jennifer Sims catalogued these examples in *Foreign Affairs*. She also listed several "good reasons for allies to spy on each other," such as monitoring divergent interests or protecting against shared vulnerabilities.[10] Mike Rogers, the Michigan Republican and chair of the House Intelligence Committee, insisted the German and French people should appreciate, rather than be angry about, America's clandestine activity. "It keeps our European allies safe" while protecting our shared national interests, Rogers insisted. He called European leaders' criticism "disingenuous," given their own surveillance programs.[11] According to John Arquilla, an intelligence expert at the Naval Postgraduate School, "Any world leader who expresses shock at being spied on should immediately fall under suspicion by his or her own people for being dangerously naive."[12]

Although foreign policy pros and elected leaders around the world understand and even expect this kind of espionage among allies, ordinary consumers of political news are likely to be surprised by it (both in the United States and Germany). And so the public indignity caused by Snowden's disclosures would surely require some delicate diplomacy. After all, the German press pumped out daily headlines which expressed anger and affront at American espionage tactics. For her part, Merkel reportedly "fed a public line that she was outraged and personally offended" even while, in reality, "she was less angry than mystified by what seemed to be the stupidity of it all."[13] The decision to expel the CIA station chief from Berlin was largely seen as a political decision by Merkel made to quell domestic political pressure. Speaking by phone (hopefully one that was no longer tapped), she and Obama agreed the White House chief of staff would travel to Berlin, largely for the signal it would send to the German people that the United States was committed to restoring a seemingly damaged relationship. However, many German officials privately admit they want us to maintain an aggressive intelligence operation, given that the United States spends about ten times as much per capita on intelligence as Germany does and this helps both countries combat common enemies like ISIS.[14]

A year and a half after Chancellor Merkel insisted that "spying between friends . . . that's just not done," the venerable German newspaper *Der Spiegel* detected a whiff of hypocrisy. It had discovered the German intelligence agency B.N.D. had worked for several years with America's NSA to spy on its "friends," including a consortium of European countries that develops military aircraft as well as "politicians and institutions" across Europe.[15] Spying between friends is just not done . . . in public.

—
ABANDONING EASTERN EUROPE

THE CHARGE

Russia menaces its Eastern European neighbors more every day. In March of 2014, Vladimir Putin annexed Crimea and sent troops into eastern Ukraine. For years, American allies like Poland and the Czech Republic have watched and worried as Putin takes a more belligerent stance toward his neighbors. Nostalgic Russians still covetously remember these "New European" countries as their Soviet satellite states. But these countries are important NATO allies and important proving grounds for reawakening democracy and capitalism in the aftermath of dictatorship. Eastern Europe was thrilled when George

Bush announced a plan to build a missile defense system in Poland and the Czech Republic. Although Bush's defense secretary Bob Gates explained the rationale for the missile defense shield was to deter or intercept *Iranian* missiles, even a foreign policy amateur knows Iranian missiles can't reach the Unites States or most all of its NATO allies . . . but *Russian* missiles can.

Our European allies were excited for a new defense system which would guard against any Russian aggression. Putin was downright annoyed and tried to pressure the Americans to rethink their plans. What did President Obama do once elected? He did exactly what Russia insisted, and scrapped the plans! According to Dick Cheney, Obama had been "pushed around" by Putin,[16] while Mitt Romney said it was a "gift to Russia."[17]

THE REALITY

The Obama administration pledged to "reset" relations with Russia but never at the expense of the national security of America and its allies. The reset was offered from a position of strength, not a posture of intimidation. NATO and Russia have a complicated relationship that sometimes involves cooperation and mutual interest (in deterring Iran's nuclear ambitions or combating ISIS) and sometimes involves competition and mutual suspicion (in keeping a check on Russia's expansionist impulses). In short, while Poland and the Czech Republic are unquestionably America's allies, Russia is not, as Romney once called it, America's "number one geopolitical foe."[18]

When President Obama scrapped the Bush-era plans for missile defense, he replaced them with an even more modern and mobile missile defense program housed on U.S. warships and therefore more readily deployable. Bob Gates, who served both George Bush and Barack Obama, oversaw the development of both plans. In his memoir, Gates recalled that, yes, as a Republican defense secretary in a Democratic administration, he sometimes felt as if he gave cover to the White House, but that it "was okay in this instance since I sincerely believed the new program was better . . . and more effective."[19] Gates wrote the new program benefited from "technological advances in airborne, space-based, and ground-based sensors" and that these "considerably outperformed the fixed-site radar originally intended for the Czech Republic."[20]

This sea-based missile defense has proven to be impressively effective indeed. Rear Admiral Alan B. Hicks, its program director, demonstrated the flexibility of the new system when a U.S. satellite strayed from orbit and began hurtling toward the earth. Hicks reported "the satellite was higher, faster, and larger than any previous target."[21] To test its capabilities, the Aegis weapons system made a few quick modifications based on the space-based sensors Gates mentioned and launched an SM-3 missile. It hit its mark and blew the fugitive satellite out of the sky. Admiral Hicks observes how the new sea-based systems "can search, detect, and track ballistic missiles of all ranges." Pretty cool, I'd say.

Recently Obama announced that the U.S. Navy would complement these antimissile ships with ballistic missile defense capabilities elsewhere in Europe, and today, the United States remains the "primary contributor to the European missile defense shield."[22] If this is, as Romney suggested, a "gift" to Russia, it's a gift Russia doesn't want. Putin continues to complain that Iran doesn't possess the kind of intercontinental ballistic missiles the system is supposedly designed to intercept. As if everyone wasn't already in on that fact. We're just being polite by mentioning Iran and North Korea and biting our tongue about Russia's ongoing violations of the Intermediate-Range Nuclear Forces (INF) treaty.[23] In fact, according to Bob Gates, Russia saw Obama's plan as more of a threat than Bush's plan. "How ironic that U.S. critics of the new approach had portrayed it as a big concession to the Russians," Gates wrote. "It would have been nice to hear a critic in Washington—just once in my career—say, 'Well I got that one wrong.'"[24]

If Russia itself wasn't happy with Obama's change in missile defense strategy, what did our NATO allies think about it? At the time, some politicians in Warsaw and Prague—those who accommodated the Bush administration's plans despite taking flack from their constituents—got annoyed. But, as Gates recalled, the political majorities in both countries would probably have blocked the presence of a new American military site, anyway, and so the "Polish and Czech governments were relieved" when the plans were pulled.[25] And many of our European allies had seen these sites as provocations toward Russia and were happy to see the plans scrapped. The secretary-general of NATO called President Obama's new direction a "positive step."[26]

Lest anyone still think the Obama administration is shaky about supporting our Eastern European allies or shy about opposing Russian aggression, consider the extraordinary pledge President Obama made in Estonia about the alliance between the United States and its Balkan partners:

> During the long Soviet occupation, the great Estonian poet, Marie Under, wrote a poem in which she cried to the world: "Who'll come to help? Right here, at present, now!" And I say to the people of Estonia and the people of the Baltics, today we are bound by our treaty Alli-

ance. We have a solemn duty to each other. Article five is crystal clear: An attack on one is an attack on all. So if, in such a moment, you ever ask again, "who will come to help," you'll know the answer—the NATO Alliance, including the Armed Forces of the United States of America, "right here, at present, now!" [Applause.] We'll be here for Estonia. We will be here for Latvia. We will be here for Lithuania. You lost your independence once before. With NATO, you will never lose it again.[27]

The speech won praise from an unlikely source. David Frum, a speechwriter for President Bush and a regular critic of President Obama, called it "the most important speech about European security . . . of the post-cold war era" and commented that it is "the ultimate commitment, given by the ultimate authority, in the very place where the commitment would be tested. . . . Today, for the first time perhaps, Eastern Europeans have reason to believe it."[28] Obama has not *abandoned* Eastern European allies. He simply *abandoned* a problematic missile defense plan and replaced it with a better one. It's high time his Republicans *abandoned* accusations to the contrary.

—

DISRESPECTING ISRAEL
THE CHARGE

The United States has had a long-standing friendship with Israel. As a democracy committed to human rights and the rule of law, Israel is an anomaly in the Middle East. Surrounded by Arab neighbors who don't even recognize it as a country, Israel relies on its military alliance with the United States for its very survival.

Yet Barack Obama has snubbed the Israelis at every opportunity. In 2014, Hamas militants viciously attacked Israeli citizens and Israel responded with rocket attacks into Gaza. Secretary of State John Kerry drew up a ceasefire plan that, according to the Israeli newspaper *Haaretz*, "placed Israel and Hamas on the same level, as if the first is not a primary U.S. ally and as if the second isn't a terror group."[29] The *Times of Israel* noted that Israeli government sources thought Kerry "completely capitulated" to Hamas.[30] When Prime Minister Netanyahu strenuously opposed the nuclear negotiations with Iran, President Obama sidelined his concerns. Speaking before the Republican Jewish Coalition, Marco Rubio said if he got elected, "The days of giving the ayatollah of Iran more respect than the prime minister of Israel will be over."[31]

THE REALITY

January 20, 2015, was a busy day for Secretary of State John Kerry. The president planned to give the State of the Union address that evening and the administration was busy with final preparations and last-minute politicking. But that didn't stop Kerry from taking two hours to meet with Israel's ambassador, Ron Dermer, and hear his concerns about the nuclear negotiations with Iran. But during that meeting, Dermer kept a secret. For about two weeks, he had been working with John Boehner to schedule a speech by Netanyahu before a joint session of Congress, much like the one Obama was about to give that evening. This was a gutsy move by congressional Republicans, since inviting a foreign leader to criticize a sitting American president in a venue typically reserved for presidential inaugurations and State of the Union addresses is a flagrant breach of decorum, if not of patriotism. Announcing the invitation on the morning after a State of the Union address, thereby distracting attention away from the president's many policy proposals with a shiny new scandal, was also poor form.

Dermer was quickly chastised for his double-dealing, and not just by the usual Obama defenders. Chris Wallace, the host of *Fox News Sunday,* reflected on the meeting with Kerry in which Dermer "never mentioned the fact that Netanyahu was in negotiations and finally agreed to come to Washington, not to see the president, but to go to Capitol Hill, speak to a joint session of Congress and criticize the president's policy. I have to say I'm shocked."[32] Martin Indyk, a former American ambassador to Israel, predicted, "Jewish leaders, Jewish voters, nobody is going to feel comfortable being put in this situation. . . . Mainstream Jewish organizations do not want Israel to become a partisan issue."[33] If they were smart, Republicans wouldn't want Israel to become a partisan issue too. That's because American Jews are overwhelmingly progressive. Three in four Jewish voters cast their ballot for President Obama[34] and, as much as they love Israel, roughly twice as many American Jews broke with Netanyahu and supported the Iran nuclear deal as opposed it.[35] Ambassador Dermer tried to redirect the incoming criticism, saying he was told by Speaker Boehner that it was "normal protocol for the speaker's office to notify the administration of the invitation."[36]

The Obama administration might have been irritated by Netanyahu's attempt to undermine it on the Iran deal, continuing to support settlement construction in the West Bank in violation of international law,[37] and going back and forth on whether he supports a "two-state solution" which would promote peace through mutual recognition between Israel and Palestine. But Barack Obama knows that the security of Israel is fundamental to our relationships in the Middle East. That's why, while the news media are busy whipping up a bunch of imaginary personal dramas between the two leaders, the United States has quietly enlarged an already generous military aid allowance to Israel. Under Obama, Israel has received more than $3 billion annually, the most of any country and twice as much as the runner-up. Obama funded programs that enhance security cooperation and bankrolled Israel's cutting-edge missile defense system, the Iron Dome.

What about that cease-fire plan that John Kerry proposed when violence broke out between Palestinians and Israelis in 2014? Didn't it draw an inappropriate moral equivalence, as the Israeli columnists seemed to suggest? The State Department responded by pointing out the plan was "nearly identical" to the Egyptian cease-fire proposal initially put forward, which had been supported by Israel and opposed by Hamas.[38] It's more likely that the judgment of some Israeli journalists was obscured in the throes of conflict. Does America project a double standard for Israel when President Obama urges restraint from "both sides"? Well, we certainly understand that Israel has a right and responsibility to defend itself. But it is also a liberal democracy committed to tolerance and inclusion, armed with an indomitable weapons system and an advanced economy—so we certainly have high standards for, and expectations of, our ally.

After the Iran nuclear deal had been signed, Netanyahu gave up on his boycott of foreign aid discussions and, in November of 2015, came to the White House to move past the disagreement with President Obama. Beginning the meeting, President Obama said, "It's no secret that the prime minister and I have had a strong disagreement on this narrow issue. But we don't have a disagreement on the need for making sure that Iran does not get a nuclear weapon." The two allies proceeded to discuss contingencies for any rule breaking on Iran's part and ways to ensure Israel's security even further with increased aid. After the meeting, Prime Minister Netanyahu spoke to Israeli reporters. He batted down suggestions there was any tension and said the "conversation was in very good spirits and very honest. . . . No one hid the disagreements between us. Rather, we focused on how to go forward."[39] The relationship between the United States and Israel—as well as between Obama and Netanyahu—is about principles, not personalities. Though it's safe to say these two guys probably aren't going to be getting brunch together anytime soon.

—

GIVING UP GAINS IN AFGHANISTAN

THE CHARGE

When he was on the campaign trail, President Obama pledged to bring the wars in Iraq and Afghanistan to an end. Even if it was all right to pull American troops out of Iraq, since its prime minister and parliament wanted us to leave, the new president of Afghanistan, Ashraf Ghani, publicly urged President Obama to "re-examine" his timeline for troop withdrawal. Insisting progress was "very real," Ghani pointed out the

Taliban's ominous and persistent presence as August 2014 approached. "Deadlines should not be dogmas," he implored us.[40] Obama repeated and repeated that American troops would be out of Afghanistan by the end of 2016. But then, in October of 2015, Obama changed course, saying the United States would be leaving 9,800 troops in Afghanistan through most of 2016. We'd then drop our troop presence to 5,500 and let the next president deal with the situation.[41]

Obama's solution broke his campaign pledge. And it pleased neither the hawks nor the doves. Isolationist Republicans like Rand Paul have asked, "Why are we still at war in Afghanistan?" and said, "The Afghans need to step it up and defend themselves."[42] Meanwhile, interventionist Republicans like Lindsey Graham and Carly Fiorina offered an opposite critique, saying the slower pace of troop withdrawal wasn't slow enough. Graham anticipated Afghanistan would become a power vacuum like Iraq, saying Obama "intentionally ignored all military advice to keep a residual force in Iraq. He paid a price and this 5,500 number is not a militarily sound number." Fiorina insisted Obama "didn't listen" to his commanders, since he arrogantly "thought he knew better."[43]

THE REALITY

Republicans understand that Americans watch the brutality of ISIS in Iraq and Syria and are afraid that, when we eventually withdraw from Afghanistan, that country will also be overrun by terrorists. It might be easy to conflate these two conflicts—but it's a trap. While ISIS is hell-bent on holy war with the West, the Taliban in Afghanistan poses no credible threat to the national security of the United

States, antidemocratic and ultraconservative though it may be. And although the Taliban continues to control about 10 percent of the (mostly rural) districts throughout Afghanistan,[44] it doesn't have international recruiting capability like ISIS, and it faces a more formidable national military.

When General John Campbell, the top U.S. military commander in Afghanistan, was asked to give testimony before the Senate Armed Services Committee, he seemed surprised at all the simplistic comparisons the senators made between Iraq and Afghanistan. Senator Joe Manchin worried aloud about Obama's troop drawdown plans, saying, "We saw the results of Iraq." But General Campbell repeatedly assured the committee that "Afghanistan is not Iraq." As he pointed out, in the wake of the U.S. departure in Iraq, an erosion in the Iraqi military and political infighting created conditions for an insurgency. This was unlikely in Afghanistan. General Campbell observed that in Afghanistan we "have a government that wants to have a counterterrorism capability. You have a fighting force that is very resilient . . . there are so many differences between Iraq and Afghanistan."[45] Yet many Republicans continue to insist that any reduction in America's presence in Afghanistan will set the stage for an encore of ISIS's rise in Iraq. Who isn't listening to our military commanders now?

Fortunately President Obama knows the situation in Afghanistan and Iraq are distinct. Although he didn't mention Iraq explicitly in his announcement that troops will remain in Afghanistan through 2017, he named three factors that are present in Afghanistan but not Iraq: a government that wants our support, a clear objective, and certain legal immunities for American soldiers.[46] The president acknowledged that he wouldn't achieve his—and many Americans'—goal of bringing all our troops home from Afghanistan before he left office. But he was willing to lose a few political points in order to "not allow Afghanistan to be used as a safe haven for terrorists to attack our nation again." He acknowledged how "weary" many Americans were of our presence there and opposed "the idea of endless war." But he also pointed out our national security interests in the region, and the way in which the Afghans are stepping up their game. American soldiers have a limited mission in training and assisting, incurring fewer and fewer casualties every year while "every single day, Afghan forces are out there fighting and dying to protect their country . . . [and are] not looking for us to do it for them."[47] In fact, in 2015, American casualties had fallen to 22[48] while the Afghan security forces had taken on more than five thousand.[49] As high as the stakes and great as the sacrifices are for the United States, they're higher and greater for the people of Afghanistan.

In President Obama's mind, the conditions on the ground and the advice of military commanders outweighed the timeline that the administration had publicized. Republicans like to bash timelines and deadlines of any sort, but they're actually important in managing the expectations of our allies, even if they remain flexible. As Obama acknowledged in October of 2015, "This isn't the first time . . . adjustments have been made; this won't probably be the last." But the specter of a future reduction in American support puts pressure on our Afghan partners to keep unifying their country and strengthening their military. Right before he told his interviewer from CBS's *60 Minutes* that "Deadlines should not be dogmas," Ashraf Ghani said that, "Deadlines concentrate the mind."[50] They probably also help him create a sense of urgency among his military commanders to make them self-reliant in protecting their country from the Taliban insurgency.

American allies and coalition partners welcomed President Obama's flexibility. The secretary general of NATO said the decision "demonstrates the continued commitment by NATO Allies and our partners toward Afghanistan."[51] President Ghani said, "We welcome and thank President Obama and the other allies including Germany, United Kingdom, Japan, and others for their historic decision to extend technical and military support to Afghanistan."[52] In Afghanistan, President Obama showed that, even when it's not politically popular, America is willing to work with its allies to ensure its—and their—security.

MUSLIM BROTHERHOOD OVER MUBARAK

THE CHARGE

Egypt's former president, Hosni Mubarak, was no democrat, but he was a critical strategic ally for the United States. He came to the presidency reluctantly, and under violent circumstances. In 1981, he was seated to the right of Egypt's then-president Anwar Sadat, viewing a military parade, when four militants leaped from a parade truck and assassinated Sadat. Mubarak rationalized his thirty-year rule by pointing out Egypt's history consisted of thousands of years of authoritarian rule. Strong leaders organized the harvests, marshaled the resources to build the pyramids, and long served as a bulwark against factionalism. His authoritarian rule allowed him to back American interests even when they weren't popular among ordinary Egyptians. He joined us in the 1991 Gulf War and was the first Arab state to sign a peace treaty with Israel.[53] The United States has returned the favor by supplying Egypt with more military aid than any other country besides Israel.

But when the Arab Spring protests sprung up, and thousands of protesters took to Tahrir Square, the Obama administration rejoiced—naively. They seemed to think Jeffersonian democracy had come at long last to the Middle East. They abandoned Mubarak and stood by while the popular uprising deposed and detained him and Egyptians voted in their first presidential election. And who did they elect, these new Jeffersonians? Mohammed Morsi, the head of the Islamist Muslim Brotherhood group. And so the Arab Spring turned out to be a short-lived experiment with democracy, indeed. A few years after the election, the Egyptian military conducted a coup (which the Obama administration wouldn't call a coup, because then they'd be legally required to withhold military aid), took power back from the Muslim Brotherhood, and installed General Abdel Fattah el-Sisi as president. El-Sisi is an "outspoken critic of Islamist extremism"[54] and is beginning to make inroads with the international community, meeting with the heads of Germany and the UK. Did President Obama extend him the same courtesy? No. His State Department invited over members of the Muslim Brotherhood, which Egyptian authorities now consider a terrorist organization. El-Sisi and his government were outraged. In the first Republican primary debate, Ted Cruz compared Obama unfavorably to the new Egyptian president, asking, "Why don't we see the president of the United States demonstrating that same courage" as el-Sisi "just to speak the truth about the face of evil we're facing right now?"[55]

THE REALITY

In 2011, Joel Beinin, a professor of Middle Eastern history at Stanford who specializes in Egypt, said with great prescience that "the United States is going to be allies with whoever is in charge of Egypt."[56] Beinin explained that, unlike other alliances which are based in part on shared values, this alliance was born of sheer opportunism. In the early 1970s, while the cold war raged, Egypt was allied with the Soviet Union, but its president, Anwar Sadat, wanted to switch sides. President Nixon's secretary of state, Henry Kissinger, didn't trust Sadat. But ever since President Carter invited him to Camp David along with Israeli prime minister Menachem Begin, in what would become known as the "Camp David Accords," Egypt has been a steadfast ally of the United States.

Just as the United States doesn't get to dictate when Afghanistan will stop battling Taliban insurgents, it also doesn't get to dictate when revolutions take place, when democracies are imposed, or when coups will occur. ("If you guys could just hurry up and finish your revolution, we have to be home to watch *Homeland* at ten o'clock.") In his first year in office, well before the Arab Spring, Obama gave a clear preview of his administration's response to democratic uprisings in the Arab world. Guess where he gave the speech? In Cairo, of course—about ten minutes from Tahrir Square. The president said, in a passage worth quoting at length for its foresight:

> *I know there has been controversy about the promotion of democracy in recent years, and much of this controversy is connected to the war in Iraq. So let me be clear: no system of government can or should be imposed by one nation by any other . . . [However] we will welcome all elected, peaceful governments—provided they govern with respect*

for all their people. This last point is important because there are some who advocate for democracy only when they're out of power; once in power, they are ruthless in suppressing the rights of others ... elections alone do not make true democracy.[57]

The key to the Obama administration's Egypt policy is summed up right there. We "will welcome" democratic movements, but we cannot "impose" them on another country. We are well aware that democratic elections can and sometimes do lead to oppression. Anyone who accused Obama of giving up on Mubarak—or, for that matter, credited him for the Arab Spring—has an inflated sense of the power of the American presidency. As President Obama said while the Arab Spring unfolded, "The policy of the United States [is] to promote reform across the region, and to support transitions to democracy."[58] "Promoting" and "supporting" are more realistic objectives than "forcing" or "coercing."

Some conservatives have scolded the Obama administration for holding meetings with former members of Egypt's parliament who were part of Morsi's democratically elected Muslim Brotherhood coalition. Those critics might be surprised to learn that the American embassy began to communicate with the group during the Bush administration, just after the Muslim Brotherhood candidates won eighty-eight seats in the national assembly. As Bush administration Middle East adviser Elliott Abrams recalled, "The Muslim Brotherhood was illegal in Egypt, but certain parliamentarians who were connected to the Muslim Brotherhood were, we felt, worth talking to."[59] The State Department in the Bush years was staffed by apolitical Middle East experts who understood the Muslim Brotherhood could be duplicitous. They conducted their conversations accordingly. The same is true during the Obama administration.

Today Egypt is in a precarious position, and things aren't always what they seem. Mohammed Morsi, a democratically elected Islamist president, couldn't quite handle the balancing act of sympathizing with Egyptian protesters angry over an American-made anti-Islamic video while simultaneously sticking up for his American ally. But he also backed up the United States on its criticism of Syrian president Bashar al-Assad and pledged to keep the peace with Israel.[60] The "first freely elected leader" of Egypt now sits in prison after the Egyptian military seized power. He was given a death sentence for escaping an "extralegal detention" during the Mubarak regime, even though this was a "form of detention that many Egyptians hoped would be eliminated by the revolution."[61] President el-Sisi, the new president whose "courage" Ted Cruz so admired, is a military dictator and an autocrat who labels legitimate political opponents "terrorists," imprisons journalists and secular activists, and oversaw the killing of 2,600 people—nearly half of them supporters of Morsi, his political rival—in the year and a half since he forcibly took power.[62] While el-Sisi has been in power, an Egyptian court has dropped all charges against Hosni Mubarak, the deposed dictator el-Sisi has come to resemble.[63] When Cruz called on President Obama to take a note from el-Sisi's courage, it'd been just two years since he criticized Obama for permitting the Egyptian military (including General el-Sisi) to "act with impunity against the Muslim Brotherhood."[64] Cruz would flatter a dictator he'd previously spoken out against—if it gave him an opportunity to criticize Obama.

Egypt is one of the world's most ancient civilizations. America is one of its most modern civilizations. It's a shame that the relationship between them—complex, dramatic, and ever-changing—should be represented in such a savage—or *uncivilized*—way.

10
—
THE
APPEASER
OF ENEMIES
—

T he world is on fire. Terrorist rampages have beset Paris, San Bernardino, and Brussels, failing nation-states aggressively pursue nuclear weapons, and in the absence of a muscular foreign policy by the United States, certain age-old adversaries have begun to contest American power. Critics contend President Obama should have advanced a grand vision for foreign policy to signal, unequivocally, how the United States wanted to reshape the post-9/11 world. Instead, they say, we got an unromantic and unimaginatively pragmatic doctrine that went something like, "Don't do stupid stuff." Even Hillary Clinton chimed in. Asked about the quote by the *Atlantic*'s Jeffrey Goldberg, candidate Clinton said, "Great nations need organizing principles, and 'Don't do stupid stuff' is not an organizing principle."[1] In trying to distance himself from the foolhardy failures of the Bush administration, some argue President Obama overcorrected. They insist he withdrew from the world at the moment America's status as the world's sole superpower began to be challenged.

An ancient riddle lies at the heart of this criticism: Do leaders shape world events or do world events shape leaders? Obama's critics relentlessly rely on the assumption that leaders shape events. The truth, however, toggles back and forth. No less a committed interventionist than Winston Churchill once said, "Never, never, never believe any war will be smooth and easy. . . . The statesman who yields to war fever must realize that once the signal is given, he is no longer the master of policy but the slave of unforeseeable and uncontrollable events."[2] We learned this lesson when Dick Cheney told us that America would "be greeted as liberators" in Iraq. We weren't. And, to be fair, we learned it when the democratic revolution Barack Obama supported in Libya had some messy and unforeseeable aftereffects.

In a more modern era, the question could be helpfully reformulated in this way: Do leaders create reality or do they respond to reality? Are they able to overhaul the real attitudes and opinions of the majority of the world's population and dismiss the interests and prejudices of other nations at their whim? Or must they develop foreign policy strategies which correspond to the world as it is? The *New York Times*'s Ron Suskind interviewed a senior Bush adviser who told us how *that administration* answered this question. Suskind recounts the adviser was upset about an *Esquire* magazine piece he had written about President Bush's communications director.

> *The aide said that guys like me were "in what we call the reality-based community," which he defined as people who*

"believe that solutions emerge from your judicious study of discernible reality." I nodded and murmured something about enlightenment principles and empiricism. He cut me off. "That's not the way the world really works anymore," he continued. "We're an empire now, and when we act, we create our own reality."[3]

We saw where trying to "create our own reality" took us. President Obama would try to steer American leadership back into the "reality-based community" and ground foreign policy in facts, even when those facts were sometimes fraught or frustrating. He would try to reinsert some humility into America's global politics, even if doing so would label him an "apologist" by conservatives whose version of American exceptionalism means never having to say we're sorry. And he would try to ensure that the American values and "enlightenment principles" for which young men and women were fighting and dying continued to distinguish America from its enemies, even if an attempt to understand our enemies might be misinterpreted, by some, as weakness rather than strength. After all, President Bush failed to see the world through our enemies' eyes, and as one Republican analyst told Ron Suskind in that same article:

This is why George W. Bush is so clear-eyed about Al Qaeda and the Islamic fundamentalist enemy. He believes you have to kill them all. They can't be persuaded, that they're extremists, driven by a dark vision. He understands them, because he's just like them. . . . This is why he dispenses with people who confront him with inconvenient facts.

Some inconvenient facts greeted Obama as he assumed the presidency. As the journalist David Sanger reminds us, "No American president since Franklin Delano Roosevelt . . . had inherited a range of problems so seemingly intractable and complex," and the Obama administration faced "a range of new threats that had festered" while the United States "had taken its eye off the ball."[4] Over the next several years, President Obama would—with great courage—shape events when he could, and espouse the serenity it took to be shaped by events when there was no other course. Deploying American service members only when a clear national interest was at stake, the president understood that the country's strength in confronting its adversaries lay in much more than its over-whelming military might.

This realism and restraint has incensed detractors. According to foreign policy columnist Bret Stephens, "Since becoming president, Obama has been engaged in a kind of conjurer's trick, pretending to make the tide recede when he's merely backing away from the waterline."[5] To Stephens, Obama's commitment to "nation building at home" and a "light footprint" overseas are admissions of a retreatist and defeatist attitude. Elsewhere, Stephens has written that the world "has already entered an era in which global disorders, spurred by American retreat, are proliferating at rates that are increasingly hard to contain, much less defeat."[6] Stephens may be an intelligent and articulate critic, but as we'll see in this final chapter, this narrative of a "retreatist" foreign policy—one that emboldens America's adversaries—is but another example of the right attempting to create its own reality.

—

THE RUSSIAN BEAR REAWAKENS

THE CHARGE

By projecting weakness and ambivalence, Barack Obama invited Russia's increasingly authoritarian president, Vladimir Putin, to bully his neighbors. In 2014, Russia annexed Crimea and began an aggressive destabilization of eastern Ukraine—but he never would have dared if the American president had seemed a more worthy adversary. At the beginning of his presidency, when Obama had committed to "reset-

ting" the relationship with Russia, he struck a chord not of cooperation, but of conciliation. The president is a pacifist who, in his Nobel
Prize victory speech, said we should have a "world without nuclear
weapons." Russia has a thousand more nukes than the United States,
and yet Obama made a voluntary one-third reduction in our own nuclear stockpile, leading Dick Cheney to complain that Obama "significantly reduced" our nuclear capabilities.

As Texas senator Ted Cruz told Fox News's Sean Hannity, "What
[Obama] does with Putin . . . is that he just surrenders and gives them
everything."[7] Instead of responding militarily to Russia's invasion of
Ukraine, the United States slapped sanctions on powerful Russians
to try to exert economic pressure. Conservative commentator Charles
Krauthammer wrote, "Why, after all, did Obama delay responding to
Putin's infiltration, military occupation and seizure of Crimea in the
first place? In order to provide Putin with a path to de-escalation."[8]
Unlike Obama, Putin is strong; economic sanctions are an ineffective
deterrent for a leader like him.

THE REALITY

Believe it or not, Russia does not set its foreign policy—and did not
get the idea to invade Ukraine—by sizing up the American president.
Obama has little to do with Putin's determination that it was the perfect time to resurrect its expansionist national agenda. One must have
a hopelessly self-centered perspective to believe another country's pursuit of national interests are determined by an appraisal of what the
United States will think. But most conservative critics don't actually
think that. They're just showing off that knack for spinning out the
reality of a "weak" Democratic president.

After all, Putin didn't only invade his neighbor when Obama was president. In 2008, he invaded Russia's *other* neighbor on the Black Sea, the sovereign country of Georgia. Like Ukraine, Georgia was being led by a pro-Western democratic government. Did Krauthammer, the same pundit who lambasted Obama's measured response, urge then-president George Bush to hold Putin to account? Krauthammer told Fox News at the time, "Well, obviously it's beyond our control. The Russians are advancing. There is nothing that will stop them. We are not going to go to war over Georgia . . . The battle will end when the Russians have achieved whatever is their objective. . . . what we can do is to put sanctions on the Russians which might induce them over time to undo a few of these steps."[9] Krauthammer's appraisal back then was lucid, before his disdain for Obama clouded his analysis. Georgia and Ukraine have both been in Russia's sphere of influence since the end of the cold war, and incremental economic sanctions on billionaire oligarchs are the most realistic and effective method for keeping Putin in check.

These sanctions are still being played out, and it's too soon to measure their full effect on Russia's longer term foreign policy. But the Carnegie Endowment for International Peace points out the extent to which the private sector in Russia relies on foreign capital. After sanctions were imposed, Russian tycoons flew to Asian financial centers seeking investments and markets that would lessen the burden President Obama placed on them. But they soon "learned . . . that there is basically no alternative to Western capital markets."[10] Obama's response of slapping sanctions on Russia was tougher and smarter than right-wing pundits would have us believe. After all, Russia did withdraw from its meddling in Ukraine and the "ceasefires and agreements negotiated in Minsk were largely the result of the sanctions."[11]

Putin rhetorically dismissed the economic sanctions, claiming the "Russian economy piled up a sufficient supply of inner strength."[12] But the reality is the Russian economy has been badly bruised. Standard & Poor's has gradually moved it from a stable rating before the sanctions to a junk rating in January 2015.[13] Foreign investment has dried up, cash stockpiles left over from Russia's oil boom are running out, and Russian businessmen are losing patience. Russian consumers are also getting annoyed with food shortages, inflation, and higher prices. According to the *Guardian*, economic growth is nonexistent in Russia—all the more ominous given the fact that Russia is still a developing country. The article observes, "Putin, who is looking to run for president in 2018, wants Russia to grow like China, with its 7.5 percent growth rate, not France, which is flatlining."[14]

Of course Putin fully appreciates the importance of economic sanctions, even if he's too busy wrestling polar bears to admit it. One of the results of the "reset" that the United States and Russia embarked upon early in Obama's tenure was the economic sanctions placed by both on Iran;[15] these eventually persuaded Iran to negotiate away its pursuit of nuclear weapons. The reset also led to the historic signing of the New START nuclear arms reduction treaty in 2010, and the opening of a supply route through Russia for American troops to get to Afghanistan.

Few people would give Obama a hard time for working to reduce the stockpiles of the two countries who, together, possess 90 percent of the world's nuclear weapons. But count Dick Cheney among them. His claim that we've "significantly reduced" our nuclear capabilities only makes sense if you believe a reduction down to 1,550 ready-to-use, long-range nuclear weapons somehow leaves America vulnerable. Cheney "drew scorn" from people who actually pay attention to these things—they refer to the $350 billion the United States is spending over the next decade to "modernize its aging strategic nuclear force."[16] Under Obama, our nuclear capabilities have improved even if our (and Russia's) stockpiles have shrunk.

There's also no reason to dismiss Obama as a pacifist peacenik because he imagines a world without nuclear weapons. The United States has pursued nuclear disarmament since the Kennedy administration.[17] Even at the height of the cold war, Ronald Reagan said, "My dream is to see the day when nuclear weapons will be banished from the face of the earth."[18]

Russia observers note the tensions between our two countries are more pitched than they've been since the cold war. And so it's a good thing these tensions are being presided over by Obama. If Putin's ambitions had unfolded under the watch of another president—one with a more impulsive mind and a shakier hand—it's unclear where the escalation between the two nuclear powers would have ended up. Calling Obama a "cold warrior indeed," the journalist Fred Kaplan writes, "Perhaps more than any president since Dwight Eisenhower, Obama defines the national interest narrowly and acts accordingly. And in following this course, he has been much more successful than his critics allow."[19] When Putin acted like a playground bully, Obama could have thwacked him upside the head. But he knew more effectual behavioral modification would result from a time-out. In this case, economic and diplomatic isolation proved to be the more effective projections of American strength, and remediated Russia's bad behavior without needlessly antagonizing. Meanwhile projections of Russian strength still don't amount to more than that famous photograph of a stoic and bare-chested Putin on horseback. Obama's realism is futilely challenged by Putin's absurd surrealism.[20] Reality-rejecting Republicans slam the former and swoon over the latter.

NUCLEAR NORTH KOREA
THE CHARGE

Early in his presidency, Barack Obama and Hillary Clinton announced the United States foreign policy would "pivot to Asia." In the face of the growing economic influence of China and the importance of the entire Asian continent, Obama signaled that he'd be "retrenching"[21]—or scaling back grand commitments in the Middle East—to pursue more targeted and flexible strategies in the Far East. The Trans-Pacific Partnership (TPP), which opened up free trade activity with Asian countries and undercut China's regional economic dominance, was a wise move (rare for Obama!). But the president overlooked one thing: North Korea. Since Kim Jong-un has taken over from his father, Kim Jong-il, North Korea's erratic young dictator improved its uranium enrichment program and reportedly tested a uranium-based nuclear weapon. Although the country had tested nuclear weapons in 2006 and 2009, those tests were with a relatively less destructive element, plutonium. But in 2013, in an underground detonation, Kim's engineers miniaturized uranium—now North Korea can boast a nuclear device so small that it fits into the warhead of a missile.[22] And we know North Korea's KN-08 missiles can reach Seattle, San Francisco, and Los Angeles.[23]

Thus, Obama's talk about reducing the U.S. nuclear arsenal when he should be focused on reducing North Korea's arsenal is—to put it bluntly—dangerous. Kim Jong-un is unpredictable and he takes advantage of the president's weakness. Witness the *Interview* affair: North Korea responded to a 2015 cinematic spoof in which two American journalists are sent to assassinate Kim Jong-un by attacking the servers of Sony Pictures. When they spilled trade secrets (and the cringe-worthy private e-mails of celebs and execs), President Obama denounced North Korea's "cybervandalism" and promised to respond "proportionately" before heading off to vacation in Honolulu. While the president left the stars of the big screen hanging, it was up to conservative stars of the small screen to come to their defense. John McCain told CNN, "It's more than vandalism. It's a new form of warfare that we're involved in and we need . . . to react vigorously."[24] Not to be outshined, Lindsey Graham complained to CBS, "The president calls this an act of vandalism. That just really bothers me greatly. It is an act of terrorism. And I hope he will respond forcefully."[25]

THE REALITY

What kind of "forceful responses" and "vigorous reactions" were Republicans calling for? Given that North Korea "threatened to strike back at the United States if Obama retaliated"[26] and given the giddy excitement its "Supreme Leader" reportedly feels about his country's nuclear weapons, it's probably a good thing we didn't respond with military force. Whether North Korea is guilty of "cybervandalism," a "cyberattack," or "cyberterrorism"—and there's no doubting that the offense was a serious one—most people would prefer the world not come to its apocalyptic end over a mediocre Seth Rogen movie.

Fortunately, in the same interview in which he called for a "forceful response," Lindsey Graham didn't advocate a military attack. He called on Obama to levy some crippling sanctions on the North Korean regime. What did the Obama administration do? It levied some crippling sanctions on the North Korean regime. Except that it took a few days, more time than it takes to call a cable news booker and write up a gripe, to develop the most effective response. Saying that "we take seriously North Korea's attack that aimed to create destructive financial effects on a U.S. company and to threaten artists and other individuals with the goal of restricting their right to free expression," the White House press secretary explained sanctions were just the first wave of our response and that future actions will "take place at a time and in a manner of our choosing."[27] In other words, in light of America's tremendous cyberwarfare capabilities and robust clandestine operations, it's likely that we civilians still don't know the full extent of our response, and that it was both punitive and preventive. (If we start to see North Korean movie stars publicly embarrassed in the coming years, we'll know revenge was ours!)

In order to understand how North Korea has been able to expand its nuclear capabilities in recent years, it's important to know the past two decades of U.S.–North Korea relations have really been a mess. In 1994, a team of American negotiators under President Clinton got North Korea to halt the construction of nuclear reactors, forgo the pursuit of nuclear weapons, and submit to international inspectors. In exchange, the United States would provide fuel oil North Korea could use for energy.[28] Even though the consensus back then was that North

Koreans would be able to produce "30 Nagasaki size nuclear weapons" by the end of the 1990s,[29] Republicans dismissed the agreement's substantive success and called it a symbolic failure. As Bob Gallucci, the chief U.S. negotiator of the agreement recalls, "We did not get ticker tape parades, as it turned out.... [conservative critics said] that we had submitted to blackmail. The North Koreans were threatening us with a nuclear program, and we gave in and gave them good things. That we were appeasers."[30]

In the aftermath of 9/11, the country shifted to a wartime footing and the Bush administration christened the "axis of evil." North Korea was one-third of this unholy trinity, and amid the heated foreign policy rhetoric, the Clinton-era agreement with North Korea got tossed out. Richard Perle, a Republican adviser to the Pentagon during the Bush administration, was asked by PBS two years after the 9/11 attacks whether Bush had moved the goalposts on the U.S.–North Korea deal. He responded, "I would hope that we would move the goalposts, because we didn't like the playing field that was established during the Clinton administration. It was a playing field on which we were expected to pay the North Koreans not to do dangerous things, and that is not a sound basis for a policy ... when Bush won the presidency, those talks [with North Korea] ceased immediately."[31] Perle was one of the critics who'd accused the Clinton administration of "appeasement" and succumbing to "blackmail" a decade earlier.

Aside from Bush crumpling up the Clinton-era agreement, some foreign policy hawks argue Bush made another mistake when he removed North Korea from the list of state sponsors of terrorism and unfroze $25 million in North Korean funds, both of which he did in an attempt to start nuclear talks up yet again. But these are quibbles.

And it's doubtful that Kim Jong-un would be willing to give up his nuclear program even if this—or the next—president can get his government to the table. As one senior Obama administration official has said, "At every turn what we've seen is a lack of sincerity and a lack of seriousness from North Korea about abandoning its nuclear program."[32]

There are two more likely scenarios: the first is that America's increased economic cooperation with China will pressure Kim Jong-un politically, since China is North Korea's only friend in the neighborhood. During the Obama administration, we've seen China go from giving "some help" to North Korea on its missile development to declaring a "red line" on North Korean nuclear activity and condemning its missile tests.[33] The second scenario is that the border-busting forces of globalized information networks will awaken ordinary North Koreans to new political possibilities and put internal pressure on the regime. If you don't think North Korea is attentive and (overly) sensitive to this eventuality, just listen to how its government spokesman responded when President Obama made such a suggestion in a YouTube interview: "The recent wild remarks made by Obama are nothing but a poor grumble of a loser driven into a tight corner in the all-out standoff with [North Korea]."[34] Apparently Republicans aren't the only ones who like to build themselves up by putting the American president down. (And if Kim Jong-un is thinking of a different career, he might do well as a Donald Trump speechwriter.)

North Korea's leader can't isolate his people—or insulate himself from criticism—forever. In the spring of 2015, Lee Min-bok, a North Korean defector living in South Korea, took eighty thousand copies of the DVD version of *The Interview,* bundled them together with political leaflets, and tied them to helium balloons. "The regime hates this film because it shows Kim Jong Un as a man, not a God," Lee said. In the middle of the night, he released them into the sky over North Korea with timers set to drop the cargo into the supposedly hermetically sealed country.[35] Side note: I hope the North Koreans don't judge all of America cinema by this rather unexceptional film. Kim Jong-un had previously called the making of the satirical film "an act of terror." For a thin-skinned dictator accustomed to punishing dissent with death, a bit of crass criticism might indeed terrorize. George Orwell put it more optimistically when he wrote that "every joke is a tiny revolution."[36] Or so we can hope.

COMFORTING CASTRO'S CUBA

THE CHARGE

Communist Cuba has been an enemy of the United States for generations. Marco Rubio, the son of Cuban immigrants, points out "this is the country that is the third most active espionage force in America today, operating against us ... they continue to provide shelter and material support for terrorist groups like the FARC in Colombia and others."[37] Yet President Obama restores diplomatic relations with Cuba, shakes hands with Raul Castro, raises a Cuban flag in the atrium of the State Department, and takes his daughters to Havana for spring break. All the while, according to a 2014 report of Human

Rights Watch, the Castro regime continues to "repress individuals and groups who criticize the government" and officials "employ a range of tactics to punish dissent and instill fear in the public, including beatings, public acts of shaming, termination of employment, and threats of long-term imprisonment."[38] Clearly, Obama is a lame duck who is looking out for his own legacy, wanting to be the president who opened up Cuba. But he's emboldening the Castro brothers in the process.

THE REALITY

There are some progressives who dismiss Senator Rubio's criticism of Cuba as a pander to his political base of Castro-hating Cuban-Americans living in Miami. But Rubio actually has a somewhat consistent record of speaking out against human rights abuses in foreign countries. And we should be concerned about Cuba's persisting human rights violations. But the fact is, the United States maintains diplomatic relations with all but four of the sixteen countries Freedom House ranks as the worst abusers of human rights.[39] The decision to open up a U.S. embassy in Havana is part of a broader diplomatic philosophy which sees engagement as, in most cases, a more effective method than isolation for combating human rights abuses. As Hillary Clinton put it, "The goal of increased U.S. engagement in the days and years ahead should be to encourage real and lasting reforms for the Cuban people."[40] This concern for human rights is, in part, what motivated Pope Francis to play a critical role in brokering the talks, and pushing for ongoing reconciliation between the two countries.[41]

It's also not true that Cuban-Americans oppose these reforms.

The conventional thinking is that American immigrants from Cuba are furious at the Castros for commandeering their businesses and private property during the 1959 revolution. Therefore they must want to punish the regime forever. But a recent poll of Cuban-Americans living in the United States overturned this conventional thinking. Most of the respondents supported, rather than opposed, President Obama's plan to normalize relations with Cuba. And of the respondents who were American-born, as more and more Cuban-Americans are, two-thirds agreed with the president's plan while only one-quarter disagreed with it.[42] Looks like the times they are a changin'.

The Castro regime is changing too. Since he took over from his brother Fidel in 2008, Raul Castro has announced various economic and social reforms. Cubans can now travel outside the country, the agricultural sector is being decentralized, real estate markets are being liberalized, and by 2014, about 20 percent of the country's workforce was involved with Cuba's new and improving private sector.[43] Unlike North Korea, Cuba has signaled a willingness to open its borders and its markets. Whereas Kim Jong-un called President Obama a "loser," Raul Castro told Cubans he believed Obama was "honest." As it emerges from this era of isolation, participating in international summits and pan-American diplomatic relations, many experts think the Cuban people stand to benefit. As the Chilean head of the Organization of American States said, "Cuba is undertaking a process of economic reforms that will, I hope, lead to political reforms."[44]

The United States stands to benefit economically as well. After George Bush reauthorized the export of American agricultural products to Cuba in 2003, a full quarter of Alabama's agricultural revenue came from selling catfish, soybeans, and poultry to the island nation.

According to Jennifer Harris of the Council on Foreign Relations, Obama's decision to normalize relations with Cuba could result in six thousand new U.S. jobs. (I bet she's not even counting professional baseball scouts!) And here's the kicker: Marco Rubio's home state of Florida is "likely to benefit economically more than any other U.S. state."[45] No less an isolationist than Republican senator Rand Paul enjoyed saying, "Senator Rubio is acting like an isolationist who wants to retreat to our borders and perhaps build a moat." Paul went on, "After fifty years of conflict, why not try a new approach? The United States trades and engages with other Communist nations, such as China and Vietnam. Why not Cuba?"[46]

Paul hit on the crux of the issue: America's foreign policy toward Cuba simply hadn't worked. The cold war strategy of isolation didn't oust the Castro regime and bring liberal democracy to Cuba. As the president pointed out, "No other nation joins us in imposing these sanctions, and it has had little effect beyond providing the Cuban government with a rationale for restrictions on its people."[47] The United States had been doing the same thing for half a century and expecting a different result. It was time to embark on a saner and smarter strategy.

Diplomatic relations—and a policy of "engagement" rather than "estrangement"[48]—were only a small part of the strategy. Increasing support for civil society and a free flow of people, information, and ideas would create the foundation for democracy among the Cuban people. Perhaps a peaceful democratic revolution with a full-throttled free-market economy won't prove to be the eventual outcomes. But at least that kooky and Communist neighbor eighty miles off the coast of Florida is now one with whom we're back on speaking terms.

"ISLAMIC TERRORISM" VS. "VIOLENT EXTREMISM"

THE CHARGE

How can the president defeat an enemy he won't even call out by name? Al Qaeda, ISIS, and the Taliban are all versions of Islamic extremism. We're fighting a war against militant Islamists and they're fighting a war against us. But the president is so concerned with political correctness he won't admit it. This is part of a long and terrible pattern. Two months after the president was elected, a memo was distributed to Pentagon staff noting "this administration prefers to avoid using the term 'Long War' or 'Global War on Terror' [GWOT]. Please use 'Overseas Contingency Operation.'"[49] Six years later, the president hosted a summit on "countering violent extremism" at the White House. The Obama administration seems to bend over backward not to use the term "Islamic." Donald Trump is right that unless President Obama uses the words "'radical Islamic Terrorism' the problem will not be solved!"[50]

THE REALITY

Democrats are too quick to dismiss this criticism as patently racist or insensitive. It might be disingenuous for smart Republicans who should know better or facile for, well, Donald Trump and his followers. But nothing is more important in a war than knowing who your enemy is and what they believe. Actually, there is one thing more important: beating them. And the Obama administration's decision to abstain from using the phrase "radical Islam" is aimed at achieving both those objectives.

The strategic debate over communicating who our enemies are—and who they are not—is an important one. The majority of Republicans who criticize the president agree that our enemies are not practicing a legitimate version of Islam. They agreed with George Bush when he said, "Ours is a war not against a religion, not against the Muslim faith. But ours is a war against individuals who absolutely hate what America stands for."[51] Like Obama, Bush saw the importance of drawing a distinction between the religion of Islam and violent extremists who abuse it. Just a week after the attacks of September 11, 2001, Bush said, "The face of terror is not the true faith of Islam. That's not what Islam is all about. Islam is peace."[52] If we start using language which associates terrorism with a group of religious people, the overwhelming majority of whom reject terrorism, we'd start alienating the millions of peace-loving American Muslims and inviting bigotry, and we'd be making a strategic wartime blunder of the first order.

That's because the Muslim-majority countries that are our allies in the war against violent extremism—such as Saudi Arabia and Jordan—are populated by many people whose brand of Islam would seem "radical" or "extreme" by Western standards. The governments of these countries do capital punishment old-school, with beheadings and the like. But they're vigorous allies in fighting terrorism, and the vast majority of their citizens aren't interested in having any kind of jihad against the West. That is, unless and until they start hearing more people echo Lindsey Graham's claim that "we are in a religious war with radical Islamists."[53] Conservative foreign policy analyst Eli

Lake highlights this paradox wherein countries that are home to some strains of radical Islam are also the allies that help us combat terrorism. "It's possible to imagine a world in the future where American presidents would speak plainly about radical Islam," writes Lake. But "it would likely be a world in which the U.S. stopped waging a global war on terror."[54]

Also unhelpful is the right-wing rhetoric of Donald Trump, who proposed a ban on all Muslims trying to enter the United States, and Ted Cruz, who suggested it was time to "patrol and secure Muslim neighborhoods." Like too many Republican primary voters, Trump casually and crudely conflates Islam with "radical Islamists." In the days following the mass shooting in San Bernardino, when Trump's anti-Islamic rhetoric was at a fever pitch, a headline appeared in the satirical newspaper *The Onion* that read, "Trump Gives Muslim on Fence About Radicalizing Just the Push He Needed."[55] As if history were repeating itself first as farce and then as tragedy, Trump told MSNBC the next morning "nobody knew [the San Bernardino killer] was radicalized. I probably radicalized him."[56] It's unclear whether the comment was sarcastic or self-aggrandizing and it's hopefully not true. But such a flip comment underscores that the way we communicate can either win us friends or alienate people—and with the highest possible seriousness.

In the words of Omar Mohammed, a Tanzanian journalist working for the BBC who was educated in Arizona, "Muslims absolutely do have a special role in this fight. And not because they need to prove anything to people like Donald Trump and his supporters. But because this fight is about protecting their communities and the preservation of Islam from those who seek to corrupt it."[57] When Republicans lump terrorists together with people like Mohammed, they help the terrorists with this corruption of Islam in the global public sphere.

Still need convincing that Obama is wise not to call out "Islamic extremism"? On the night Osama bin Laden was killed, the special forces team which raided his compound in Abbottabad seized piles of the Al Qaeda leader's documents and plans for terrorist plots. One such plan was to attack Air Force One since, as bin Laden wrote, "Obama is the head of infidelity and killing him automatically will make [Vice President] Biden take over the presidency. . . . Biden is totally unprepared for that post, which will lead the U.S. into a crisis." (Bin Laden must have been on the e-mail distribution list of the Republican Party's Biden-related talking points.) What else did American intelligence analysts find (aside from, no joke, a stash of VHS pornography tapes)? According to an analysis of the documents by the *Washington Post*'s David Ignatius:

> *Bin Laden's biggest concern was Al-Qaeda's media image among Muslims. . . . The Al-Qaeda brand had become a problem, bin Laden explained, because Obama administration officials "have largely stopped using the phrase 'the war on terror' in the context of not wanting to provoke Muslims," and instead promoted a war against Al-Qaeda.*[58]

Like Al Qaeda, ISIS is obsessed with its image abroad. Its entire recruitment strategy is based on Internet propaganda, sending violent videos of its attacks to supporters and even developing a secret set of terrorist emojis—depicting swords and jihadists and executions—that ISIS sympathizers can download.[59] It's kind of hard to imagine a world in which a homicidal zealot and a twelve-year-old girl are communicating with their besties in the same way. ISIS can't stand when people refer to the group as "Daesh," which is how many European leaders and some foreign policy experts refer to the group. It's an acronym for the official name of the organization: "al-Dawla Al-Islamiya fi al-Iraq wa al-Sham." But uttered phonetically, it sounds like the Arabic word for "a bigot who imposes his views on others" or "one who crushes something underfoot." Do ISIS leaders really care about the names they're called? Yes! So much so that they threaten to cut out the tongue of anyone who uses the term. Which is why, after the 2015 terrorist attacks in Paris, the French president "defiantly attributed" the attacks to Daesh.[60]

It's not necessary to ignore the radical religious component that underpins terrorists' warped ideologies. And it's important to understand the beliefs and motivations of our enemies. But the more the American president can do to separate the majority of the world's billion or so Muslims from the terrorists who maintain a deranged view of Islam, rather than tie them together, the better.

—

WHAT'S THE DEAL WITH IRAN?

THE CHARGE

Nothing poses more of a threat to the safety of Americans than Iran armed to the hilt with nuclear warheads. We're all too familiar with images of Iranians being led by their ayatollahs in chants of "death to America" while American flags are lit on fire. When John Kerry, who once chaired the Senate Foreign Relations Committee, was called into the Senate to testify about the deal, he was told by the committee's current chairman, Bob Corker, "I believe you've been fleeced."[61] The nuclear deal negotiated between Iran and the P5+1 nations (United States, Great Britain, France, Russia, China, and Germany) was a raw one. Jeb Bush lambasted it, comparing Obama to Neville Chamberlain, the British prime minister who appeased Adolf Hitler in the lead-up to World War II. "The people of Iran, the region, Israel, America, and the world deserve better than a deal that consolidates the grip on power of the violent revolutionary clerics who rule Tehran with an iron fist," said Bush.[62]

THE REALITY

No one wants Iran to expand its nuclear capabilities. Nuclear weapons in the hands of an unfriendly or irresponsible country pose an existential threat to Western Civilization. And there are—believe it or not—other and more complicated geopolitical problems involved in the very idea of Iran getting the bomb. We'd start to see allies like Saudi Arabia, Turkey, and Egypt try to develop one as well. An all-out nuclear arms race in the Middle East isn't in America's interest or the world's. And the development of nuclear weapons can lead a country to behave more aggressively with its neighbors (as we've seen in Pakistan's relationship with India), bolster its alliances and sell nuclear technology to its allies, or fend off international pressure for political reform.[63]

Before the international agreement on the nuclear program of Iran was reached in July 2015, Iran had enough enriched uranium to produce eight to ten nuclear bombs and nearly twenty thousand centrifuges spinning at its enrichment facilities in the cities of Natanz and Fordow. It had the ability to produce a bomb within just two to three months. So how does the Iranian deal, the bureaucratically named "Joint Comprehensive Plan of Action," actually block Iran from getting a nuclear weapon? Under the deal, Iran agreed to reduce its stockpile of enriched uranium by 98 percent, reduce its centrifuges to just over six thousand, and keep uranium enrichment at 3.67 percent, "significantly below the level needed to create a bomb."[64] It also loses its ability to enrich plutonium, the other element needed to make a nuclear weapon. Iran's "breakout time," the amount of time it would take to get the fissile material together for one nuclear weapon, would be extended from the previous time period of two or three months to a full year.[65] And Iran will be required to let international inspectors snoop around at every single stage of nuclear development, from the mining to the enrichment to the fuel manufacturing to the nuclear reactors themselves. This is not an agreement based on trust. Administration officials are fond of saying it's a policy of "distrust but verify."

If this is such an intrusive inspection process and a deal that's good for the United States, why would Iran have agreed to it? Well, the one thing Iran wants more than world-destroying weaponry is to expand its regional economic and political influence. President Rouhani was the first Iranian leader in a decade to visit the annual meeting of the World Economic Forum in Switzerland in 2014. He told the global gathering of influential business and political leaders that "Iran's economy has so far the potential to be among the world's top ten in the next three decades" and, soliciting foreign investment, expressed an intention "to reopen trade, industrial and economic relations, with all of our neighbors."[66] Is this just the sweet talk of a duplicitous leader who wants to do battle with the West or the natural ambition of a leader trying to increase his country's economic dominance? A former U.S. ambassador to Saudi Arabia was initially skeptical of the deal but then detected a real reason Iran would comply: Iran may just have "a chance to become an economic superpower. . . . The Iranian people may have unrealistic expectations of how soon they'll see economic benefits, but when they come, it will be substantial."[67]

We should note too that Iran only came to the negotiating table because the economic sanctions President Obama had levied on it early in his administration had their intended effect. The bipartisan advocacy group United Against Nuclear Iran had supported these sanctions. When it ultimately objected to the nuclear deal, its president, Gary Samore, stepped down. An expert with deep knowledge of Iran and nuclear nonproliferation, Samore concluded the deal was well within our national interest. "I think President Obama's strategy succeeded. He has created economic leverage and traded it away for Iranian nuclear concessions," he said.[68] Who took over the organization? In a symbol of the politicization of the nuclear negotiations, it was former Connecticut senator Joe Lieberman, a longtime Obama critic who had actively campaigned for John McCain, Obama's opponent in the 2008 election.

Lieberman doesn't just dislike Obama, he also really likes Israel. And some of the opposition to the Iran deal among American lawmakers was motivated by the fact that Israeli Prime Minister Benjamin Netanyahu so opposed it. Responding to Netanyahu's objections, President Obama said, "I do not doubt his sincerity. But I believe he is wrong. . . . And as president *of the United States*, it would be an abrogation of my constitutional duty to act against my best judgment simply because it causes temporary friction with a dear friend and ally." The president also pointed out that every other nation on earth which had commented publicly about the nuclear deal, besides Israel, supported it.[69]

Former national security adviser Sandy Berger expressed empathy for Israel given that "they have, sitting next to them, a country [Iran] that is rabidly anti-Israel." But Berger concluded "I'm for the nuclear agreement. Not in spite of Iran's ambitions. I'm for a nuclear agreement because of Iran's ambitions."[70] What other Americans have come out in support of the deal? Oh, just more than a hundred former ambassadors, more than sixty people who'd worked as senior U.S. national security officials, the twenty-nine physicists from our nuclear weapons program, and five former U.S. ambassadors to Israel.[71]

What could be a reasonable alternative to the Iranian nuclear deal? Ask any critic and they'll argue we could slap even harder sanctions on Iran. But the purpose of sanctions in the first place was to get Iran to curb its nuclear activity. They'll say Iran's government is extremist and anti-Semitic and unreliable. But this is precisely the reason for subjecting them to international inspectors trained to be intrusive and distrustful. Similar appraisals were made about the government of China when Nixon started negotiating with it or about the government of the Soviet Union when Reagan started negotiating with it. The only alternative left is war or, as John McCain joked in 2007[72]—and President Bush's UN ambassador John Bolton seriously suggested in a 2015 *New York Times* op-ed[73]—to "bomb, bomb Iran." You'd have to have been living under a rock for the past decade to think that preemptive, unilateral military action in the Middle East is a good idea. And here's something foreign policy hawks have noticed and which the Obama administration isn't saying out loud: the nuclear deal actually gives international legitimacy to airstrikes, should they be required to deter Iran. Adam Schiff, the ranking Democrat on the House Intelligence Committee said, "It's certainly an argument I've heard made. . . . We'll be better off with the agreement were we to need to use force."[74]

Although the United States and Iran remain staunch adversaries, the aspiration for peace between the citizens of the two countries is not a trivial one. While right-wing extremists in both the United States and Iran have tried to block a nuclear deal, majorities in both countries support the deal.[75] And despite the incessant news coverage of radical clerics shouting "death to America," the Iranian public has mostly positive attitudes toward Americans.[76] The results from Iran's election in February 2016 shows a loosening of control by the anti-Western hardliners and an emphatic vote of confidence for Rouhani and reformist candidates. In fact, almost two-thirds of Iranians want to reestablish diplomatic relations with the United States and "Americans are more widely liked in Iran than anywhere else in the Middle East," even more widely than in the U.S. allies Turkey and India.[77] Of course, that would probably change if we started to bomb Iran.

Beneath the romantic notions about grand "clashes of civilizations," long "religious wars," and ideological "global struggles," reality patiently persists. The next administration is going to have a choice to make: it can either sensibly confront our shared reality or it can sensationally create its own. We will continue to face real challenges over the next four years. We will continue to energetically debate public policies which affect the lives of real people. And we will continue to deal with very real enemies in the world. The idea that Barack Obama has been one of them is pure fantasy.

EPILOGUE

P resident Obama's critics have tried not only to turn our country's political realities into their own fantasies. They've also tried to turn our productive political fantasies into stodgy realities, and this might be as great a sin.

The first impression we often get from our politicians relates less to their dreams for the country and more about how neatly they fit our dreams for it. The son or daughter of a mailman, or a bartender . . . a small-town waitress or a salesman: a candidate for elected office could come from the most modest means and, with a little industriousness and ingenuity, rise through the ranks of his or her fellow Americans to answer the call of public service. We're told these tales of upward mobility less because they speak to the character of a candidate than because they speak to the immortal longings of a country. Our leaders' origin stories comfortingly reflect and refract our nation's origin story. From rags to riches; from many, one. By publicly displaying their inglorious inheritances, these candidates implicitly propose themselves as American dreams come true.

But dreams are dreams and reality is reality. The American dream is a motivating muse and not a testable—what scientists call a "falsifiable"—hypothesis. They say faith is defined as "the substance of things hoped for, the evidence of things unseen." In a country that is, at once, buoyed by diverse religious traditions and bogged down by divisive political polarization, the American dream arms us with a kind of universal political faith. And so political leaders who try to use this dream to focus on fears rather than on what's "hoped for," or who try to reassure voters by putting themselves forward as observable proof of its existence, rather than leaving it "unseen," kind of miss the point.

In an otherwise cynical era, one of the most difficult and significant things a political leader can do is cultivate hope. When Sarah Palin taunted the president by asking at a Tea Party convention, "How's that hopey, changey stuff working out?" and Donald Trump operatically intoned at one of his campaign rallies, "The American dream . . . is dead," they broke with deeply rooted American values. Palin and Trump might have been tapping into the temporary frustrations of a thin slice of the electorate, but America is populated mostly by optimists—liberal and conservative alike—who sensed a tinge of blasphemy in Trump's and Palin's rhetoric of despair.

It's not a coincidence that America's most beloved modern presidents—from Roosevelt to Reagan and Eisenhower to Kennedy—have also been its most optimistic. In 1988, University of Pennsylvania psychologists Marty Seligman and Harold Zullow discovered that, within the previous forty years, the more optimistic candidate won every presidential campaign except one.[1] They defined optimism as the ability to see problems as "temporary or correctable" and pessimism as a tendency to focus on blame and the way in which problems can be "intractable."

Campaigning for the presidency back in 2008, Barack Obama

got annoyed at something. Speaking at a rally in New Hampshire, he said, "One of my opponents suggested that we should stop giving the American people false hopes about what could be . . . accomplished." It was a pessimistic sentiment and Obama was a congenital optimist. He continued on, saying that this idea "bugs the heck out of me" before finally making a modest—but striking—philosophical statement: "There's no such thing as false hope."[2] As it's the stuff of national aspirations and not logical propositions, hope can't be false. Barack Obama was affirming that hope, in general, and the American dream, in particular, were not falsifiable.

Benedict Anderson famously defined a nation as "an imagined political community." He explained that it is "imagined" because, without the ability to directly interact with the millions of other members of our national community, we rely on newspapers and books (and now, the Internet) to help mediate our national discussions and national identity. Monarchies became passé and modern democracies became possible when the printing press emerged. Newspapers and books (like this one) began to be mass-produced, and information and ideas began to circulate. Fueled by the commercial pursuit of new markets, these new publications had the ability to attract—and in so doing, construct—nationwide audiences. William Lloyd Garrison's abolitionist newspaper, *The Liberator,* and Harriet Beecher Stowe's novel *Uncle Tom's Cabin,* helped forge a sense of national community that led many young white men in Maine to fight in a civil war for the emancipation of slaves in Georgia whom they had never met. Similarly, today, a Latino kid in Santa Fe is willing to put on a uniform and parachute into a war zone to protect the freedoms of an unknown Arab-American family in Detroit.

The fact that our national community is imagined doesn't mean it's fictitious or fraudulent. Anderson wrote, "Communities are distinguished not by their falsity or genuineness, but by the style in which they are imagined."[3] As you've seen throughout these pages, the critics of Barack Obama's presidency have imagined the United States as a country in "decline" or "retreat." One of the casualties of our recent transition from a mass media to more niche-driven media outlets has been, on some level, a drift from an imagined community to a set of imagined cliques. One of the most refrained ridicules lobbed at Obama was that he began his career as a "community organizer." The job title was as foreign to many Americans as the president himself seemed to be. When we consider the nation as a kind of community— a community that has been facing decades of mounting political polarization and economic inequality, a community that is being fractured and fragmented into ideological echo chambers, a community where a vigorous competition of ideas is devolving into uncompromising standoffs between political factions—we see how the job of an American president is in essence, that of a community organizer. And, as we've seen, Barack Obama has done that job much more skillfully than many have imagined.

Some readers may have come to this book with a gloomy, misguided narrative of President Obama's legacy. I hope this book has put forward an alternate narrative, packed with facts and evidence in the spirit of those quaint, little enlightenment principles. I hope it has enabled those readers to reexamine and renew their assessment of President Obama's legacy and, as we consider the challenges before our next president, the current state of the union. I hope you enjoyed it. And regardless of whether you actually did, that's not a false hope.

ACKNOWLEDGMENTS

For years I've had the nagging thought that President Obama wasn't getting the credit he was due. There's truth to the old maxim, "everyone's a critic," and, in a democracy, we *should* be critical of the leaders we elect. But good criticism shows a capacity for appreciating the best—not just deprecating the worst—in something or somebody. So I became increasingly annoyed as one-sided criticism seemingly blinded us to the president's important accomplishments. It was ugly and made us look like an ungrateful nation.

Fortunately for me, Carrie Thornton, the editorial director at Dey Street Books, felt the same way when she hatched the idea for this book and entrusted me with it. It's been a true joy working with Carrie and her team at Dey Street/HarperCollins, including: Sean Newcott, Lauren Janiec, Kendra Newton, Ashley Tucker, David Palmer, and Nyamekye Waliyaya. I'm grateful to Dey Street's publisher, Lynn Grady, for giving this book her support.

Gillian MacKenzie is the kind of agent who cares deeply about her authors and their ideas, and I'm fortunate to have her in my corner. She was instrumental in pulling this project together, and pairing me up with Bob Staake, an extraordinarily talented illustrator whose work I've long admired (and whose children's books I'll be stocking up on in the months and years ahead).

This book was improved by the editorial wisdom of Annie Julia Wyman and comedic wit of Matt Ritter, two friends who took time to look at early drafts and help me make some segues smoother and some funny parts funnier. Two other friends, Teresa Wells and Mona Mouallem, generously donated their strategic thinking to some of the book's promotional effort. Brittany Taylor skillfully helped me tidy up the references. And Jill Swenson applied her copy editing talents to help tighten up a later draft.

A book like this leans heavily on the research done by—and institutional wisdom of—many different advocacy groups. I'm grateful to my friends in the Truman National Security Project for their support and camaraderie. Especially to Graham West, Brendan Gilfillan, and Caitlin Howarth for giving helpful feedback on the three foreign policy chapters. Truman's president, Mike Breen, and its advisory board chairman, Doug Wilson, were kind to lend their encouragement and endorsement. I was also referred to some of my sources by various reports and articles produced by progressive groups such as the Center for American Progress, Media Matters for America, and New America. So I'm indebted to many of these smart and purpose-driven people working behind the scenes.

I've also benefited from the advice of some conservative friends including Rich Lowry, who gave helpful feedback on a few chapter outlines, helping me prioritize the conservative criticism accurately. I'm deeply grateful to the hosts, producers and bookers who have given me a platform for developing and expressing some of the ideas in this book throughout the past several years. Especially: Megyn Kelly,

Neil Cavuto, Howie Kurtz, Larry Kudlow, Al Sharpton, Megan Brown, Karrah Kaplan, Jovian Wei, Tom Lowell, Matt Saal, Ben Finley, Ben Thompson, and Laura Petti.

To write this book, I had to take a break from a Ph.D. program at the Annenberg School for Communication & Journalism at the University of Southern California. I'm appreciative that the three faculty members on my dissertation committee—Larry Gross, Geoffrey Cowan, and Manuel Castells—offered me an uncommon amount of flexibility in doing so. I also want to recognize a few of the professors who've helped spur my interest in politics along the way, including: Kathleen Hall Jamieson and David Eisenhower (at the University of Pennsylvania), and Shawn McIntosh and Stephen Sigmund (at Columbia University).

My very first teachers were, of course, my mother and father, Janice and Stephen Hannah. The love and selflessness they've shown me—and pretty much everyone in their lives—has been a valuable example. I wouldn't have had the confidence to take on such a prominent subject in such a public way without their support in those early years. My brothers Jamie and Eric constantly make me proud, and let me bounce my political commentary off them to make sure it's not too "inside baseball." Jennifer, my wife, has affectionately and enterprisingly championed this book and its author. She keeps me truer to myself than I'd ever known how to be before. I am so fortunate this book isn't the only thing she let me dedicate to her.

NOTES

PROLOGUE

1. Jill Zuckman and David Mendell, "Obama to Give Keynote Address," *Chicago Tribune*, July 15, 2004.
2. Todd Leopold, "The Day America Met Barack Obama," *CNN.com*, November 5, 2008.
3. Louis Jacobson, "Julian Castro Says Seven Presidents Before Barack Obama Sought Universal Health Care," *PolitiFact*, September 5, 2012.

1: THE DICTATOR

1. David Nakamura and Debbi Wilgoren, "Caught on Open Mike, Obama Tells Medvedev He Needs 'Space' on Missile Defense," *Washington Post*, March 26, 2012.
2. "Obama Tells Russia's Medvedev More Flexibility after Election," *Reuters*, March 26, 2012.
3. David Nakamura and Debbi Wilgoren, "Caught on Open Mike, Obama Tells Medvedev He Needs 'Space' on Missile Defense," *Washington Post*, March 26, 2012.
4. Aaron Blake, "The Obama Presidency, from 'Socialist' to 'Dictator,'" *Washington Post*, January 20, 2015.
5. Katie Zezima and Robert Costa, "Republicans Challenge Obama's Executive Actions, File Lawsuit over Obamacare," *Washington Post*, November 21, 2014.

6. "Sen. Sessions: Obama Has 'No Authority' to Suspend Deportation of Illegal Immigrants," *The Kelly File*, Fox News, November 12, 2014.

7. Matt Wilstein, "Beck: Obama Became 'America's First Dictator' during State of the Union," *Mediaite*, January 29, 2014.

8. Hunter Walker, "Republicans Blast 'Emperor' Obama's Immigration Order," *Business Insider*, November 19, 2014.

9. Drew DeSilver, "In Late Spurt of Activity, Congress Avoids 'Least Productive' Title," Pew Research Center, December 29, 2014.

10. Stephen F. Hayes, "A Do-Nothing Congress?" *Weekly Standard*, January 25, 2015.

11. Michael O'Brien, "Obama: US 'Does Not Stand Still' and 'Neither Will I,'" *NBCNews.com*, January 28, 2014.

12. Dhrumil Mehta, "Every President's Executive Orders in One Chart," *FiveThirtyEight*, November 20, 2014.

13. The White House, *President Obama Is Taking Steps to Fix Our Broken Immigration System*, November 20, 2014.

14. The White House, *Year of Action*, December 19, 2014.

15. John J. Patrick, *Understanding Democracy: A Hip Pocket Guide* (Oxford: Oxford University Press, 2006).

16. John Berlau, "Auto Bailout Gives Away Chrysler," *Newsmax*, January 13, 2014.

17. Paul Steinhauser, "Six in 10 Oppose Auto Bailout, Poll Shows," CNN, December 3, 2008.

18. Center for Automotive Research, *New Study Estimates the Effect on the U.S. Economy of Successful Restructuring of General Motors*, December 9, 2013.

19. John Cassidy, "An Inconvenient Truth: It Was George W. Bush Who Bailed Out the Automakers," *New Yorker*, March 16, 2012.

20. Cassidy, "An Inconvenient Truth."

21. Brent Snavely, "Final Tally: Taxpayers Auto Bailout Loss $9.3B," *USA Today*, December 30, 2014.

22. Steve Contorno, "Obama Says Automakers Have Paid Back All the Loans It Got from His Admin 'and More,'" *PolitiFact*, January 22, 2015.

23. Center for Automotive Research, *New Study*.

24. Snavely, "Final Tally."

25. Bloomberg News, "At Detroit Auto Show, Joe Biden Praises Ford, GM, Chrysler Post-Bailout Operations," *Newsday*, January 16, 2014.

26. Reuters, "Darrell Issa Reprising Familiar Role in IRS Probe," *Huffington Post*, June 3, 2013, updated August 4, 2013.

27. David Weigel, "Darrell Issa's Big New IRS Revelation about the White House Was Actually Reported Two Months Ago," *Slate*, July 18, 2013.

28. Peggy Noonan, "Where Was the Tea Party?," *Peggy Noonan's Blog*, June 21, 2013.

29. Sam Stein, "Obama on IRS Scandal: 'I Have Got No Patience' for It," *Huffington Post*, May 13, 2013.

30. Marco Rubio, *Rubio to Lew: American People Deserve Answers, IRS Head Must Resign*, U.S. Senate, May 13, 2014.

31. Jennifer Bendery, "IRS Inspector General, Darrell Issa Communicated Multiple Times in 2012," *Huffington Post*, May 21, 2013, updated May 22, 2013.

32. Richard Rubin and Julie Bykowicz, "IRS Look at Progressive Groups Complicates Controversy," *Bloomberg Business*, June 25, 2014.

33. Sander Levin and Elijah Cummings, *Republican IRS Investigations Have Cost at Least $14 Million ... and Counting*, U.S. House Ways and Means Committee and Oversight and Government Reform Committee, February 26, 2014.

34. "Transcript of Lois Lerner's Remarks at Tax Meeting Sparking IRS Controversy," *Election Law Blog*, May 11, 2013.

35. Associated Press, "IRS Chief Says Tax-Exemption Screening Went Wider Than Tea Party Groups," *Guardian*, June 24, 2013.

36. Bernie Becker, "IG: Audit of IRS Actions Limited to Tea Party Groups at GOP Request," *The Hill*, June 26, 2013.

37. Josh Israel and Adam Peck, "New Records: IRS Targeted Progressive Groups More Extensively Than Tea Party," *ThinkProgress*, April 23, 2014.

38. Ryan Chittum, "The IRS Scandal Unwinds," *Columbia Journalism Review*, June 25, 2013.

39. Kevin Drawbaugh and Kim Dixon, "IRS Kept Shifting Targets in Tax-Exempt Groups Scrutiny: Report," *Reuters*, May 13, 2013.

40. Greg Sargent, "The Morning Plum: Darrell Issa Backtracks on IRS Scandal," *Washington Post*, June 26, 2013.

41. I devote an entire chapter (Chapter 5) of this book to Obamacare and the charges levied against it by Obama's critics. This section focuses on the charge that the law was foisted upon Americans in a dictatorial/undemocratic fashion.

42. Carl Hulse and Adam Nagourney, "Senate G.O.P. Leader Finds Weapon in Unity," *New York Times*, March 16, 2010.

43. Julie Rovner, "Republicans Spurn Once-Favored Health Mandate," *Morning Edition*, NPR, February 15, 2010.

44. Ezra Klein, "Unpopular Mandate," *New Yorker*, June 25, 2012.

45. Howard Markel, "69 Years Ago, a President Pitches His Idea for National Health Care," *PBS NewsHour*, November 19, 2014.

46. Edward Kennedy, "Speech on Health Care," *Good Morning America*, ABC, December 9, 1978.

47. Nedra Pickler, "Obama Calls for Universal Health Care," *USA Today*, January 25, 2007.

48. "The First Presidential Debate," John McCain and Barack Obama, PBS, September 26, 2008.

49. "Gowdy: Obamacare Passed w/o a Single Republican Vote; Let's See if Dems Can Fund It w/o a Single Republican Vote," *The Right Scoop*, August 14, 2013.

50. Seth Motel, "Opinions on Obamacare Remain Divided along Party Lines as Supreme Court Hears New Challenge," Pew Research Center, March 4, 2015.

51. Henry J. Kaiser Family Foundation, *Kaiser Health Tracking Poll: March 2013*, 2013.

52. Henry J. Kaiser Family Foundation, *Republicans Have an Edge in Voter Enthusiasm Heading into Fall, But Few Cite ACA as Motivating Factor,* September 9, 2014.

53. Steve Contorno, "Which Is More Unpopular: Obamacare or Repealing Obamacare?," *PolitiFact*, April 21, 2014.

54. Sam Levine, "Republicans Slam Obama over Immigration Executive Order," *Huffington Post*, November 20, 2014.

55. Seung Min Kim, "Senate Passes Immigration Bill," *Politico*, June 27, 2013, updated June 28, 2013.

56. Ann Colwell and Tom Watkins, "CNN Fact Check: Illegal Border Crossings at Lowest Levels in 40 Years," *CNN.com*, February 13, 2013.

57. Joanna Dreby, How Today's Immigration Enforcement Policies Impact Children, Families, and Communities, American Progress, August 2012.

58. The White House, *President Obama.*

59. Danny Vinik, "Reagan and Bush Acted Unilaterally on Immigration, Too—for the Same Reason That Obama Will," *New Republic*, November 19, 2014.

60. American Immigration Council, *Executive Grants of Temporary Immigration Relief, 1956–Present*, October 2014.

61. Sam Stein, "Legal Panel at Federalist Society Begrudgingly Accepts Obama's Immigration Powers," *Huffington Post*, November 19, 2014.

62. Kate M. Manuel and Todd Garvey, *Prosecutorial Discretion in Immigration Enforcement: Legal Issues*, Congressional Research Service, December 27, 2013.

63. Leigh Ann Caldwell, "Breaking Down the Debate over Obama's Immigration Plan," *NBCNews.com*, November 21, 2014.

64. Ellie Sandmeyer, "Conservative Media Cite Widely Discredited Research to Falsely Claim Immigration Executive Action Will Cost $2 Trillion," *Media Matters*, November 25, 2014.

65. Alex Nowrasteh, "Heritage Immigration Study Fatally Flawed," Cato Institute, April 2, 2013.

66. Jordan Fabian, Twitter post, May 6, 2013, 1:05 p.m.

67. Silva Mathema, "Assessing the Economic Impacts of Granting Deferred Action through DACA and DAPA," *Center for American Progress*, April 2, 2015.

68. The Office of the President of the United States, *The Economic Effects of Administrative Action on Immigration*, November 2014.

69. Ruben Navarrette Jr., "The GOP Immigration Flip-Flop," *USA Today*, April 12, 2015.

70. James Rainey, "Fox News Star Sean Hannity Suddenly Likes Immigration Reform," *Los Angeles Times*, November 9, 2012.

71. Michael Wear, "Is Immigration Reform Dead? Not If Evangelicals Can Do Anything about It," *The Atlantic*, July 18, 2013.

2: THE SOCIALIST

1. Jim Galloway, "Paul Broun: 'I Was the First to Call Obama a Socialist,'" *Atlanta Journal-Constitution*, February 12, 2013.

2. Stanley Kurtz, "Romney, Obama, and Socialism," *National Review*, September 23, 2011.

3. Mitt Romney, *No Apology: Believe in America* (New York: St. Martin's Griffin, 2011).

4. Louis Jacobson, "In Context: Obama's 'You Didn't Build That' Comment," *PolitiFact*, July 18, 2012.

5. Eugene Kiely, "'You Didn't Build That,' Uncut and Unedited," *FactCheck.org*, July 23, 2012, updated July 24, 2012.

6. Associated Press, "Is Obama a Socialist?" *CNBC.com*, June 4, 2012.

7. Floyd Norris, "Under Obama, a Record Decline in Government Jobs," *New York Times*, January 6, 2012.

8. Floyd Norris, "Government Getting Smaller in the U.S.," *New York Times*, May 4, 2012.

9. Andy Medici, "Obama Wants to Reorganize, Merge Federal Agencies," *Federal Times*, February 2, 2015.

10. Louis Jacobson, "Paul Ryan Says Barack Obama 'Has Doubled the Size of Government Since He Took Office,'" *PolitiFact*, April 10, 2012.

11. Danny Vinik, "Government Employment Is Way Down under Obama," *New Republic*, August 4, 2014.

12. Derek Thompson, "Barack Obama, Austerity President," *The Atlantic*, February 1, 2012.

13. Jeanne Sahadi, "How Spending Has Fallen under Obama," *CNNMoney*, January 27, 2014.

14. Justin Wolfers, Twitter, March 16, 2012, 4:09 p.m.

15. Reuters, "U.S. Fiscal Year Budget Deficit Narrows to $439 Billion," October 15, 2015.

16. The White House, *Campaign to Cut Waste*, accessed November 27, 2015.

17. Cass R. Sunstein, "Why Regulations Are Good—Again," *Chicago Tribune*, March 19, 2012.

18. Nicholas Wells and Mark Fahey, "Here's What's Going on with the Dodd-Frank Act," *CNBC.com*, July 24, 2015.

19. Paul Krugman, "Wall Street Voodoo," *New York Times*, January 18, 2009.

20. Jeffry A. Frieden, "Nationalizing the Bank Problem: Socialism It's Not," *New York Times*, January 22, 2009.

21. Timothy F. Geithner, *Stress Test: Reflections on Financial Crises* (New York: Broadway Books, 2015).

22. Deborah Solomon, "Timothy Geithner Book 'Stress Test' Defends Financial-Crisis Decisions," *Wall Street Journal*, May 10, 2014.

23. Terry Moran, Interview with Barack Obama, ABC News, February 10, 2009.

24. The White House, Office of the Press Secretary, *News Conference with Ronald Reagan*, August 12, 1986.

25. Jonathan Weisman, "U.S. Declares Bank and Auto Bailouts Over, and Profitable," *New York Times*, December 19, 2014.

26. Jake Berry, "Barack Obama Says Banks Paid Back All the Federal Bailout Money," *PolitiFact*, October 25, 2012.

27. Ryan Tracy, Julie Steinberg, and Telis Demos, "Bank Bailouts Approach a Final Reckoning," *Wall Street Journal*, December 19, 2014.

28. http://www.perdue.senate.gov/content/senator-perdue-introduces-bill-make-consumer-agency-accountable-american-people.

29. Ted Cruz, *Sen. Cruz and Rep. Ratcliffe Introduce Bill to Abolish the Consumer Financial Protection Bureau*, July 21, 2015.

30. Elizabeth Warren, "Unsafe at Any Rate," *Democracy Journal 5* (Summer 2007).

31. Lydia DePillis, "A Watchdog Grows Up: The Inside Story of the Consumer Financial Protection Bureau," *NerdWallet*, January 11, 2014.

32. Anisha Sekar, "The Consumer Financial Protection Bureau Explained," *NerdWallet*, November 24, 2012.

33. Sekar, "The Consumer Financial Protection Bureau Explained."

34. Consumer Federation of America, *Reducing Regulatory Burdens on Smaller Financial Institutions: Requirements the Consumer Financial Protection Bureau Must Meet*, June 17, 2011.

35. Consumer Financial Protection Bureau, *CFPB, 47 States and D.C. Take Action Against JPMorgan Chase for Selling Bad Credit Card Debt and Robo-Signing Court Documents*, July 8, 2015.

36. Consumer Financial Protection Bureau, *Special Bulletin for Current and Former Students Enrolled at Corinthian-Owned Schools*, February 3, 2015.

37. Consumer Financial Protection Bureau, *By the Numbers*, July 15, 2015.

38. Arthur Delaney and Alissa Scheller, "Who Gets Food Stamps? White People, Mostly," *Huffington Post*, February 28, 2015.

39. Ana Marie Cox, "The Ring of Truth behind the Right's 'Obamaphone' Line," *Guardian*, December 14, 2012.

40. Ian Millhiser, "Tea Party Group Launches Racist 'Obama Phone' Ad," *ThinkProgress*, October 15, 2012.

41. Elspeth Reeve, "Just How Racist Is the 'Obama Phone' Video?" *The Wire*, September 27, 2012.

42. Molly Moorhead, "Adam Putnam: Obama Campaign Gives Free Cell Phones to Supporters," *PolitiFact*, October 31, 2012.

43. Federal Communications Commission, Lifeline: Affordable Telephone Service for Income-Eligible Subscribers, Updated August 28, 2015.

44. Justin Bank, "The Obama Phone?" *FactCheck.org*, October 29, 2009, updated November 5, 2009.

45. U.S. Department of Agriculture, *Supplemental Nutrition Assistance Program Participation and Costs,* accessed November 26, 2015.

46. George Zornick, "The GOP's No Good, Very Bad Food Stamp Cuts," *The Nation*, September 20, 2013.

47. Dottie Rosenbaum, "SNAP Is Effective and Efficient," Center on Budget and Policy Priorities, March 11, 2013.

48. Rosenbaum, "SNAP."

49. U.S. Department of Agriculture, *What Is SNAP Fraud?*, April 16, 2014.

50. Eugene Kiely, "Does Obama's Plan 'Gut Welfare Reform'?," *FactCheck.org*, August 9, 2012.

51. Dylan Matthews, "Welfare Reform's Architect: You Call That a Gutting?," *Washington Post*, August 7, 2012.

52. Travis Waldron, "Romney Claims Waivers He Used to Support Will 'Gut Welfare Reform,'" *ThinkProgress*, August 7, 2012.

53. Associated Press, "Gov. Jindal Sues Obama Administration over Common Core," *USA Today*, August 27, 2014.

54. Ted Cruz, Twitter post, March 15, 2015, 7:53 p.m.

55. Sail Kapur, "Tom Cotton: 'Obamacare Nationalized the Student Loan Industry,'" Talking Points Memo, October 14, 2014.

56. David Weigel, "What Ted Cruz Talks about When He Talks about Common Core," Bloomberg Politics, March 19, 2015.

57. Common Core State Standards Initiative, *About the Standards: Development Process*, 2015.

58. For more on the difference between "standards" and "curricula," see the comparison provided in "The Common Core FAQ," *NPR.org*, June 6, 2014.

59. Amy Golod, "Common Core: Myths and Facts," *U.S. News*, March 4, 2014.

60. U.S. Department of Education, *Arne Duncan Remarks at the American Society of News Editors Annual Convention*, Capital Hilton, Washington, D.C., June 25, 2013.

61. Casey Quinlan, "Hillary Clinton Has to Be Very Careful When Talking about Common Core," *ThinkProgress*, April 23, 2015.

62. Bill Bennett and Greg Abbott, "Debating Common Core," *Fox News Sunday*, February 1, 2015.

63. Lori Robertson, "Student Loan Stretching," *FactCheck.org*, October 20, 2014.

64. Douglas W. Elmendorf, *Letter to Nancy Pelosi*, Congressional Budget Office, March 20, 2010.

65. Glenn Kessler, "Are College Students Are [sic] Being Overcharged on Loans to Pay for 'Obamacare'?," *Washington Post*, July 17, 2013.

66. Ry Rivard, "New Higher Ed Federalism," Inside Higher Ed, January 12, 2015.

67. Michael Mitchell, Vincent Palacios, and Michael Leachman, "States Are Still Funding Higher Education Below Pre-Recession Levels," Center on Budget and Policy Priorities, May 1, 2014.

68. David Hudson, "The President Proposes to Make Community College Free for Responsible Students for 2 Years," *The White House Blog*, January 8, 2015.

69. Jillian Berman, "These Schools Could Lose Federal Funding If Graduates Don't Get Jobs," *MarketWatch*, July 1, 2015.

3: THE OUTSIDER

1. Jim Rutenberg, "The Man behind the Whispers about Obama," *New York Times*, October 12, 2008.

2. Alex Pareene, "The Obama Madrassa Emailer's First Insane Chain Letter," *Gawker*, October 14, 2008.

3. Seamus McGraw, "Trump: I Have 'Real Doubts' Obama Was Born in U.S.," *Today News*, April 7, 2011.

4. Peter Roff, "Lessons From the Iron Lady," *U.S. News*, April 16, 2013.

5. Alex Pareene, "The Birthers: Who Are They and What Do They Want?," *Gawker*, July 22, 2009.

6. "Statements about Obama Birth Certificate," *PolitiFact*, September 2015.

7. Michael Isikoff, "Ex-Hawaii Official Denounces 'Ludicrous' Birther Claims," *NBCnews.com*, April 11, 2011.

8. Markos Moulitsas, "Birthers Are Mostly Republican and Southern," *Daily Kos*, July 31, 2009.

9. Mark Twain, "Advice to Youth," 1882.

10. CNN Wire, "Obama Lampoons Trump, Releases 'Birth Video' at Annual Dinner," *CNN.com*, May 2, 2011.

11. Darren Samuelson, "Giuliani: Obama Doesn't Love America," *Politico*, February 18, 2015.

12. Jake Miller, Rudy Giuliani: "Let Me Explain Why I Said Obama Doesn't Love America," *CBSNews.com*, February 23, 2015.

13. Michael Barbaro and Michael D. Shear, "President Obama Has, in Fact, Expressed Love for His Country," *New York Times*, February 22, 2015.

14. The White House, Office of the Press Secretary, *News Conference by President Obama*, April 4, 2009.

15. The White House, *News Conference.*

16. Steve Contorno, "Rudy Giuliani: Barack Obama Said American Exceptionalism No Better Than Other Countries,'" *PolitiFact*, February 23, 2015.

17. Sam Leith, *Words Like Loaded Pistols: Rhetoric from Aristotle to Obama* (New York: Basic Books, 2012).

18. Jeremy Diamond, "Rudy Giuliani: Obama Doesn't Love America," *CNN.com*, February 20, 2015.

19. "Obama Says U.S., Turkey Can Be Model for World," *CNN.com*, April 6, 2009.

20. Trip Gabriel, "Ryan Says Obama Policies Threaten 'Judeo-Christian' Values," *New York Times*, November 5, 2012.

21. Jonathan Martin and Amie Parnes, "McCain: Obama Not an Arab, Crowd Boos," *Politico*, October 10, 2008.

22. "Smears 2.0," *Los Angeles Times*, December 03, 2007.

23. Rutenberg, "The Man behind the Whispers."

24. Alex Theodoridis, "Scott Walker's View of Obama's Religion Makes Him a Moderate," *Washington Post*, February 25, 2015.

25. Stephen Prothero, "A Secret Muslim President? Been There. Done That," *USA Today*, September 22, 2015.

26. Ali Gharib, "Dick Cheney Still Thinks Saddam Hussein Was Involved in 9/11," *ThinkProgress*, September 7, 2011.

27. Dan Balz and Robert Costa, "Gov. Scott Walker: 'I Don't Know' Whether Obama Is a Christian," *Washington Post*, February 21, 2015.

28. Juliet Eilperin, "Critics Pounce after Obama Talks Crusades, Slavery at Prayer Breakfast," *Washington Post*, February 5, 2015.

29. Selzer and Company, *Bloomberg Politics Poll*, December 7, 2014.

30. "Innis: Obama the 'Most Racially Divisive' President Since Wilson," *Breitbart*, November 25, 2014.

31. Byron Tau, "Obama: 'I'm Not the President of Black America,'" *Politico*, August 7, 2012.

32. Barack Obama, "A More Perfect Union," NPR.org, March 18, 2008.

33. Evan Agostini, "Glenn Beck: Obama Is a Racist," *CBSNews.com*, July 29, 2009.

34. Jennifer Epstein, "Obama Urges 'Care and Restraint,'" *Politico*, November 24, 2014.

35. Krishnadev Calamur, "'Criminals' Taking Advantage of Situation in Baltimore, Obama Says," *NPR.org*, April 28, 2015.

36. The White House, Office of Faith-Based and Neighborhood Partnerships, *Promoting Responsible Fatherhood and Strong Communities*, 2015.

37. The White House, Office of the Press Secretary, *Opportunity for All: President Obama Launches My Brother's Keeper Initiative to Build Ladders of Opportunity for Boys and Young Men of Color*, February 27, 2014.

38. Sunlen Serfaty, "Brother's Keeper Enters New Phase amid Baltimore Tension," *CNN.com*, May 4, 2015.

39. Jamelle Bouie, "Why I Am Optimistic about the Future of Race Relations in America," *Slate*, December 31, 2014.

40. *Saddleback Presidential Candidates Forum*, CNN, August 17, 2008.

41. Robin Roberts and Barack Obama, "Interview on Gay Marriage," ABC, May 9, 2012.

42. Humphrey Malalo, "MP Tells Anti-Gay Rally: Obama Should Not Push Gay Agenda in Kenya," *Reuters*, July 6, 2015.

43. Jennifer Agiesta, "Majority Oppose 'Religious Freedom' Laws That Could Discriminate," *CNN.com*, April 24, 2015.

44. Ben Kamisar, "Poll: Orientation Should Be a Protected Class," *The Hill*, April 17, 2015.

45. *Saddleback*, CNN.

46. Becky Bowers, "President Barack Obama's Shifting Stance on Gay Marriage," *PolitiFact*, May 11, 2012.

47. "More Support for Gun Rights, Gay Marriage Than in 2008 or 2004," Pew Research Center, April 25, 2012.

48. Andrew Sullivan, "Barack Obama's Gay Marriage Evolution," *Newsweek*, May 13, 2012.

49. "Obergefell v. Hodges," SCOTUSblog.com, updated July 28, 2015.

4: THE ECONOMY DESTROYER

1. Jeffrey M. Jones, "Economy Trumps Foreign Affairs as Key 2016 Election Issue," Gallup, May 15, 2015.

2. Lauren Carroll, "Jeb Bush: Obama Caused 'Massive' Tax Increase on Middle Class," *PolitiFact*, June 23, 2015.

3. Andrew Soergel, "Where Are All the Workers?," *U.S. News*, July 16, 2015.

4. Carroll, "Jeb Bush."

5. The White House, *Tax Relief for Middle-Class Families and Small Businesses*, accessed November 23, 2015.

6. Angie Drobnic Holan and Louis Jacobson, "Barack Obama Said He's Cut Taxes for 'Middle-Class Families, Small Businesses,'" *PolitiFact*, September 7, 2012.

7. The White House, *U.S. National Debt*, July 26, 2011.

8. John Kartch, "Obamacare's Top Five Middle Class Tax Hikes," Americans for Tax Reform, April 15, 2014.

9. This is called the "Mitt Romney Loophole," since it was discovered, in the 2012 presidential campaign, that Governor Romney had stashed more than $20 million.

10. Democratic Policy & Communications Center (DPCC), "72 Straight Months of Private Sector Job Growth," March 4, 2016.

11. Brooks Jackson, "Obama's Numbers (April 2015 Update)," *FactCheck.org*, April 6, 2015.

12. Adam Hartung, "Obama Outperforms Reagan on Jobs, Growth and Investing," *Forbes*, September 5, 2014.

13. Hartung, "Obama Outperforms."

14. Ibid.

15. Matt Phillips, "The Chart Obama-Haters Love Most—and the Truth behind It," *Quartz*, November 4, 2014.

16. *Economic Report of the President, Together with the Annual Report of the Council of Economic Advisers*, United States Government Printing Office, March 2014.

17. Peter Schroeder, "Lew: Obama's Economic Critics Have Been 'Proven Wrong,'" *The Hill*, February 9, 2015.

18. Gerald F. Seib, "In Crisis, Opportunity for Obama," *Wall Street Journal*, November 21, 2008.

19. Victoria Finkle, "Is Dodd-Frank Really Killing Community Banks?," *American Banker*, August 18, 2015.

20. Steven J. Markovich, "CFR Backgrounders," Center on Foreign Relations, December 10, 2013.

21. Louise Story and Eric Dash, "Banks Prepare for Big Bonuses, and Public Wrath," *New York Times*, January 9, 2010.

22. Mark Koba, "Dodd-Frank Act: CNBC Explains," *CNBC.com*, May 11, 2012.

23. U.S. Commodity Futures Trading Commission, *Dodd-Frank Act: Volcker Rule*, April 16, 2012.

24. Linda Qiu, "Marco Rubio Slams Dodd-Frank, Gets His Numbers Wrong," *PolitiFact*, August 12, 2015.

25. Steve Culp, "Financial Institutions Start to See Some Upside in Dodd-Frank," *Forbes*, March 20, 2013.

26. Lucy Madison, "From Romney Camp, Conflicting Remarks on Fair Pay Act," *CBSNews.com*, October 18, 2012.

27. Joan Walsh, "Sunday Best: Marco Rubio Blasts the Lilly Ledbetter Fair Pay Act," *Salon*, October 21, 2012.

28. Jamie Peck, "What Is the Lilly Ledbetter Fair Pay Act, and What Are Its Strengths and Weaknesses?," *The Gloss,* November 6, 2012.

29. Robert Pear, "Justices' Ruling in Discrimination Case May Draw Quick Action by Obama," *New York Times,* January 4, 2009.

30. The White House, Council of Economic Advisers, *Gender Pay Gap: Recent Trends and Explanations*, April 2015.

31. Christina Hoff Sommers et al., "Should the Senate Pass the Paycheck Fairness Act?" *U.S. News*, May 4, 2012.

32. Catherine Hill and Christianne Corbett, *Graduating to a Pay Gap: The Earnings of Women and Men One Year after College Graduation*, American Association of University Women, October 2012.

33. Jessica Arons, *Lifetime Losses: The Career Wage Gap*, Center for American Progress Action Fund, December 8, 2008.

34. Jonathan Masters, "Debt, Deficits, and the Defense Budget," *PBS NewsHour*, February 25, 2013.

35. J. Taylor Rushing, "Obama Signs Pay-Go Law but Also Raises Federal Debt Ceiling," *The Hill*, February 13, 2011.

36. Michael O'Brien, "Senate Passes Pay-Go Rule on Party-Line Vote," *The Hill*, January 28, 2010.

37. Jim Puzzanghera, "In Search of a Way to Defuse the Debt Limit Brinkmanship," *Los Angeles Times*, October 19, 2015.

38. Annie Lowry, "White House Puts Price on Government Shutdown," *New York Times*, November 8, 2013; Executive Office of the President of the U.S., *Impacts and Costs of the October 2013 Federal Government Shutdown*, October 2013.

39. Jane C. Timm, "Does Cruz Understand 'Green Eggs and Ham'?" *MSNBC.com*, September 25, 2013.

40. Angie Drobnic Holan, "Ronald Reagan Talks about the Debt Ceiling," *PolitiFact*, July 22, 2011.

41. Simn Maloy, "Mitch McConnell's Debt Limit Bluff: The Senate Leader Knows He Has No Leverage, but He Has to Pretend," *Salon*, October 15, 2015.

42. Amy Gutman and Dennis Thompson, *The Spirit of Compromise: Why Governing Demands It and Campaigning Undermines It* (Princeton: Princeton University, 2014).

43. Puzzanghera, "In search of a way."

44. Ibid.

45. Paul Krugman, "Nobody Understands Debt," *New York Times*, February 9, 2015.

Dave Boyer, "That's Rich: Poverty Level under Obama Breaks 50-Year Record," *Washington Times*, January 7, 2014.

46. Dave Boyer, "That's Rich: Poverty Level under Obama Breaks 50-Year Record," *Washington Times*, January 7, 2014.

47. Charlie Gile and Justin Peligri, "Fact-Checking the GOP Debate," *NBCNews.com*, September 17, 2015.

48. Susan Milligan, "Poverty, Wages Remain Stagnant Despite Economic Recovery," *U.S. News*, September 16, 2015.

49. Arloc Sherman, "Stimulus Keeping 6 Million Americans Out of Poverty in 2009, Estimates Show," *Center on Budget and Policy Priorities,* September 9, 2009.

50. "Nearly 90 Percent of Americans Have Health Coverage," *CNN.com*, April 13, 2015.

51. Danielle Kurtzleben, "50 Years Later, a War over the Poverty Rate," *U.S. News*, January 6, 2014.

52. Danielle Kurtzleben, "Fact Check: Is It Obama's Fault That Poverty Has Grown?," *NPR.org*, August 17, 2015.

53. Ibid.

54. Barbara Mantel, "Minimum Wage: Would Raising the Rate Be Good for the Economy?," *CQ Researcher*, volume 24, issue 4 (2014).

55. Michelle Ye Hee Lee, "Obama's Claim That Raising the Minimum Wage Helps Low-Wage Workers 'Make Ends Meet,'" *Washington Post*, February 2, 2015.

56. Paul Lewis and Karen McVeigh, "Obama: 'Nobody Who Works Full-Time Should Have to Live in Poverty,'" *Guardian*, February 12, 2014.

57. Aimee Picchu, "Is a Higher Minimum Wage a Job Killer? Not in These States," *CBSNews.com*, April 1, 2014.

58. Bryce Covert, "States That Raised Their Minimum Wages Are Experiencing Faster Job Growth," *ThinkProgress*, July 3, 2014.

59. David Cooper and Douglas Hall, *Raising the Federal Minimum Wage to $10.10 Would Give Working Families, and the Overall Economy, a Much-Needed Boost,* Economic Policy Institute, December 19, 2013.

60. *Opinion Poll: Small Businesses Support Increasing the Minimum Wage to $10.10,* Small Business Majority, March 6, 2014.

61. National Poll: Small Business Owners Favor Raising Federal Minimum Wage, Business for a Fair Minimum Wage, July 2014; Corey Fedde, "Employers

Support Raising the Minimum Wage, Survey Finds," *Christian Science Monitor*, September 18, 2015.

62. Bruce Drake, "Polls Show Strong Support for Minimum Wage Hike," Pew Research Center, March 4, 2014; Jesse Byrnes, "Poll Finds Support for Minimum Wage Increase, Paid Leave," *U.S. News*, February 19, 2015.

5: THE HEALTH CARE USURPER

1. Ashley C. Allen, "Countries Spending the Most on Health Care," *USA Today*, July 7, 2014; Lenny Bernstein, "Once Again, U.S. Has Most Expensive, Least Effective Health Care System in Survey," *Washington Post*, June 16, 2014.

2. Max Fisher, "Here's a Map of the Countries That Provide Universal Health Care (America's Still Not on It)," *The Atlantic*, June 28, 2012.

3. Jenna Levy, In U.S., "Uninsured Rate Dips to 11.9% in First Quarter," *Gallup*, April 13, 2015.

4. Deirdre Walsh, "House Votes—Again—to Repeal Obamacare," *CNN.com*, February 3, 2015.

5. Associated Press, "Obama: 'I Have Become Fond of This Term 'Obamacare,'" *CBS DC*, October 3, 2012.

6. Lucy Madison, "On Bus Tour, Obama Embraces 'Obamacare,' Says 'I Do Care,'" *CBSNews.com*, August 15, 2011.

7. Rush Limbaugh, "Rush's Morning Update: Budget," *The Rush Limbaugh Show*, February 27, 2009.

8. Adam Liptak, "Supreme Court Allows Nationwide Health Care Subsidies," *New York Times*, June 25, 2015.

9. Paul R. La Monica, "Thanks, Obamacare! Health Insurer Stocks Soar," *CNNMoney*, January 21, 2015.

10. Bruce Japsen, "Obamacare Will Bring Drug Industry $35 Billion in Profits," *Forbes*, May 25, 2013.

11. Dan Diamond, "Healthcare Jobs Just Grew at Fastest Pace Since 1991," *Forbes*, June 5, 2013.

12. The White House, *Health Care That Works for Americans*, accessed November 24, 2015.

13. Steven Brill, "Bitter Pill: Why Medical Bills Are Killing Us," *Time*, April 4, 2013.

14. John Tozzi, "Obamacare: The Third-Fastest Expansion of Health Insurance in U.S. History," *Bloomberg Business*, March 16, 2015.

15. Paul Starr, *The Social Transformation of American Medicine: The Rise of a Sovereign Profession and the Making of a Vast Industry* (New York: Basic Books, 1984), 283.

16. John D. Morris, "Fight Looms over Medical Plan; Kennedy Message Stirs Partisans in the Strongly Opposed Camps," *New York Times*, February 12, 1961.

17. "The Nation," *New York Times*, July 11, 1965.

18. Devin Dwyer, "Memo Reveals Only 6 People Signed Up for Obamacare on First Day," *ABCNews.com*, October 31, 2015.

19. Jonathan Chait, "Ted Cruz's Obamacare Nightmare Comes to Life," *New York*, September 9, 2014.

20. Robin A. Cohen and Michael E. Martinez, *Health Insurance Coverage: Early Release of Estimates from the National Health Interview Survey, January–March 2015*, U.S. Department of Health and Human Services, August 2015; Dan Diamond, "Thanks, Obamacare: America's Uninsured Rate Is Below 10% for First Time Ever," *Forbes*, August 12, 2015.

21. Rachel Garfield, Rachel Licata, and Katherine Young, *The Uninsured at the Starting Line: Findings from the 2013 Kaiser Survey of Low-Income Americans and the ACA*, Kaiser Family Foundation, February 6, 2014.

22. Ibid.

23. Namrata Uberoi, Kenneth Finegold, and Emily Gee, "Health Insurance Coverage and the Affordable Care Act, 2010–2016," ASPE Issue Brief, Department of Health & Human Services, March 3, 2016.

24. Kevin Quealy and Margot Sanger-Katz, "Obama's Health Law: Who Was Helped Most," *New York Times*, October 29, 2014.

25. Sarah Ferris, "ObamaCare Sign-ups Swell to 17.6 million," *The Hill*, September 22, 2015.

26. Office of the Assistant Secretary for Planning and Evaluation. Department of Health & Human Services, "At Risk: Pre-Existing Conditions Could Affect 1 in 2 Americans: 129 Million People Could be Denied Affordable Coverage Without Health Reform," November, 2011.

27. Matthew Buettgens, John Holahan, and Hannah Recht, *Medicaid Expansion, Health Coverage, and Spending: An Update for the 21 States That Have Not Expanded Eligibility*, The Kaiser Foundation, April 29, 2015.

28. Dan Diamond, "The 3-Minute Story behind Medicaid Expansion," The Advisory Board Company, July 1, 2014.

29. *Public Approval of Health Care Law*, RealClearPolitics, accessed November 24, 2015.

30. *Kaiser Health Tracking Poll: March 2013*, Kaiser Family Foundation, March 20, 2013.

31. Ezra Klein, "Obamacare's Most Popular Provisions Are Its Least Well Known," *Washington Post*, March 22, 2013.

32. "74 Percent of Republicans Are Happy with Their New ObamaCare Plans," *The Week*, July 10, 2014.

33. Erik Wemple, "Ted Cruz Admits He'll Be Getting Insurance through Obamacare," *Washington Post*, March 24, 2015.

34. Peter Sullivan, "The GOP's New Case against ObamaCare," *The Hill*, May 6, 2015.

35. Steve Contorno, "John Boehner Says More People Are Uninsured Since Obamacare Took Effect," *PolitiFact*, March 18, 2014.

36. "Understanding Why Americans' Insurance Plans Are Being Canceled," *PBS NewsHour*, PBS, November 12, 2013.

37. Juliet Eilperin, "President Obama Apologizes to Americans Who Are Losing Their Health Insurance," *Washington Post*, November 7, 2013.

38. *Health Care Costs: A Primer*, Kaiser Family Foundation, May 01, 2012.

39. Julie Appleby and Kaiser Health News, "How Quickly Are Health Insurance Premiums Rising?," *PBS NewsHour*, August 21, 2013.

40. Glenn Kessler, "The GOP Attack on a Dubious Obama Health Care Pledge," *Washington Post*, September 11, 2013.

41. Kessler, "The GOP Attack."

42. Lori Robertson, "Health Savings Still Optimistic," *FactCheck.org*, May 15, 2009.

43. Ezra Klein, "Obama Guesses His Way to Trillions in Health Savings," *Bloomberg View*, June 12, 2013.

44. Jonathan Chait, "Obamacare Haters Freaking Out over New Report," *New York*, September 24, 2015.

45. Jason Millman, "Lower Premiums (Yes, Really) Drive down Obamacare's Expected Costs, CBO Says," *Washington Post*, April 14, 2014.

46. Reed Abelson, "Health Insurance Deductibles Outpacing Wage Increases, Study Finds," *New York Times*, September 23, 2015.

47. Kaiser, *Health Care Costs*.

48. Justin Haskins, "Obamacare Waste Continues to Pile Up," *Townhall*, September 24, 2015.

49. John Tozzi, "How Healthcare.gov Botched $600 Million Worth of Contracts," *Bloomberg Business*, September 15, 2015.

50. Tom Cohen, "Rough Obamacare Rollout: 4 Reasons Why," *CNN.com*, October 23, 2013.

51. Liz Klimas, "Rumor Check: Obamacare Website Might Be Glitchy, But It Didn't Cost $634 Million," *The Blaze*, October 10, 2013.

52. Kaitlin Devine, "How Much Did Healthcare.gov Actually Cost?," *Sunlight Foundation*, October 22, 2013.

53. Glenn Kessler, "How Much Did HealthCare.gov Cost?," *Washington Post*, October 24, 2013.

54. Louis Jacobson, "Donald Trump Says the '$5 Billion Website for Obamacare … Never Worked. Still Doesn't Work,'" *PolitiFact*, July 14, 2014.

55. Steven Levy, "Why the New Obamacare Website Is Going to Work This Time," *Wired*, June 5, 2014.

56. David Lauter, "Redesigned Obamacare Website Is Faster and Easier to Use," *Los Angeles Times*, October 8, 2014.

57. Benjamin Bell, "Nancy Pelosi: Obamacare Rollout Glitches 'Unacceptable,'" *ABCNews.com*, October 20, 2013.

58. Jon Greenberg, "Fox News Pundit Says Health Care Law Will Cost $50,000 Per Enrollee," *PolitiFact*, January 28, 2015.

59. Greenberg, "Fox News."

60. "Conflating Costs of the ACA," *FactCheck.org*, February 6, 2015.

61. David Martosko, "Obamacare Program Costs $50,000 in Taxpayer Money for Every American Who Gets Health Insurance, Says Bombshell Budget Report," *Daily Mail*, January 26, 2015.

62. *Updated Budget Projections: 2015 to 2025*, Congressional Budget Office, March 2015.

63. Max Ehrenfreund, "Obamacare's Projected Cost Falls Due to Lower Premiums under Health Care Law, CBO Says," *Washington Post*, March 9, 2015.

64. *Deficit-Reducing Health Care Reform*, The White House, accessed November 24, 2015.

65. Ibid.

66. *Budgetary and Economic Effects of Repealing the Affordable Care Act*, Congressional Budget Office, June 19, 2015.

67. Glenn Kessler, "Obama's Claim the Affordable Care Act Was a 'Major Reason' in Preventing 50,000 Patient Deaths," *Washington Post*, April 1, 2015; Louis Jacobson, "Barack Obama Says Health Care Law Has Led to 50,000 Fewer Preventable Hospital Deaths," *PolitiFact*, March 31, 2015.

68. Benjamin D. Sommers, Sharon K. Long, and Katherine Baicker, "Changes in Mortality after Massachusetts Health Care Reform: A Quasi-Experimental Study," *Annals of Internal Medicine*, volume 160, number 9 (2014).

6: THE PLANET "HEALER"

1. Barack Obama, "Victory Speech," June 3, 2008.

2. Anne C. Mulkern and ClimateWire, "Scientists Seek Strategy to Convey Seriousness of Sea-Level Rise," September 10, 2012.

3. Katie Glueck, "Jeb Bush Knocks Pope on Climate Change Push," *Politico*, June 16, 2015.

4. *Colorado, Iowa, Virginia Voters Back Pope on Climate, Quinnipiac University Swing State Poll Finds; Voters Say Leave Same-Sex Marriage Alone*, Quinnipiac University, July 23, 2015.

5. Laura Barron-Lopez, "'I'm Not a Scientist, Either,' President Says," *The Hill*, January 20, 2015.

6. Kelsey Warner, "Economic Bite of Climate Change Could Be Even Bigger Than We Thought," *Christian Science Monitor*, October 21, 2015.

7. Dan Lamothe, "Climate Change Threatens National Security, Pentagon Says," *Washington Post*, October 13, 2014.

8. *DOE Announces Final Rule for Loan Guarantee Program*, United States Department of Energy, October 4, 2007.

9. Henry Fountain, "Researchers Link Syrian Conflict to a Drought Made Worse by Climate Change," *New York Times*, March 2, 2015.

10. James Ayre, "SolarCity Leasing 200,000-Sq-Ft Former Solyndra Manufacturing Facility in Fremont," *Clean Technica*, February 18, 2015.

11. Ted Gayer and Emily Parker, *Cash for Clunkers: An Evaluation of the Car Allowance Rebate System*, Brookings Institute, October 30, 2015.

12. Patrick O'Connor, "DeMint Not a 'Cash-for-Clunkers' Fan," *Politico*, August 2, 2009.

13. Daniel Gross, "Cash for Clunkers Helped Car Dealers, But ...," *Slate*, August 24, 2009.

14. Jeff Bennett, "Car Makers Upbeat as Sales Rebound," *Wall Street Journal*, September 2, 2009.

15. Ibid.

16. Bill Vlasic, "Invigorated by Clunker Cash, Ford Moves to Increase Output," *New York Times*, August 13, 2009.

17. Jeff Bennett, "Car Makers Upbeat."

18. Emphasis added. Andrew Greiner, "American Cars Were the Clunkiest of the Bunch," *NBCChicago.com*, August 26, 2009.

19. Executive Office of the President, Council of Economic Advisers, *Economic Analysis of the Car Allowance Rebate System*, September 10, 2009.

20. Joe Romm, "Cash for Clunkers Is a Double Economic Stimulus That Pays for Itself in Oil Savings So CO_2 Savings Are Free," *ThinkProgress*, August 27, 2009.

21. Ibid.

22. Sean Tucker, "Cash for Clunkers—What Was the Payoff?," *U.S. News*, August 5, 2009.

23. Andrew Greiner, "American Cars."

24. Brian Merchant, "Cash for Clunkers Passes—Auto Industry Saved? Blue Skies Ahead?," *TreeHugger*, June 19, 2009.

25. Anne Lutz Fernandez and Catherine Lutz, "After Years of Resistance, Auto Industry Agrees to New Mileage Standards," *StreetsBlog*, August 2, 2011.

26. The White House, *President Obama Announces Historic 54.5 mpg Fuel Efficiency Standard*, July 29, 2011.

27. Eric Holthaus, "'America Is Not a Planet': The Only Thing Marco Rubio Got Right on Climate Change," *Slate*, September 17, 2015.

28. The White House, Office of the Press Secretary, *U.S.-China Joint Announcement on Climate Change and Clean Energy Cooperation*, November 11, 2014.

29. Julie Hirschfeld Davis and Coral Davenport, "China to Announce Cap-and-Trade Program to Limit Emissions," *New York Times,* September 24, 2015.

30. Steven Mufson, "With Cap and Trade Plan, China Adopts Emissions Policy That Couldn't Get through U.S. Congress," *Washington Post*, September 28, 2015.

31. Fergus Green and Nicholas Stern, *China's "New Normal": Structural Change, Better Growth, and Peak Emissions*, Grantham Research Institute, June 2015.

32. Michael Grunwald, "5 Reasons Obama's Transformative Power Plan Won't Transform Anything," *Politico*, May 2015.

33. Steve Hargreaves, "What's to Blame for Lost Coal Jobs," *CNN.com*, September 9, 2012.

34. U.S. Supreme Court, *New State Ice Co. v. Liebmann*, 285 U.S. 262 (1932).

35. Gina McCarthy, "6 Things Every American Should Know about the Clean Power Plan," *Medium*, August 3, 2015.

36. Karthick Arvinth, "Obama Unveils Ambitious 'Clean Power Plan' to Combat Climate Change," *International Business Times*, August 4, 2015.

37. Southern Environmental Law Center, *Clean Power Plan Impact Analysis Support*, September 4, 2014.

38. The White House, *Climate Change and President Obama's Action Plan*, accessed November 24, 2015.

39. Christopher Dean Hopkins, "Republicans' Responses Take Shots at Obamacare, Push Keystone XL," *The Two-Way,* NPR, January 21, 2015.

40. Evelyn Bateman and Adam Haley, "Keystone Pipeline XL," *Rhetoric and Civic Life*, March 2, 2013.

41. Nicholas Bergin, "Landowners Continue Fight with TransCanada," *Journal Star*, October 19, 2015.

42. "Environmental Consequences" in *Final Supplemental Environmental Impact Statement,* Keystone XL Project, 2015.

43. U.S. Environmental Protection Agency, *National Environmental Policy Act*, accessed November 25, 2015.

44. Suzanne Goldenberg, "Keystone Pipeline: Obama Given Boost from EPA Report Revising Climate Impact," *Guardian*, February 3, 2015.

45. David Turnbull, "Cooking the Books: The True Climate Impact of Keystone XL," *Oil Change International*, April 16, 2013.

46. Brooks Jackson, "Pipeline Primer," *FactCheck.org*, March 10, 2014.

47. Joshua Green, "State Department Says Keystone Pipeline Will Create Just 50 Jobs," *Bloomberg Business*, January 31, 2014.

48. Jackson, "Pipeline Primer."

49. Richard Pallardy, "Deepwater Horizon Oil Spill of 2010," *Britannica.com*, accessed November 25, 2015.

50. Campbell Roberts and Clifford Krauss, "Gulf Spill Is the Largest of Its Kind, Scientists Say," *New York Times*, August 2, 2010.

51. Pallardy, "Deepwater."

52. Tom Cohen, "Obama Administration Lifts Deep-Water Drilling Moratorium," *CNN.com*, October 13, 2010.

53. Hannah Breul and Linda Doman, *U.S. Expected to Be Largest Producer of Petroleum and Natural Gas Hydrocarbons in 2013*, U.S. Energy Information Administration, October 4, 2013.

54. The White House, *Advancing American Energy*, accessed November 25, 2015.

55. Rebecca Leber, "Five Years Ago, Obama Promised to Phase Out Government Subsidies for Oil and Gas Exploration. Instead, They've Doubled," *New Republic*, November 11, 2014.

56. Chris Tackett, "Bill McKibben on the Failure of Obama's Energy Policy," *TreeHugger*, October 30, 2013.

57. Rachel Waldholz and Liz Ruskin, "Obama Administration Cancels Offshore Lease Sales, Citing Lack of Interest," *AlaskaPublic.org*, October 16, 2015.

58. The White House, Office of the Press Secretary, *President Barack Obama's State of the Union Address*, January 28, 2014, h.

7: THE FREEDOM WRECKER

1. John Sopel, "Interview with Barack Obama," BBC, July 24, 2015.

2. Pew Research Center, *Continued Bipartisan Support for Expanded Background Checks on Gun Sales*, August 13, 2015.

3. Bob Dreyfuss, "The NRA Wants You," *The Nation*, May 11, 2000.

4. Sarah Wheaton, "Obama Urges 'Single Issue' Voting on Guns," *Politico*, October 2, 2015.

5. The White House, Office of the Press Secretary, *Statement by the President on the Shootings at Umpqua Community College, Roseburg, Oregon*, October 1, 2015.

6. Lauren Carroll, "Obama: More Gun Laws Means Fewer Gun Deaths," *PolitiFact*, October 6, 2015.

7. Malcolm Gladwell, "Thresholds of Violence," *New Yorker*, October 19, 2015.

8. Allie Bidwell, "American Students Fall in International Academic Tests, Chinese Lead the Pack," *U.S. News*, December 3, 2013.

9. A. Barton Hinkle, "The Case for School Vouchers," *Reason.com*, June 10, 2015.

10. William Bruce Cameron, *Informal Sociology: A Casual Introduction to Sociological Thinking* (New York, Random House, 1963).

11. Bill Chappell, "U.S. Students Slide in Global Ranking on Math, Reading, Science," *NPR.org*, December 3, 2013,

12. Alain de Botton, *Status Anxiety* (New York: Vintage, 2005).

13. William O'Reilly, "Interview with Barack Obama," Fox, February 3, 2014.

14. Stephanie Simon, "Louisiana Makes Bold Bid to Privatize Public Education," *Reuters*, June 1, 2012.

15. Jarvis DeBerry, "Louisiana Lawmaker Needs Lesson in Religious Freedom," *Times-Picayune,* July 8, 2012.

16. Danielle Dreillinger, "Louisiana Supreme Court Rules Voucher Funding Violates the State Constitution," *Times-Picayune*, May 7, 2013.

17. Zack Kopplin, "Creationism Spreading in Schools, Thanks to Vouchers," *MSNBC.com*, January 13, 2013.

18. Jonathon Fagan, "Voucher Bill Could Fund Muslim Schools," *Murphreesboro Post*, March 31, 2013.

19. James Harrison, "Haslam's Voucher Bill Pulled," *Nooga.com*, April 4, 2013.

20. Thomas Jefferson, letter to Joseph C. Cabell, January 14, 1818.

21. "The President on Mass Surveillance," *New York Times*, January 17, 2014.

22. The White House, Office of the Press Secretary, *Remarks by the President on Review of Signals Intelligence*, January 17, 2014.

23. Jennifer Agiesta, "Poll: 6 in 10 Back Renewal of NSA Data Collection," *CNN.com*, June 1, 2015.

24. Bill Scher, "The Liberal Case for High-Tech NSA Surveillance," *The Week*, June 13, 2013.

25. U.S. Senate, *Church Reports, Book III: Supplementary Detailed Staff Reports on Intelligence Activities and the Rights of Americans*, April 14, 1976.

26. Verne Lyon, "Domestic Surveillance: The History of Operation CHAOS," *Covert Action Information Bulletin*, Summer 1990.

27. U.S. Federal Bureau of Investigation, Letter to Martin Luther King, Jr., November 1964.

28. Peter Bergen, David Sterman, Emily Schneider, and Bailey Cahall, *Do NSA's Bulk Surveillance Programs Stop Terrorists?*, New America Foundation, January 2014.

29. Bruce Schneier, "NSA Doesn't Need to Spy on Your Calls to Learn Your Secrets," *Wired*, March 25, 2013.

30. "Habeas Corpus," Legal Information Institute, accessed November 26, 2015.

31. Elise Foley, "Rand Paul: Obama's Drone Policy Involves 'Looking at Some Flashcards' Instead of Due Process," *Huffington Post*, May 26, 2013.

32. Cora Currier, Peter Maass, "The Drone Papers: Firing Blind," *The Intercept*, October 15, 2015.

33. Tom Junod, "The Lethal Presidency of Barack Obama," *Esquire*, August 2012.

34. Billy Kenber, "Nidal Hasan Sentenced to Death for Fort Hood Shooting Rampage," *Washington Post*, August 28, 2013.

35. Sudarsan Raghavan, "Cleric Says He Was Confidant to Hasan," *Washington Post*, November 16, 2009.

36. Raghavan, "Cleric Says."

37. Michael Isikoff, "Justice Department Memo Reveals Legal Case for Drone Strikes on Americans," *NBC Nightly News*, February 4, 2013.

38. Benjamin Wittes, "In Defense of the Administration on Targeted Killing of Americans," *Lawfare*, February 27, 2013.

39. Scott Shane, "The Moral Case for Drones," *New York Times*, July 14, 2015.

40. Daniel L. Byman, "Why Drones Work: The Case for Washington's Weapon of Choice," Brookings Institute, July/August 2013.

41. Julian Hattem, "Sanders: I Wouldn't End Drone Program," *The Hill*, August 30, 2015.

42. Joel Simon, "Barack Obama's Press Freedom Legacy," *Columbia Journalism Review*, April 3, 2015.

43. Jake Miller, "Obama: Press Freedom 'Vital' to Democracy," *CBSNews.com*, May 1, 2015.

44. O'Reilly, "Interview."

45. Associated Press, "Former CIA Officer Convicted of Leaking Secrets to Reporter James Risen," *Guardian*, January 26, 2015.

46. Charlie Savage, "Court Tells Reporter to Testify in Case of Leaked C.I.A. Data," *New York Times*, July 19, 2013.

47. Matt Apuzzo, "Times Reporter Will Not Be Called to Testify in Leak Case," *New York Times*, January 12, 2015.

48. Charlie Savage, "Criticized on Seizure of Records, White House Pushes News Media Shield Law," *New York Times*, May 15, 2013.

8: THE BUNGLER OF FOREIGN POLICY

1. Philip Rucker and Robert Costa, "Mitt Romney Gives a Brutal PowerPoint Critique of Obama's Foreign Policy," *Washington Post*, June 12, 2015.

2. Frank Newport, "Obama Averages 47% Job Approval in May," *Gallup*, June 5, 2012.

3. Greg Myre, "Taking U.S. Politics beyond 'The Water's Edge,'" *NPR.org*, March 10, 2015.

4. Romesh Ratnesar, "Libya: The Case for U.S. Intervention," *Time*, March 7, 2011.

5. Michael Hastings, "Inside Obama's War Room," *Rolling Stone*, October 13, 2011.

6. Ibid.

7. Jayshree Bajoria, *Libya and the Responsibility to Protect*, Council on Foreign Relations, March 24, 2011.

8. Samantha Power, *"A Problem from Hell": America and the Age of Genocide* (New York: Basic Books, 2013), 13.

9. The White House, Office of the Press Secretary, Remarks by the President in Address to the Nation on Libya, March 28, 2011.

10. "Libya Peace Process Stumbles as Crisis Looms," *Al Jazeera*, October 23, 2015.

11. Jonathan Karl, "Benghazi Talking Points Underwent 12 Revisions, Scrubbed of Terror Reference," *Good Morning America*, ABC, May 10, 2013.

12. "Republican primary debate," CNBC, October 29, 2015.

13. Karl, "Benghazi."

14. Glenn Kessler, "Is Hillary Clinton a 'Liar' on Benghazi?," *Washington Post*, October 30, 2015.

15. "CNN's Cuomo Pushes Back Against Sen. Rubio's Already-Debunked Benghazi Falsehoods," *New Day*, CNN, October 29, 2015.

16. U.S. Senate, *Report of the U.S. Senate Select Committee on Intelligence Review of the Terrorist Attacks on U.S. Facilities in Benghazi, Libya, September 11–12, 2012*, January 15, 2014.

17. Clayton Youngman, "Clinton: 7 Benghazi Probes So Far," *PolitiFact*, October 12, 2015.

18. Lauren French, John Bresnahan, and Jake Sherman, "Gowdy Gets into Benghazi," *Politico*, May 4, 2014.

19. Ken Dilation, "House Intelligence Committee Investigation Debunks Many Benghazi Theories," *PBS.org*, November 21, 2014.

20. Andrea Mitchell, "Witnesses Discuss Actions during Benghazi Attack," *Andrea Mitchell Reports*, MSNBC, May 08, 2013.

21. Jake Miller, "Gates: Some Benghazi Critics Have "Cartoonish" View of Military Capability," *CBSNews.com*, May 12, 2013.

22. Andrew Rosen, "The Benghazi Circus," *New York Times*, November 16, 2012.

23. "Hillary Clinton's Live Testimony before House Benghazi Committee," CNN, October 22, 2015.

24. Kessler, "Is Hillary."

25. David D. Kirkpatrick, "Brazen Figure May Hold Key to Mysteries," *New York Times*, June 17, 2014.

26. Sophia Tesfaye, "Kevin McCarthy's Nasty Benghazi Hangover: Speaker-in-Waiting Torched by His Own Party for Letting the Mask Slip," *Salon*, October 1, 2015.

27. Michelle Ye Hee Lee, "Trey Gowdy to GOP Colleagues: 'Shut Up' If You're Not on Benghazi Panel," *Washington Post*, October 18, 2015.

28. Kevin Cirilli, "Cruz: Prisoner Swap Negotiations 'Disturbing,'" *The Hill*, June 1, 2014.

29. Kendall Breitman, "Cheney: A Bad Deal," *Politico*, June 3, 2014.

30. Donald Trump, "Our Country Needs a Truly Great Leader," speech, June 16, 2015.

31. Department of Defense, *Code of the U.S. Fighting Force*, American Forces Information Services, 1988.

32. William Saletan, "Don't Desert Bergdahl," *Slate*, June 4, 2014.

33. Arun Rath and Paul Springer, "How Bergdahl's Release Fits in the History of Prisoner Exchanges," *Around the Nation*, NPR, June 7, 2014.

34. Cited in John Knefel, "Four Myths about the Bowe Bergdahl Swap That Must Be Destroyed," *Rolling Stone*, June 5, 2014.

35. Robert Farley, "Sorting Murky Issues on the POW Swap," *Factcheck.org*, June 6, 2014.

36. Marie Harf, "Daily Press Briefing," U.S. Department of State, June 5, 2015.

37. NSC Press Office, "Statement by NSC Spokesperson Caitlin Hayden on the Transfer of Taliban Detainees from Guantanamo," June 3, 2014.

38. Wesley Lowery, "Senators Shown Bergdahl Video That Taliban Provided White House before Trade," *Washington Post*, June 4, 2014.

39. "Defense Bill Includes Ayotte Priorities to Support Troops," Military Readiness, Office of U.S. Senator Kelly Ayotte, May 22, 2014.

40. "Sen. Ayotte Criticizes Taliban-U.S. Prisoner Swap," *Union Leader*, June 2, 2014.

41. Anderson Cooper, "Deadly Uprising in Ukraine," *Anderson Cooper 360*, CNN, February 18, 2014.

42. Peter Nicholas, "Republicans Criticize Swap with Taliban for Sgt. Bowe Bergdahl," *Wall Street Journal*, June 1, 2014.

43. David Fahrenthold and Jaime Fuller, "The Bergdahl Boomerang: Some Lawmakers Who Long Urged a Rescue Now Sour on the Idea," *Washington Post*, June 6, 2014.

44. Anthony Zurcher, "The 'Republican Strategist' behind the Bergdahl Story," *BBC.com*, June 3, 2014.

45. The White House, Office of the Press Secretary, "Government Assessment of the Syrian Government's Use of Chemical Weapons on August 21, 2013," August 30, 2013.

46. Julian Hattem, "Obama Refugee Plan Targeted after Attacks," *The Hill*, November 15, 2015.

47. U.S. Congress, *House Resolution 1828, Syria Accountability and Lebanese Sovereignty Restoration Act of 2003*, December 12, 2003.

48. Josh Feldman, "Stewart Slams Syrian Red Line, Begs Cable News 'Idiot Parade' to 'Shut the F*ck Up,'" *Mediaite*, September 3, 2013.

49. The White House, Office of the Press Secretary, "Remarks by the President in Address to the Nation on Syria," September 10, 2013.

50. Ted Cruz, "Why I'll Vote No on Syria Strike," *Washington Post*, September 9, 2013.

51. Scott Clement, "Opposition to Syria Airstrikes Rises as Republicans Shift Sharply against Action," *Washington Post*, September 9, 2013.

52. Aaron Blake, "The Eight Important Quotes from Obama's Syria Interviews," *Washington Post*, September 9, 2013.

53. Maayana Miskin, "Syrian Officials Gloat: Obama Defeated before War Began," *Arutz Sheva*, September 1, 2013.

54. Arshad Mohammed and Andrew Osborn, "Kerry: Syrian Surrender of Chemical Arms Could Stop U.S. Attack," *Reuters*, September 9, 2013.

55. Elizabeth Sherwood-Randall, "A Major Milestone in Our Effort to Eliminate Syria's Chemical Weapons Program," *Whitehouse.gov*, November 4, 2013.

56. Justin Fishel, "Top Anti-ISIS Envoy Confident US Could Defend against Possible Refugee Infiltration," *ABCNews.com*, September 11, 2015.

57. Julian Hattem, "Obama Refugee Plan Targeted after Attacks," *The Hill*, November 15, 2015.

58. Dara Lind, "The US Is So Paranoid about Syrian Refugees That It's Letting Barely Any In," *Vox*, November 16, 2015.

59. Mahal Toosi, "Christian Groups Break with GOP over Syrian Refugees," *Politico*, November 17, 2015.

60. Julian Hattem, "Cheney: Obama's Iraq Withdrawal Created ISIS," *The Hill*, August 31, 2015.

61. "'ISIS Is an Obama Creation': Giuliani Blasts President's 'Vacuous' Foreign Policy," *Hannity*, Fox, November 16, 2015.

62. "De-Baathification," *Frontline*, *PBS.org*, October 17, 2006.

63. Reina Flores, "What Does an Iran Nuclear Deal Have to Do with ISIS?," *CBSNews.com*, March 11, 2015.

64. Arash Karami, "Iran Officials Call for International Response to ISIS Violence," *Al Monitor*, June 10, 2014.

65. Mike DeBonis, "For Marco Rubio and 2016 Republicans, It All Comes Back to Iran," *Washington Post*, March 11, 2015.

66. Simon Rogers, "War in Iraq: The Cost in American Lives and Dollars," *Guardian*, December 15, 2011.

67. Daniel Trotta, "Iraq War Costs U.S. More Than $2 Trillion: Study," *Reuters*, March 14, 2013.

68. Angie Drobnic Holan, "Obama Orders 'Responsible' Withdrawal from Iraq," *PolitiFact*, January 21, 2009.

69. Joshua Gillin, "Obama Refused to Sign Plan in Place to Leave 10,000 Troops in Iraq, Bush Says," *PolitiFact*, May 18, 2015.

70. David S. Cloud and Ned Parker, "U.S. Willing to Leave 10,000 Troops in Iraq Past Year's End, Officials Say," *Los Angeles Times*, July 06, 2011.

71. Zack Beauchamp, "Obama's 6-Point Plan for Defeating ISIS," *Vox*, September 10, 2014.

72. Cathy Otten, "Exclusive: Inside America's ISIS Air Strike Center in Iraq," *The Daily Beast*, November 19, 2015.

73. Rebecca Kaplan, "Grim Future for Obama's Request to Fight ISIS," *CBSNews.com*, May 20, 2015.

9: THE ALIENATOR OF ALLIES

1. Pete Kasperowicz, "Ted Cruz Rips Obama's Foreign Policy: 'Friends No Longer Trust Us, and Our Enemies No Longer Fear Us,'" *The Blaze*, December 10, 2014.

2. Brooks Jackson, "Obama's Numbers (July 2015 Update)," *FactCheck.org*, July 7, 2015.

3. *Confidence in the U.S. President*, Pew Research Center, August 2015; *Opinion of the United States*, Pew Research Center, August 2015.

4. WikiLeaks, "US Spied on Angela Merkel's Ministers Too, Says German Newspaper," *Guardian*, July 1, 2015.

5. Madeline Chambers, "Berlin Tells CIA Station Chief to Leave in Spy Scandal," *Reuters*, July 10, 2015.

6. "Embassy Espionage: The NSA's Secret Spy Hub in Berlin," *Der Spiegel*, October 27, 2013.

7. Dustin Volz, "Obama Asks Germany to Stop 'Assuming the Worst' about NSA Spying," *National Journal*, February 9, 2015.
8. Dustin Volz, "Edward Snowden Is More Admired Than President Obama in Germany and Russia," *National Journal*, February 5, 2015.
9. Mark Landler, "One Casualty of Eavesdropping on Merkel: A Warm Rapport," *New York Times*, November 1, 2013.
10. Jennifer Sims, "I Spy…," *Foreign Affairs*, November 6, 2013.
11. Ben Wolfgang, "Hey Europe, You're Welcome: Allies Made Safer by U.S. Snooping, Lawmakers Insist," *Washington Times*, October 27, 2013.
12. Michael Hirsh, "Why America Spies on Its Friends," *National Journal*, October 31, 2013.
13. Matthew Karnitschnig and Edward-Isaac Dovere, "How Obama Wooed Back Merkel," *Politico*, June 6, 2015.
14. Ibid.
15. "America's Willing Helper: Intelligence Scandal Puts Merkel in Tight Place," *Der Spiegel*, May 4, 2015.
16. Dick Cheney, "Obama Has 'Demonstrated Repeatedly' That He Can Be Pushed Around," *Fox News Sunday*, Fox, May 18, 2014.
17. "Romney Slams Both Obama and Clinton for Handling of Russian Threat," *NBCNews.com*, March 23, 2014.
18. Mitt Romney, "Russia Is Our Number One Geopolitical Foe," *The Situation Room with Wolf Blitzer*, CNN, March 26, 2012.
19. Katie Sanders, "Romney: Obama Stopped Missile Defense Shield 'As a Gift to Russia,'" *PolitiFact*, March 23, 2014.
20. Eugene Kiely, "Cheney's Misguided Missile Attack," *FactCheck.org*, May 20, 2014.
21. "Is Obama Throwing Eastern Europe under the Bus?," Center for Strategic International Studies, September 2009.
22. Steven Beardsley, "Navy to Create Missile Defense Task Force in Europe," *Stars and Stripes*, July 28, 2015.
23. Fiona Keating, "Russia Successfully Launches 'Missile Defence Killer' Despite Warnings from Pentagon," *International Business Times*, June 9, 2015.
24. Kiely, "Cheney's Misguided Missile Attack."

25. Glenn Kessler, "The GOP Claim That Obama Scrapped a Missile Defense System as 'a Gift' to Putin," *Washington Post*, March 28, 2014.

26. "Obama Scraps Bush-Era Europe Missile Shield," *NBCNews.com*, September 17, 2009.

27. Barack Obama, "U.S. Relations with Baltic States," C-SPAN, September 3, 2014.

28. David Frum, "Obama Just Made the Ultimate Commitment to Eastern Europe," *The Atlantic*, September 3, 2014.

29. Barak Ravid, "Kerry's Latest Cease-fire Plan: What Was He Thinking?," *Haaretz*, July 27, 2014.

30. "Kerry 'Completely Capitulated' to Hamas in Ceasefire Proposal, Say Israeli Sources," *Times of Israel*, July 26, 2014.

31. David Jackson, "Rubio: Obama Has Weakened U.S. and Israel," *USA Today*, December 3, 2015.

32. Thomas Friedman, "A Bad Mistake," *New York Times*, February 4, 2015.

33. Steven Mufson, "Netanyahu's Panned Congress Speech Splits U.S. Jewish Organizations," *Washington Post*, February 28, 2015.

34. Hilary Leila Krieger, "Jewish Support for Obama Slipped, but Still Strong," *Jewish Post*, November 8, 2012.

35. http://www.jewishjournal.com/IranSurvey.

36. Jeffrey Goldberg, "Israeli Ambassador: Netanyahu Never Meant to Disrespect Obama," *The Atlantic*, January 30, 2015.

37. Jodi Rudoren and Jeremy Ashkenas, "Netanyahu and the Settlements," *New York Times*, March 12, 2013.

38. Rebecca Shabad, "Rogers: Kerry Has Led Israel to Think It's Alone," *The Hill*, July 28, 2014.

39. Julie Hirschfeld Davis, "Obama and Netanyahu Seek to Move Past Rift over Iran Nuclear Deal," *New York Times*, November 9, 2015.

40. Chloe Sommers, "Afghan President: Obama Should 'Re-examine' Troop Withdrawal for 2016," *CNN.com*, January 5, 2015.

41. Matthew Rosenberg and Michael D. Shear, "In Reversal, Obama Says U.S. Soldiers Will Stay in Afghanistan to 2017," *New York Times*, October 15, 2015.

42. Jeremy Diamond, "Rand Paul: Why Are We Still in Afghanistan?," *CNN.com*, October 6, 2015.

43. Heather Goldin, "2016 GOPers Sound Off over Obama's Afghanistan Decision," *CNN.com*, October 15, 2015.

44. Sarah Almukhtar and Karen Yourish, "14 Years after U.S. Invasion, the Taliban Are Back in Control of Large Parts of Afghanistan," *New York Times*, October 16, 2015.

45. Felicia Schwartz, "U.S. General Urges Slower Drawdown of Troops in Afghanistan," *Wall Street Journal*, October 6, 2015.

46. Rosenberg and Shear, "In Reversal."

47. Barack Obama, "Remarks on Afghanistan Troop Withdrawal Shift," *Wall Street Journal*, October 15, 2015.

48. Operation Enduring Freedom, "Coalition Military Fatalities by Year."

49. Gayle Tzemach Lemmon, "Eyes on the Prize in Afghanistan," *Foreign Affairs*, October 21, 2015.

50. Sommers, "Afghan President."

51. http://www.ft.com/cms/s/0/89397942-733b-11e5-a129-3fcc4f641d98 .html#axzz3tJqbeAeL [PAYWALL]

52. Ashram Ghani, "Translation of the Transcript of President Ghani's Speech on ANSDF and Announcement of Continued Support of the International Partners," Office of the President, Islamic Republic of Afghanistan, October 20, 2015.

53. Caryle Murphy and Howard Schneider, "After 3-Decade Rule, Mubarak Will Be Remembered for How It Ended," *Washington Post*, February 12, 2011.

54. John Hayward, "Egypt, Saudi Arabia Outraged by State Dept. Reception of Muslim Brotherhood Delegation," *Breitbart*, February 18, 2015.

55. Taylor Wofford, "In Republican Debate, Cruz Praises Egyptian Dictator Al-Sisi," *Newsweek*, August 6, 2015.

56. Justin Elliott, "How Did the U.S. Get in Bed with Mubarak?," *Salon*, January 29, 2011.

57. Barack Obama, "Remarks by the President at Cairo University, 6-04-09," The White House, Office of the Press Secretary, June 4, 2009.

58. Barack Obama, "Speech on Middle East," *Guardian*, May 19, 2011.

59. Eli Lake, "Look Who's Talking," *New Republic*, March 3, 2011.

60. P. J. Crowley, "Is Egypt an Ally of the U.S.?," *Foreign Policy,* September 16, 2012.

61. Jared Malsin, "Egyptian Court Sentences Ousted President Morsi to Death," *New York Times*, May 16, 2015.

62. Hamza Hendawi, "Egypt: 2,600 Killed after Ouster of Islamist President," *Associated Press*, May 31, 2015.

63. David D. Kirkpatrick and Merna Thomas, "Egyptian Judges Drop All Charges against Mubarak," *New York Times*, November 29, 2014.

64. Ted Cruz, "Statement on Egypt," The Office of U.S. Senator Ted Cruz, August 16, 2013.

10: THE APPEASER OF ENEMIES

1. Jeffrey Goldberg, "Hillary Clinton: 'Failure' to Help Syrian Rebels Led to the Rise of ISIS," *The Atlantic*, August 10, 2014.

2. Brian Adam Jones, "Winston Churchill Gave One of the Most Poignant Quotes Ever about Warfare," *Task & Purpose*, April 6, 2015.

3. Ron Suskind, "Faith, Certainty and the Presidency of George W. Bush," *New York Times Magazine*, October 17, 2004. I was reminded of this *New York Times Magazine* article by Stephen Duncombe's excellent book *Dream: Re-imagining Progressive Politics in the Age of Fantasy*, which informs some of the ideas I lay out in this chapter.

4. David E. Sanger, *The Inheritance* (New York: Broadway Books, 2010), viii.

5. Bret Stephens, *America in Retreat: The New Isolationism and the Coming Global Disorder* (New York: Sentinel, 2014).

6. Bret Stephens, "What Obama Gets Wrong," Foreign Affairs, September 2015.

7. "'He Just Surrenders & Gives Them Everything': Cruz Rips Obama on Russia, Iran," *Hannity, FOXnews.com*, November 4, 2015.

8. Charles Krauthammer, "Obama's Pathetic Response to Putin," *Washington Post*, March 20, 2014.

9. "'Special Report' Panel on Russian-Georgian Conflict and How Obama, McCain Are Responding to It," *Special Report with Brit Hume*, Fox News, August 11, 2008.

10. Oleg Buklemishev, "Myths and Realities of Sanctions in Russia," Carnegie Endowment for International Peace, August 13, 2015.

11. Ibid.

12. Reuters, "Vladimir Putin: Russia Has 'Inner Strength' to Weather the West's Sanctions," *Telegraph*, June 19, 2015.

13. Lauren Gensler, "Russia Downgraded to Junk by S&P," *Forbes*, January 26, 2015.

14. Jennifer Rankin, "Russian Sanctions Start to Bite as Growth Forecasts Are Downgraded," *Guardian*, August 17, 2014.

15. Steve Holland, "With Eye on U.S. Election, Republicans Assail Russia's Putin," *Reuters*, June 8, 2015.

16. Katie Sanders, "Cheney: Obama Wants to Get 'Rid of All Nuclear Weapons,' Has Reduced U.S. Capability 'Significantly,'" *PolitiFact*, July 17, 2015.

17. Ibid.

18. Ronald Reagan, "Address to the Nation and Other Countries on United States-Soviet Relations," January 16, 1984.

19. Fred Kaplan, "The Realist," *Politico*, February 2014.

20. Peter Pomerantsev, *Nothing Is True and Everything Is Possible: The Surreal Heart of the New Russia* (New York: PublicAffairs, 2014).

21. Paul MacDonald and Joseph M. Parent, "Graceful Decline? The Surprising Success of Great Power Retrenchment," *International Security*, volume 35, issue 4, 7–44.

22. "How Advanced Is North Korea's Nuclear Programme?," *BBC.com*, September 15, 2015; Luis Martinez, "North Korea Can Put a Nuke on a Missile, U.S. Intelligence Agency Believes," *ABCNews.com*, April 11, 2013.

23. Sue Chang, "North Korea's Missiles Are No Longer a Punchline," *MarketWatch*, April 23, 2015.

24. Jeremy Diamond, "McCain Hits Obama on North Korea Hack, Russia," *CNN.com*, December 21, 2014.

25. "Republicans Critical of Obama Response to Sony Attacks, 'Cybervandalism' Remark," *FOXNews.com*, December 21, 2014.

26. Ibid.

27. "Obama Administration Imposes Sanctions on North Korea, after Sony Hack," *FOXNews.com*, January 2, 2015.

28. *The U.S.-North Korean Agreed Framework at a Glance*, Arms Control Association, August 2004.

29. Robert L. Gallucci and Joel S. Wit, "Nuclear Knowledge," *Foreign Affairs*, May 5, 2015.
30. "Examining the Lessons of the 1994 U.S.-North Korea Deal," *Frontline*, PBS, March 2003.
31. Richard Perle, "Kim's Nuclear Gamble," *Frontline*, PBS, March 2003.
32. Nahal Toosi, "Obama's True Nuclear Test: North Korea," *Politico*, May 6, 2015.
33. *Chronology of U.S.–North Korean Nuclear and Missile Diplomacy*, Arms Control Association, May 2015.
34. David Jackson, "North Korea: Obama Is a 'Loser,'" *USA Today*, January 26, 2015.
35. Paula Hancocks, "Defector Sends Thousands of 'The Interview' DVDs to North Korea," *CNN.com*, April 11, 2015.
36. George Orwell, *Funny, But Not Vulgar and Other Selected Essays and Journalism* (London: Folio Society, 1968).
37. Mark Hensch, "Rubio: Obama's Cuba Thaw 'Ridiculous,'" *The Hill*, April 11, 2015.
38. *World Report 2014: Cuba*, Human Rights Watch, 2014.
39. Igor Bobic, "GOP Opposes Diplomatic Relations with Cuba, But Not Other Human Rights Abusers," *Huffington Post*, December 17, 2014.
40. Lauren Leatherby, "Republicans Stand against Cuba Change Despite Public Opinion Shift," *NPR.org*, July 27, 2015.
41. John Hooper, "Pope Francis and the Vatican Played Key Roles in US-Cuba Thaw, Leaders Reveal," *Guardian*, December 2014.
42. "Polling Results on Cuban Americans' Viewpoint on the Cuba Opportunity," *National Journal Hotline*, March 2015.
43. Danielle Renwick and Brianna Lee, "U.S.-Cuba Relations," Council on Foreign Relations, August 4, 2015.
44. Ibid.
45. Jennifer M. Harris, "The Winners of Cuba's 'New' Economy," *Fortune*, January 14, 2015.
46. Leatherby, "Republicans Stand against."
47. The White House, Office of the Press Secretary, "Statement by the President on Cuba Policy Changes," December 17, 2014.

48. Michael Crowley, "On Cuba and Iran, Obama Defies His Critics," *Politico*, July 20, 2015.

49. Scott Wilson and Al Kamen, "'Global War on Terror' Is Given New Name," *Washington Post*, March 25, 2009.

50. David Kurtz, "Trump: Terrorism Won't Be Solved Until Obama Says 'Radical Islamic Terrorism,'" *Talking Points Memo*, November 15, 2015.

51. Domenico Montanaro, Lisa Desjardins, Rachel Wellford, and Simone Parthe, "Who Said It? Bush vs. Obama on Islam," *PBS.org*, February 19, 2015.

52. George W. Bush, "'Islam Is Peace' Says President," The White House, September 17, 2001.

53. Jeremy Diamond, "Why Obama Won't Call Terror Fight a War on Radical Islam," *CNN.com*, February 1, 2015.

54. Eli Lake, "Why Obama Can't Say 'Radical Islam,'" *Bloomberg View*, January 19, 2015.

55. "Trump Gives Muslim on Fence about Radicalizing Just the Push He Needed," *The Onion*, December 7, 2015.

56. "Donald Trump on Ban, Obama and 2016," *Morning Joe*, MSNBC, December 8, 2015.

57. Omar Mohammed, "As a Muslim, I Believe It's My Responsibility to Help Defeat ISIL," *Quartz*, December 8, 2015.

58. David Ignatius, "The bin Laden Plot to Kill President Obama," *Washington Post*, March 16, 2012.

59. Gilad Shiloach, "ISIS Loyalists Can Download a Secret Set of Terrorist Emojis," *Voactiv*, November 24, 2015.

60. "ISIS Hates Being Called 'Daesh.' Here's Why," *TestTube*, December 4, 2015.

61. Fred Kaplan, "Bad Posture," *Slate*, July 23, 2015.

62. Ben Jacobs, "Jeb Bush Denounces Iran Nuclear Deal as Appeasement," *Guardian*, July 14, 2015.

63. Mark S. Bell, "Okay, So What if Iran Does Get Nuclear Weapons?," *Washington Post*, August 20, 2015.

64. The White House, *Read the Iran Deal Facts*, accessed December 9, 2015.

65. The White House, "Parameters for a Joint Comprehensive Plan of Action Regarding the Islamic Republic of Iran's Nuclear Program," April 2, 2015.

66. Michel Euler, "Iran's Rouhani Sets Lofty Goals at Davos Forum," *CBSNews. com*, January 23, 2014.

67. Robert W. Jordan, "Iran Could Become an Economic Superpower," *Time*, July 16, 2015.

68. Michael R. Gordon, "Head of Group Opposing Iran Accord Quits Post, Saying He Backs Deal," *New York Times*, August 11, 2015.

69. James Fallows, "The President Defends His Iran Plan," *The Atlantic*, August 7, 2015, Emphasis added.

70. Andrew Helms, "Sandy Berger on U.S.-Israel Relations, the Iran Nuclear Deal and More," *Frontline*, PBS, December 4, 2015.

71. James Fallows, "A Reader Condemns the Iran Deal—and Other Readers Respond," *The Atlantic*, August 11, 2015.

72. Don Gonyea, "Jesting, McCain Sings: 'Bomb, Bomb, Bomb' Iran," *Election 2008*, NPR, April 20, 2007.

73. John R. Bolton, "To Stop Iran's Bomb, Bomb Iran," *New York Times*, March 26, 2015.

74. Michael Crowley, "The Ultimate Argument in Favor of the Iran Deal," *Politico*, August 24, 2015.

75. Teresa Welsh, "Iranian Public Opinion Clashes with Supreme Leader on Nuclear Deal," *U.S. News*, June 24, 2015.

76. *Iranians Favor Diplomatic Relations with US But Have Little Trust in Obama*, World Public Opinion, September 19, 2009.

77. Christopher Thornton, "The Iran We Don't See: A Tour of the Country Where People Love Americans," *The Atlantic*, June 6, 2012.

EPILOGUE

1. Daniel Goleman, "For Presidential Candidates, Optimism Appears a Winner," *New York Times*, May 8, 1998.

2. Maria Gavrilovic, "Obama Rails on 'False Hope,'" CBS News, January 6, 2008.

3. Benedict Anderson, *Imagined Communities: Reflections on the Origin and Spread of Nationalism*, Revised Edition (London: Verso, 2006), 6.

MARK HANNAH (author) is a veteran of John Kerry's and Barack Obama's presidential campaigns and a Democratic political analyst who has appeared regularly on Fox News, MSNBC, and CNBC. He has written political analysis for PBS.org, the *Huffington Post,* and *Politico* and currently teaches at New York University and The New School. A partner at the Truman National Security Project, he holds degrees from the University of Pennsylvania, Columbia University, and the University of Southern California. He is from Cape Cod, Massachusetts, and now lives in Brooklyn, New York.

BOB STAAKE (illustrator) is the author and/or illustrator of more than sixty books that have been translated into over twelve languages around the world. His artwork has been published in the *Washington Post,* the *Chicago Tribune,* the *Los Angeles Times,* the *New York Times, Vanity Fair, Time,* and the *Wall Street Journal*. He's created numerous covers for *The New Yorker,* including their best-selling cover of all time, "Reflection," rendered for the occasion of Obama's first inauguration. His children's book *The First Pup* (2010) tells the story of the puppy President Obama adopted during his stay at the White House.